William Thomas Walker

Notes of Seven Decades

ANTAL DORÁTI

Notes of
Seven Decades

Revised edition
Wayne State University Press
Detroit, 1981

Library of Congress Cataloging in Publication Data

Dorati, Antal.
  Notes of seven decades.

  Includes index.
  1. Dorati, Antal. 2. Conductors (Music) – Biography.
I. Title.
ML422.D66A3 1981   785′.092′4[B]   80-27568
ISBN 0-8143-1685-9

Revised edition published in the United States of America by Wayne State University Press, Detroit, Michigan 48202, 1981. Originally published in Great Britain by Hodder and Stoughton, Ltd., London, 1979. Copyright © 1979, 1981 by Antal Doráti.

Illustrations

(Picture credits: *AD*, author's collection; *DSO*, Detroit Symphony Orchestra; *FW*, Fayer Wien; *MM*, Raymond Mander and Joe Mitchenson Theatre Collection; *P*, Popperfoto; *WSU*, Wayne State University)

Antal Doráti at Orchestra Hall, Detroit *(DSO)*
Gwyneth Jones and Antal Doráti *(DSO)*
Maestro Doráti and the Detroit Symphony Orchestra at Carnegie
  Hall *(DSO)*
Aaron Copland and Antal Doráti *(DSO)*
Al Kaline, William Schuman, Antal Doráti and Charlie Gehringer
  (DSO)
Antal Doráti *(AD)*
Manzù's *Nymph and Faun (WSU)*
Manzù's *Porte della morte (AD)*
Maestro and Mrs. Doráti *(AD)*

1

A SMALL BOY IN A GARDEN, DRAWING LINES ON THE SANDY PATH with a twig. He looks at what he has drawn, tramples on it furiously, then goes at it again. The result is the same. Again he tramples on the dust, again he draws, now other criss-cross lines. He does not like that one either, erases it, trampling, kicking. He starts to cry.

This is the earliest memory I have of myself; altogether the first thing I remember.

My mother later confirmed that this scene really did take place, in a small Hungarian village, in 1907, when I could not yet speak. She also told me that she finally tried to help me and drew all sorts of figures in the sand: a dog, a cat, a flower. Nothing was to my liking, I yelled louder and louder. Finally she guessed right, and I was quiet and happy with the right drawing in the sand.

Perhaps it has some meaning that I did not recall that happy ending. In a way the little story has continued throughout my life: I have tried and tried to draw what would please at the end. I am still trying.

2

HUNGARY AT THE START OF THE TWENTIETH CENTURY WAS A seething, fermenting place. The war of liberation of 1848, with which Austria could not cope by itself, was quelled by the Russian Army, called in by the Emperor Franz Joseph in 1849. The thirty years that followed were those of the "Iron Fist" of the Austrian government. When a reconciliation was brought about in 1876, the country burst forth into its newly-won constitutional freedom like a river released from the narrows.

The expansion was feverish, as old ways were cast aside, and the speed with which a modern state began to emerge was incredible. It was also ominous. For as the new wine was fermenting, the old grapes were rotting away, and the traditional structures of Central Europe were being destroyed too swiftly for natural change.

1896 marked the thousandth anniversary of the founding of the Kingdom of Hungary and it was in this year of delirious celebration that Budapest, the capital city, emerged as a small metropolis.

The site of the city is indestructibly lovely. The Danube, approximately half a mile broad, flowing southward, separates the plain to its left from the hilly country to its right like a knife. At a point where the river divides twice in succession to flow around islands, lie the two settlements: old Buda, already a township (Aquincum) under the Romans to the right; and the newer Pest to the left. The two cities were united into the present Budapest as late as 1873.

Exactly fifty years later, on the evening of November 19th, 1923, a remarkable event took place in the "Vigadó" (or "Redouten-saal", to use the Austro-Hungarian term for a place of entertainment) – an orchestral concert to celebrate the first half century of "Budapest". There were world premières of three works commissioned for the occasion. The first work of the evening was a Festive Overture by Ernö von Dohnányi, who was at that time the musical leader of the city. A man of enormous talent and great energy, he virtually took care of music in Budapest all by himself. He was a great pianist who, after some virtuoso concert tours, settled in his city and played hundreds of recitals there in the course of many years, all sold out, all admired – justly so – by a grateful, adoring populace. He also played a great deal of chamber music in public. For many years he was the chief conductor of the Budapest Philharmonic Orchestra, and while his prowess as a conductor was somewhat disputed, he did provide his audience constantly with fine, interesting programmes, not neglecting the old and keeping up with the new. This achievement was the more remarkable as he was not a modernist himself. A prolific composer of the finest technique and noble taste, he represented the German element in Hungary's heady new nationalistic mix. His music was derived from the Brahmsian romanticism (Brahms, to whom he showed his Piano Quintet, Op. 1, said about it: "I could not have done it better myself") and took in marginal "Magyarisms" only later.

What he wrote for the event was a structurally huge piece – Festive Overture for two Orchestras – in which a number of Hungarian anthems and patriotic songs were combined contrapuntally, often in antiphonal treatment, with great skill and superb knowledge of instrumentation but little originality. The piece burst in the air like a firecracker. It shone, glowed with all the colours of the rainbow, then – pouf! – it was gone, disappeared immediately after it ended into limbo, emerging now and then for other joyous jubilees only – and as these are rather rare in our lives, and in today's Hungary especially, presumably not too often.

The next number on the programme, the second première of the evening, was Béla Bartók's *Dance Suite*. It was a shocking failure. We were impressed, but also depressed, by it. We did not know what to think of the piece, what to do with it. Dohnányi, who conducted – he was the conductor for the whole evening – could not find his way in this music, and so of course the players did not find theirs either. It was with this work that I was most involved, playing the celesta in it, and I was astonished and grieved, with all the innocence of my youth, not so much by the ugly playing I heard around myself as by the lack of any attempt to do better.

It was an example of how a poor performance of a complex work can hinder its understanding but – luckily – cannot ruin it

9

for ever. If a work of art has enough creative strength, it will survive, and will come out victorious in the end.

The *Dance Suite* was coldly received by the audience, and mistreated by the press.

Bartók, who was present both at rehearsal and at the performance, was rather depressed. He said, softly and with sad irony: "Well, it seems I cannot orchestrate."

During the next few years one or two people tried to resuscitate the work, but failed. None of the conductors of that time in Hungary could cope with it. But the day of truth did arrive.

A few years later – it must have been before 1928 because I still lived in Hungary then – the Czech Philharmonic came on a tour to Budapest, with its conductor, Vaclav Talich. It was, I believe, the first visit of that orchestra to the Hungarian capital – the neighbourly relations between the postwar states of Central Europe were none too good at that time, and it took the power of the one really international language, music, to make such visits across borders welcome or even possible – and was attended with great curiosity, genuine interest and a complete readiness to lash out into hostile and wounding criticism.

One of the pieces on the programme was Bartók's *Dance Suite*. The audience sat back, prepared to hiss at the first opportunity. However, Talich obviously knew how to perform that piece (he was probably the first conductor who did) and thus the very fine orchestra also knew how to play it. Its success was enormous. The applause, yelling and stamping went on and on. The piece stopped the show. Talich tried to continue the programme in vain. The show remained stopped.

When he lifted his arms for the start of the next piece there was silence, but after the first note pandemonium broke out. There was no way out: the entire *Dance Suite* had to be played again.

Bartók, who was present, bowed awkwardly, modestly, from his seat. Later he said only and, as always, very softly: "Well, it might seem that I *can* orchestrate."

But to complete the picture of that anniversary concert: the third and closing work on the programme was Kodály's *Psalmus Hungaricus*, which there and then began its uninterrupted career of success. This was new music expressed in terms which were easily understandable, and while it was deeply, touchingly Hungarian, its musical language was universal. No wonder the public at this first

10

performance jumped from their seats and shouted their ferocious acclaim. Nor is it surprising that the effect of the piece has not diminished over the years: nor that this lasting popularity has been world-wide. Its ideas are strong and superbly focused.

On that great day, perhaps the proudest group of young people were the pupils of Kodály's composition class. We – I was one of the class – expected great things. Some of us saw pages of the score on their way to or from the copyist. We had talked – those who dared, the cheeky ones – to the tenor soloist, Székelyhidy, to get an inkling of what was in store. But the effect of the actual performance was overwhelming. Imagine being all of a sudden a pupil of Jupiter!

Kodály never mentioned this or any other work of his either in class or out of it. Much later, in his eighty-first year, we were together in Salzburg, where he heard a rather uninteresting performance of his *Psalmus*. He said to me later in the soft voice Bartók and he always cultivated: "It cannot be destroyed."

The same was said about Hungary by all of my countrymen at the start of the century. Little did we know about the forces of destruction already gathering under the surface of that euphoric life.

When thinking of a city, there is always one image that instinctively comes to mind. At first it may be superficial, the Eiffel Tower for Paris, the Empire State Building for New York. Later, and on better acquaintance, it becomes more specifically personal.

The image I have of my native city is a blossoming chestnut tree. That, for me, is the incarnation of Budapest. Many streets were lined with those splendid big chestnut trees, and their white or pink blossoms like little candelabras or petal trees gave a fresh splendour to each springtime. Those were incomparable days: walking to and from school under those trees was a feast to sing about.

Other pictures of the town emerge: in particular the fine street known as the Andrássy út, named after a Hungarian nobleman, prime minister at the turn of the century, a Habsburg partisan and a great favourite of the beautiful Queen Elizabeth. It leads out from a fine square harbouring statues of a row of kings, in the centre of which stands the Millennial Column with a bronze angel on its top; and at the sides two large neo-Greek-style buildings, museums of the fine arts. From this square, a mile long and dead straight, the Andrássy út runs to the centre of the city. Three quarters of the way along, on the right-hand side as one walks towards the centre, stands a building of great importance in my life: the one-time "Royal" Opera House.

The centre – the so-called "inner city" – is the oldest part of Pest, compact and complex, with narrow and crooked streets. Walking around in it felt like walking in a fist.

Crossing the inner city took but a few minutes on foot and the walker arrived at the Danube, which flows from north to south in an elegant, slightly curved line. The left bank – at which he now arrived – is dominated by a steel-grey, neo-Gothic building, the Parliament, constructed at the turn of the century and inspired by the Houses of Parliament in London, just as the nobly conceived (but alas, short-lived) Constitution was inspired by Magna Carta. A row of fine bridges lead across the river, where, immediately, the hills of Buda emerge, the nearest of which are the site of the old city, with its ancient Citadel, Royal Palace and St. Mathias Church, and behind that skyline rise the green-blue hills of Transdanubia.

Indeed, a city profile of great and rare beauty.

It is the tragedy of Queen Budapest that she was de-throned – and not, as it would be easy to imagine, by the lost wars and the Communist régime. The process began much earlier, as through the years I became convinced, with the ill-chosen, ill-conceived political and cultural adherence of Hungary to Western Europe, which it sought and fought for assiduously for several centuries.

By nature, Hungary and the Hungarians belong to Eastern Europe – to the Balkans, if you will – and not to the West. It can be argued that the European balance was gravely disturbed by Hungary's refusal to accept its geographical, political and humanistic role as the westernmost outpost of the East, rather than the West's eastern bulwark.

That *Drang nach dem Westen* or westward pull – "Westward, Ho!" – is a strangely strong instinct. Almost all major migrations of people are in a westward direction. Practically all conquests of territories have been westward directed. (This is not the same as colonisation; colonisation is not conquest.) The Huns, Persians, Tartars went westward. So did Columbus and all the conquerors of the new worlds. And so did the tiny tribe of Finno-Ugrians. And the Ugrian (Hungarian) part of this tribe, while it stopped, physically, in the Danube basin, could not stop thinking about, and yearning for, the West.

Of the Hungarians it is said that they saved Europe by stopping the Turkish invasion. But it is not certain that Europe was saved by that deed. Neither is it certain that Europe would have been finished if the Turks had marched beyond Hungary. After all, the Huns did, the Mongols did – and went back whence they came, without having destroyed the West which they invaded for brief periods.

It is difficult to describe the Hungarian people – difficult even to imagine it as one people and not several. There are so many small groups, all differing, quarrelling and arguing with each other yet maintaining, in spite of it, one strange, multi-coloured unity.

The best way to describe it is through epigrams or anecdotes, which are innumerable.

"The Hungarian is a person who goes into a revolving door behind you and comes out ahead of you."

"The secret of the economic life of Hungary is that there is only one gold coin in the country but it is owned every twenty-four hours in turn by the entire populace."

The Hungarians' daily prayer: "God, please order things so that I shall be able to permit myself to live the way I do."

And so on.

The Hungarian is a born leader. Every Hungarian is, that's the trouble. Perhaps this is why Hungary so seldom wins wars, since no army could succeed if entirely composed of generals. And perhaps it is why so many Hungarians emigrate, and why so many of them do so well wherever they go.

The Hungarian is also a born fantast and a born talker. These qualities, if not backed by intelligence, energy and talent, can be truly tiresome, but when so backed can have a sparkle all their own: the same sort of sparkle that makes the difference between wine and champagne.

The time of my childhood was the last happy period of Hungary. I was born in Budapest which was then growing by leaps and bounds. A whole generation of "Budapestiens" was born in that decade whose parents had come from the country into the big city.

13

Until my eighth year (I was born on April 9th, 1906), I lived in the atmosphere of what we now call "peace" – a state of mind, a kind of life, that in its essence ended for the whole world in 1914.

My recollections of those prewar years are those of a normal child of a small, impecunious, middle-class family, but with the difference that it was a family of artists. I felt even then, as a small boy, that it is a privilege to be an artist, something very precious for which one has to be very grateful, and I regarded myself as one of the "clan".

It is incredible how deeply and strongly the roots of a man's spiritual life are imbedded in the soil of his youth. Therefore it might not be useless if I dig out a few memories of that time. Some may have become fantasies, but in their essence all are true.

Very early years: a double-life spanning city and countryside. Mysterious preparations for journeys between the two. A large yellow house – where we stayed in the country – with a huge yard, cellar, trees, flowers, much nicer than the dark grey stone house in the city, with its three flights up to the corridor at the end of which lay our apartment.

Oh, the country, the Lake Balaton, the summers! This was long before the chestnut-tree memories, which reconciled me to the city. Those came with my school years, games, and explorations with my sister, two years younger than I.

Then dreams, like this one: I walk a path in the forest, collecting berries. The flowers suddenly change into shiny stones, crystals, and make lovely sounds in the wind.

A beautiful lady in white – a real grown-up lady – is suddenly at my side and helps me pick the berries; but she also plucks the crystal flowers. She bends down and holds one large and beautiful crystal flower close to my face. A small lizard appears among the glass petals. She picks it up, the little animal struggles, winds itself around her hand. She laughs and says: "Oh, we know that the snakes make sounds like . . ." With the tremendous shriek that follows I wake up, rather scared, crawl into my parents' bed and tell my dream.

Other memories:

My little sister bends over a candle and her hair catches fire. I yell: "Mami, Gizi is burning!" My mother is there and with one slap of her hand extinguishes the firebrand.

Or I am sculpting a Turkish face on a tree trunk – turban, beard and all. It causes great comings and goings amongst the grown-ups. They look at it from near and far, kneel down, close one eye – to see better. Funny: they ask me questions which I don't understand. Two days later an overnight rain washes the sand figure from the tree and the event is forgotten.

The first walk alone. My mother permits me to go unaccompanied to the post office to get the mail. This is a great day. It makes my heart beat faster. I leave the house, look back at my mother who is standing at the gate of our garden, cross the railway track, look back again, walk up a little hill to the forest, look, enter the shade and the cool, and start downwards on the forest path. After a few steps I stop and look back again. There are only the trees to see, but it is comforting to turn around. I walk another hundred steps, then turn again – no mother now, no house. I am definitely on my own. The long walk downwards to the village goes on and on. Then come the white houses, the mud streets. A few corners, and there is the small, white, red-roofed post office. The mail is there, and the way homewards uphill is much shorter than the one downwards.

The walks: the hilltop with special benches to sit and enjoy the view – it was the much-loved look-out point, the highest spot of the environs, which after a long, tiring, uphill walk yielded a splendid, wide horizon of superb, hilly, woody landscape, with Lake Balaton in the centre.

"Is this the whole world?" I asked my father when I first saw the view.

"It is your world, my son," he said.

The neighbours: to the left, a lovely, big, new stone house: behind, a large hillside of grapes. Old people: the father had a very large nose which we much admired. My sister, worried perhaps by some parental admonishment, enquired: "Uncle Bató, did your nose get that large because you picked it a lot when you were little?" To Uncle Bató's credit, I must report that he nodded sadly and said: "Yes, my little girl, yes!" The children of Uncle Bató were "grown-ups", one of them a painter, whom I often watched at work, fascinated.

The packing. An almost religious ceremony, during which we children were benevolently exiled into some corner – and it lasted a week or more. Suitcases, packages, enormous hand-made

15

baskets, were filled with practically everything we possessed. Later, in the midst of my travelling life, I often wondered how a small family of six – parents, two children and two servants – could accumulate so much. The big pieces were called for by horses and carts, then the family left for the railway station in two horse-drawn carriages, the taxis of those days. The embarking into the train was a long and exciting process, involving much yelling, discussion, stormy scenes over unsuitable seats, temper about almost-lost luggage, temporarily lost children, and so on. Finally the baggage and children were all accounted for: the stationmaster blew his whistle, the locomotive blew its steam-pipe; and the train began to roll. The journey lasted three hours. Then the excitement repeated itself, enhanced by the circumstances that now it was night-time and things and children got lost more easily in the dark. Then, after another carriage ride, we were at one or the other end of the journey – in a house, anyway. To be in a house was safe – the adventure was the trip itself. Especially after nightfall. Then, with the light fading, the mystery of night sounds took hold of the imagination. Each station, where the slow train stopped, was a new miracle. A deep voice: "The eleven-thirty train is twenty minutes late"; a dog barking close by; the horses' hooves; a child crying; people whispering; trees rustling in the breeze; steps of an animal; these and a thousand more noises all atoms of a vast, wondrous silence.

This memory, much later, found its way into music, as the "mood-programme" of the fourth movement of my symphony.

The memories of our life in the city through the winter season are of a different kind. The sounds of winter were sounds of music, which was ever-present in our life. The music-making of my sister and myself started very early, with singing. We sang with passion, to our mother's piano accompaniment or without, in unison or in two parts, changing parts according to our whim. Our repertoire was large and bilingual, Hungarian and German. The music we heard was of great variety, violin and piano music played by our parents and their pupils; also chamber music, string quartets, or music for piano and stringed instruments, as taught by my father. Even glimpses of orchestral music reached us at those rare moments when we could sneak during rehearsal into the pit of the Opera House, where my father was violinist in the orchestra.

16

Those were moments of unspeakable wonder of sound, colours – and smell.

Last but not least I remember watching and loving the numerous bands in the city parks.

As I could read and write very early – I learned by pestering my parents to tell me the meaning of the letters of the alphabet and putting them together into words – my parents had me skip the two first terms of grade school, so I did not go to school before I was seven years old. However, they made me start having piano lessons when I was five.

3

I REMEMBER THE OUTBREAK OF THE FIRST WORLD WAR VERY WELL. The family was, as it was every year, in the country near Lake Balaton. What my eight-year-old brain registered was confusion, change, anxiety.

I heard: Crown Prince – Ferdinand – murder – ultimatum – mobilisation. I did not know what all these words meant, but I knew they brought menace.

People came and went, talking in groups; the tempo, the pulse of life had changed abruptly.

My father suddenly left and was absent for days, and my mother was not her old self. Then my father returned, and my mother was again as before.

One day the peasants of the village wore blue-grey suits, all alike, much different from their peasant dress, and marched in rows and sang.

The next day the young men of our circle – the painter son of our big-nosed neighbour, and many others – came around, in blue, grey or brown garb, with gold braid and other extravagant things on their collars and shoulders. Some even wore swords, which they left on the verandah as they went into the house to see our parents.

It was an irresistible compulsion to try to pull the blade out of the sheath of one of those swords. Several resisted; one finally yielded, and there I was with the naked sabre in my hand. Triumph! The embarrassment started when I couldn't push the blade back again. After a while it went in halfway, but not further, and would not come out again. I was trying and trying, pushing and pulling, red and later blue in the face, short of breath, panting – and was found in that agony by the young officers coming out from the house. I thought that I would be put to death there and then. I wasn't. But my execution, although probably horrible, bloody and painful, would not have been as humiliating by far as was the short laugh, the snap of movement with which the mishap was corrected, and the subsequent complete disregard.

The declaration of war was "drummed about" in the village. The "drumming about" or "drumming out" was the rural news-service, the equivalent of a town-crier. When something important happened, or an important order was announced, the village drummer went round, with his drum hanging over his shoulder on a belt. At every second or third corner he stopped and began a "tattoo" on his drum until he was well surrounded by listeners. Then he read the message, and went on to the next corner or square. That day he read the very words of His Majesty the King.

More marching, more men in the light blue, green, brown, red fancy dresses which, as by then I knew, were called uniforms and were worn in wars, such as the one which had just begun. It did not take long to learn that the blue-grey meant infantry, which went afoot; the brown jackets meant artillery, which did the shooting; and the blue and red meant hussars like the ones in our story books. And we knew the soldiers were fighting because the Serbs were bad people. They had shot the Crown Prince and were abominable anyway.

Some days later it was decided that the summer stay had to be cut short; we would return to the city because things were "uncertain". The great big packing exercise was performed again. Meanwhile, many messages were received, discussions held about the trip back to the city. The trains did not function on schedule, some didn't function at all, because they had to carry the soldiers. So the infantry didn't walk after all, and what about the hussars? They were the top: even the horses were loaded into the trains, and the freight-cars were not freight-cars any longer. One could read on them in big letters: "Six horses or forty men."

Finally we did travel to the city, our longest trip ever, and the most uncomfortable (so far). Instead of the usual three hours, it took us ten to arrive in Budapest, and we had to change trains several times.

But we were home. Tired and full of misgivings, but home.

School started soon, and all the children, boys and girls, had to knit, for a few hours daily, things for the soldiers, in preparation for winter. Out of the blue-grey wool strings we knitted misbegotten bonnets, socks, pulse warmers. Looking back in my mind upon those pitiful objects, I see them as the crippled heralds of a war to be lost.

19

The human cripples appeared soon enough. The first sight – less than a month after the war was "drummed out" – of blue-grey-dressed men with white bandages on their heads, eye-patches, arms in slings, on crutches or in wheel-chairs, was traumatic. The nightmarish, horrible sight was made worse by the broken, unintelligible talk of the grown-ups. Words flew back and forth: "front", "retreat", "advance", "Kaiser Wilhelm", "Russia", "Entente", "England", "France", "attack", "break-through", "wounded", "fallen". And large numbers. The figures meant nothing, but the wounded one could see. And each limping step, each bandaged face was a new shock, a new horror, unexplainable and unexplained, a nauseating reality that soon invaded my dreams and occupied them long after the war was over.

The end of the war was a special horror, not so much in a physical sense, as mentally. Not even a twelve-year-old could escape the monstrosity of a war lost – especially, perhaps, of *that* war lost, which changed the face of Europe for ever. All during the war we still continued to live in the Habsburg Empire, in which we were – to some extent anyway – safe under the great wings of the two-headed eagle. At least, a child could *feel* safe. Life went on, in spite of the shocking intrusions. We saw more and more wounded and crippled men, we had less and less to eat, but school continued, the Opera – where my father played the violin – remained open, music was made at home and everywhere else that I went. Even the death of King Franz Joseph meant a continuation rather than an end; the coronation of Karl IV was a great event and made an indelible impression. It was then that I saw, for the first and last time, the real pomp of the past, and especially the great and colourful Hungarian past, with its splendid velvet costumes, jewelry, trains and plumes.

The crowning of the King of Hungary was not the same ceremony as that of the Austrian Emperor, although it was the same head that was crowned. It took place, traditionally, in the old part of Buda, in a square called the Square of the Holy Trinity. There a small hill was formed from earth brought from all the provinces of the land. As part of the coronation ceremony the new king had to mount this hill on horseback and point with his sword to north, south, east and west to symbolise his promise to protect the country.

20

One little spectator found it rather comical that the crown was far too large for the King's head and hung, ridiculously, down to his nose. (Tragically it did prove too large for him soon afterwards.) Another amusing moment was when the young Crown Prince Otto, then four years old, who followed the King's horse in a carriage with his mother, Queen Zita, suddenly had to be taken out of the carriage and disappeared from the scene for a few minutes, to follow a call of nature that was more important and more urgent than Papa's coronation. He was brought back soon afterwards, with no dignity lost, and at least one young friend won.

The world to which all this pageantry belonged collapsed like a paper-tiger in the autumn of 1918. A new life emerged, naked and ugly, yelling and helpless like a newborn baby.

Even a child could feel the complete, blind insecurity of that birth, pitifully masked in words, slogans, senseless-looking actions.

The people I pitied most in that period and for some time after, were my teachers. I started the middle school (high school, called "gymnasium") in the autumn of 1917, and began my second year when the war was over and the series of revolutions began. I deduced there was something phoney, because my teachers, in whose wisdom I had unlimited faith, displayed complete ignorance of the things that happened, and showed the greatest difficulty not only in coping with them, but even more in explaining them in some way to us boys, who were just as bewildered but, perhaps, more curious, less defeated, than our elders.

Things by which one can recognise a lost war: packed trams with people hanging from them like clusters of grapes; packed trains; people running, everybody carrying large parcels; people being rude to each other.

Things by which to notice a revolution: people shouting; lorries cruising the streets at great speed, full of men carrying rifles; people wearing ribbons; posters appearing on the walls with gruesome pictures, incomprehensible texts and many exclamation marks; people being even more rude to each other than after a lost war.

One thing by which one can notice both a lost war and a

21

revolution is that there is less and less to eat. First one has to hand in a little piece of paper – torn off a bigger piece – in order to get some food. Queues form, several blocks long, first to get the paper, then to get the food. People replace each other in the queues in cleverly thought out systems. But no matter how clever the systems, other people shout at the clever ones, sometimes beat them up. Then there is no more food to exchange for the paper, then no more paper, and then one has to go into the country to scavenge for food. Children are good at that.

But worse still is to come.

It was difficult to understand the sudden transformation, and even more difficult, perhaps, for the grown-ups than for the young. We learned that Hungary – finally – was "independent". This was a matter of great pride, for Hungary had striven for independence since the great Renaissance days. So we tried to rejoice in that achievement. But this was no simple matter, for at the same time we heard that our country was occupied by foreign armies. This had not happened during the four years of the war; not for a single day had an enemy soldier set foot on Hungarian soil. So it was puzzling that this occupation came about just when peace had "broken out" and we had become "independent". Soon foreign soldiers gathered in the capital – the most picturesque of them were the French Zouaves – and not long after that we heard that the foreign occupation of about two-thirds of the country was to be permanent.

The embarrassment of our teachers and their desperate efforts to explain, to make the unavoidable accepted and at the same time to create a revolt against it, was heartbreaking, humiliating.

The government was all of a sudden democratic, whatever that meant. It could have meant, first of all, that from now on ordinary people would govern, "misters" like my father, instead of princes and counts.

However, the prime minister was a count – Count Michael Károlyi. How come? Oh, he is a different count! A democratic count. Hm. Tisza was a count too, and he was shot – will Károlyi be shot too? No, because he is different. He is democratic. Tisza was not. But he was brave and his death was a great loss for the country. What about Károlyi? He is a great gain for the country. He likes the people, and the French like him.

22

The only thing I was able to perceive about Károlyi was that he spoke very indistinctly. In fact, he mumbled horribly. That did not impress me favourably. My father always told me to speak up, loud and clear, not to mumble.

True, in his Cabinet there were no other titles, they were all "misters", save one: Count Albert Apponyi. I admired him greatly. That was a count to my liking, out of the history books and novels. I had to pass his house twice every day, to and from school. It was like a small castle: dark brown, somewhat forbidding, with a heavy wrought-iron fence and gate. He often came out of his house as I passed it, and then I walked carefully at the same pace as he, sometimes a few steps behind him, sometimes even at his side, a few yards away, until the next corner, where I had to make my turn. He was old, very tall, over six feet, gaunt, his profile strong and aquiline, and he had a white, squarely cut beard. His overcoats had velvet lapels, he wore a felt hat that was in between a bowler and a top hat, and yellow leather gloves.

All this, evidently, did not belong to democracy. But it was lovely to behold. Some time later it was the same Count Apponyi who signed the peace treaty at Trianon, which created the new map of Central Europe, distributing great chunks of the old Hungarian Kingdom to the new states of Czechoslovakia, Yugoslavia and Rumania, the beneficiaries of World War I.

Of these countries only Rumania sent troops into Budapest. Their appearance was brief and I never learnt what purpose it served. I have never seen soldiers marching that fast, before or since. They were practically running, and the music they marched to was like a square tarantella. Their coats were overlong and made them look very funny.

Everyone wore the red, white and green Hungarian tricolour as ribbons, buttons, cockades, whatever. My father decided that we – the men of the family – must not fall behind the others and bade me make two cockades from whatever red, white and green material I could find at home. It so happened that there was no white and green material in our house, so I made two beautiful, big buttons entirely in red. My father was as unaware as I of the political significance of these; they were just something to wear on our lapels, so we wore them proudly, the only two red buttons among the thousands of red-white-green ones, attracting many an astonished, critical and even menacing glare from beneath raised eyebrows.

When, soon after, the real "red period" came, we knew better. We did not wear those buttons any longer.

The Károlyi government did not last long, his so-called "primula revolution" quickly lost ground, and the also short-lived Communist régime of Béla Kun took over.

Our teachers again had a bad time: now they had to explain Communism to us. Strange geometrical shapes appeared on the blackboard, accompanied by strange words: a big square was "capital", an oblong parallelogram was "profit", a circle was the capitalist who swallowed all the profit, and a strange conglomeration of thin, knife-like figures in a row – not unlike a comb – was the proletariat, which had nothing but was entitled to everything. We learned that Marx wrote a book called *Das Kapital*, which was very important, and so was he. Of the latter we had no doubt, seeing his beard. Other names were floating about: Lasalle, Engels, Lenin, and many more. An entirely new set of posters appeared on the walls, with pictures not unlike the ones before, but with new texts, featuring the newest of the new words: proletarian, proletariat; a new song was sung: "Get up you prisoners of the earth, get up you hungry proletarian."

All of a sudden the word was everywhere. We had never heard it before. Now practically everyone we met was a "proletarian". Pretty soon we noticed what it was about: the poor people so far known simply as "poor people" were given this title. They were, so to say, "knighted" – they became "*proletari*". This was great. But our enthusiasm waned very fast, because it soon became apparent that the new and celebrated "*proletari*" – to which most of us more or less belonged, because most of us were poor – did not profit from their new rank. They didn't get any richer. In fact, no one did. The interesting and depressing truth was that everybody got poorer. The rich boys' fathers no longer had automobiles, but the poor boys' fathers did not acquire any either. The rich ones ate less but the poor ones did not eat more than before.

This was much discussed by us boys, while our teachers, desperate, scribbled their diagrams on the blackboard.

Thus was a generation of anti-Communists initiated.

24

This initiation was not entirely theoretical.

The Parliament building of Budapest has a broad flight of stone steps leading to its entrance from street level. These steps began to show a curious row of indentations, or shallow holes in the stone. It was soon found out that these were bullet-marks, the only reminders to be seen at daylight of the fusillades and executions that took place on these steps during the night. Many of us, grown-ups and children alike, made regular, grisly pilgrimages to those steps to look at the growing destruction of stone, the cold symbols of destroyed lives. For us young ones this was utterly beyond comprehension; we lived in the atmosphere of unexplained anguish.

During these times my father sought refuge in the Museum of Fine Arts, which was only a few minutes' walk from our home. He spent every minute of his free time there and took me along, whenever I was not in school. My music studies went along at a leisurely pace at that time; besides we never had so many school holidays as during that epoch, so I had free hours galore.

These months at the museum, with the great beauty and great silence of the paintings, drawings and sculptures, were my solace, a wonderful reassurance given to me there, a refuge of the soul, more intense, more intimate, more devout and above all, more human than any church could give. Dear, dear silent friends, who shall remain with me as long as I live!

That first Communist régime in Hungary was as short-lived as the October Revolution. It yielded to a rightist system headed by Admiral Horthy. The Admiral made his entry into Budapest on a white horse, which I thought a rather incongruous form of transportation for an officer of the Navy. But then I had to admit that he could scarcely have paraded down the main street in a battleship.

By that time the entire population was in a bad way, sadly demoralised as well as undernourished. Some of the lucky neutral countries undertook at least to help feed us, and among the many charitable actions of those nations was the invitation from Denmark to a group of Hungarian children to live with Danish families for a few months and be fed. My sister and I were amongst those children, selected at random. That voyage was to be the turning point of my life.

The family I was sent to lived in a small town, called Frederickssund. They were simple, very kind people. Their name was Jensen, the Danish equivalent of the English Johnson. Of their many children, I remember only the daughter, Karen, blonde, blue-eyed, ever smiling, with whom I had a childish flirtation, on my side with a bad conscience, because I had left home with my first great, wondering, helpless love deeply in my heart.

The Jensens were not well-to-do people and it was clear to me immediately that it was a considerable sacrifice for them to take care of an extra young person, and one with a tremendous appetite. Thus I felt very much indebted to them, and while I was absolutely unable to eat less than I did, I thought hard about what I could do to show my gratitude, which was very deep.

In their house there was an upright piano, old and battered, and indescribably out of tune. Nobody ever touched it in that family; it was probably bought at a junk yard by one of their ancestors as a piece of decorative furniture. I tried it and fled from it. But, just because that instrument was obviously outside the orbit of the Jensens, I returned to it cautiously, and examined it to see if and how it could be made workable. In their shed I got hold of a tool which I could use as a tuning-key and started out on the seemingly hopeless task. With great determination I succeeded. After about two weeks of sweat and toil I had the piano reasonably well tuned. It was now in good enough shape to be called no more than "out of tune". It never got better; the string's screws simply didn't hold. I had to tune it all the time, as one tunes a violin or a harp.

Anyway, there it was, ready at last to be played upon. So after the next evening meal I asked the family if they would like to hear some music. They said they would – very politely. I played (I was rather proficient on the piano already at that time and I knew many pieces from memory) and the effect was the most refreshing imaginable. Apparently they were very musical people who were never exposed to music; they loved it and could not have enough of it. My repertoire was, after a while, exhausted and I continued improvising far into the small hours, when finally performer and listeners stumbled into their beds.

The performance was asked for again the next evening, and a neighbour was invited in. Evening after evening I played for practically everybody in the little town; as time went on, I played in other houses as well (where there were, occasionally, better pianos), two or three times each day. Every evening, however, was reserved for the Jensens.

Later, in my life of a performing artist, I experienced exhilaration and success and many exciting evenings, but never anything like those months in Frederickssund. What we all lived through then was not an "artistic success" or an "event"; it was simply music affectionately offered, happily accepted, nothing more, nothing less. Hours of simple, wordless, complete human communication. Utopia.

I felt that my music did some good, that it was useful, that I was able to provide something valid for people. I walked upright, felt on an even standing with my hosts whose kindness, in some degree at least, I was able to reciprocate with a welcome service.

By the time I returned home, a few pounds heavier in weight from the food and richer by the decisive experience of my life, there was no need to make up my mind. I *was* a professional musician.

4

BUT WHILE I TREASURE THAT FREDERICKSSUND MEMORY, IT WAS, OF course, not the only factor which made me a musician. Very probably I would have become one even if I never had been in Denmark. My entire life has been very deeply rooted in music. Since my earliest childhood the strongest impressions and influences which pointed my way, emanated from my father and mother. Both were musicians through and through.

They are present in my life, not as transfigured phantoms, but as real, dear and faithful companions. I love them very much. When I say that they were remarkable people, I am trying to dismiss the thoughts of an admiring son and to use my old-man's brain.

My father, christened Sándor (Alexander), was a "wild" man. Very short of temper, endowed with an overdose of temperament and fantasy, he had his problems with himself.

He came from a small village, Mándok by name, in North-East Hungary, now part of Rumania. The circumstances of his family were less than modest. His father – whom I never knew – was, as far as I could gather, some sort of superior lumberjack, whose job it was to transport the freshly cut logs down the rivers as crafts. My father told me of some such trips on which he was taken in his childhood. He had a number of sisters and brothers who all died as young children in an epidemic of diphtheria. That he survived is little less than a miracle, because he was not separated from the other children during their illness. His account of his last conversation with his favourite little sister was very deeply moving – and the evident danger of infection, the complete lack of hygiene, frightening.

How it happened that in the completely unmusical atmosphere of his home – he told me his father did sing folksongs, but which father didn't in a Hungarian village? – he discovered and developed his musical talent is a mystery.

Somehow he got hold of a violin and a violin teacher to boot. The rural instruction he received was not deep. About keys and scales he was told: "In G major there is one sharp, in D major there are two, in A major three. There is also E major with four sharps but very seldom."

In spite of this he managed to be accepted at the Franz Liszt Academy for music in Budapest – the same school that I myself attended later – and from there he went as violinist to the orchestra of the then Royal Opera House, which was also, on the Viennese pattern, known as the Philharmonic and for a long time was the best and most prestigious orchestra in the land. It was his only post. He retired from it after something over thirty years' service. But his was more than the simple and modest career that it appears.

During these years he developed into an extraordinary musician and personality.

Endowed with a very keen sense of observation and an exceptional memory, he was a veritable storehouse of orchestral experience. His accounts of the conductors under whose direction he had played were masterly and unforgettable. His descriptions of the working methods, manners, virtues and weaknesses of Mahler, Balling, Richter, Weingartner, Loewe, Schuch and others gave me precious insights into the past. Others, like Schalk, Richard Strauss, Clemens Kraus, I heard myself as I grew up, and we could discuss them together. True, the discussions were rather one-sided, and whenever a difference of opinion occurred there was never any doubt as to whose would prevail – my father's mind was stocked with an inexhaustible supply of impressions which he found no difficulty in pouring out with persuasive eloquence.

All this knowledge was built upon a single base: my father's own great, but unfulfilled, talent as a conductor.

He did conduct sometimes – school orchestras and amateurs – and I heard him now and then. I thought him very competent, but only in the course of my own years as a conductor could I slowly reconstruct a picture of his talent, his undeveloped potential, and the problems he must have had as a man with his own gift, of which he was becoming increasingly aware, while being all his life on the other side of the fence.

How did he survive? Possibly by the over-abundance of his fantasy, which was so great that it could live on and remain fresh without the experience of realisation. His imagination had few limits. And what he imagined became real in his own mind, so strongly, so compellingly was it conceived. The double life he thus created for himself – *his* reality and the reality of other

29

people – was not easy to cope with. A scrupulously honest man who would never stoop to uttering even a white lie, he was baffled that certain things which existed in his own mind had, as he discovered, no "reality" in the world outside.

"His book" for instance. He was "writing" a big essay, or treatise, on orchestral conducting. In his desk a special drawer was reserved for this book, with a lot of white paper. He would go on quoting from it for hours, from memory; and I am the loving witness that the quotations were pertinent, interesting, penetrating, original, and "well written". That the pages in the drawer remained blank he chose to ignore.

Or his letters to music-critics. After his retirement from the Opera orchestra he became a most avid concertgoer. (He was altogether very active – musically, and in every other way. Life with him was complicated.) After each concert he read the reviews in the morning papers. Of course he disagreed with every one of them most violently, and immediately sat down to pen passionate replies. These letters of protest he did actually write. But he never sent them. They accumulated for years.

One morning, still fuming after having just finished such a letter, he called my sister: "Listen to this! Here is one he will never forget!"

And he read: "Sir! – This handwriting is already well known to you . . ."

That letter, like all the others, remained buried for ever in the drawers of his desk.

His memory was fabulous, and not only for music. He often amazed us, his children, with sudden bursts of incredible knowledge. Suddenly he knew everything. Slowly, very slowly, it began to dawn on me that what my father knew was not everything, but almost everything; and furthermore that his facts had one curious thing in common – a letter of the alphabet. For instance, Paragraph, Parsimony, Parthenon, Paris, Paracelsus, Paragon, Parergon, and so forth. For out of sheer interest, as we ultimately found out, he read at random from encyclopaedias. And what he once read, he never forgot.

Likewise in music, what he once learned he always remembered. As his interest did not stop at operatic and orchestral literature but embraced – very emphatically – many varieties of chamber music, his field of information was vast.

30

But more important was the penetrating originality of his approach to what he knew. For this reason his explanations of musical works, his introductions to them, given both verbally and musically on his violin, were of immeasurable value.

This I came to realise in its full extent much later, when I was able to compare his ideas with my own.

My only wish is that he had been more patient with me, but this he never was. In later years, when we met as men, he often harked back to those earlier times, when he taught me this and that. A memory he was particularly proud of was that he and I studied and played together all Beethoven's sonatas for violin and piano. I did not tell him then – having not his fanatical honesty – but I record it now, that in fact we played only about four bars of each movement of each sonata. After several repeats of these, accompanied by comments of increasing strength and vehemence, he invariably chased me from the piano as being insufficiently prepared.

My father will, I hope, forgive me for telling this tale in public. And perhaps he will find it easier to forgive if I add that it did not matter. In those four bars of shouting, singing, urging, gesticulating, cajoling, I learned enough for a lifetime. Of course I had to live with it all inside me for a bit to "assimilate it", to really learn to apply its values. But I should have had to do the same even if my father had diligently taken me through every measure of every movement – and that might have been dull. Whereas the way I was injected with his wisdom was the reverse of dull. All the same, how I wished for one movement – just one! – to be played through peacefully.

My father, enlightened conservative in his musical tastes, was steeped in the German tradition. This led to difficulties when I began my studies under Zoltán Kodály who was, with Bartók, the aggressive leader of Hungarian national music. The problem was that the tradition I grew up in continued in my parental house, while in school I was infected by the new movement. Yet my father, though he did not co-operate with the new trend, sensed its values and respected them.

I remember a family luncheon at our home, after the first performance of Bartók's *Prince Bluebeard's Castle* at the Opera House. The work was far too advanced for the general public and was received, except by an exhilarated small group, with hostility.

In Hungary every event is made the subject of jokes, stories, anecdotes which spring up from nowhere and are suddenly all around, like grains of dust that sparkle and make one sneeze. I took the liberty of repeating a disparaging quip about *Prince Bluebeard* (which I cannot quote here because it wouldn't work in English). Whereupon I was sent away from the table to finish my lunch in the kitchen, because "it is shameful to say derogatory things about anything one does not understand".

While his great problem was his terrible temper, my father's salvation was a deep-rooted, human and humane sense of humour. I know only too well the curse, and the delivery from it, for I have inherited both. "Ill-temper is nothing but lack of discipline." That is easy to say. But the short circuit in the nervous system which causes that momentary breakdown seldom comes from the flimsy equivalent of faulty wiring. Mostly it is caused by deeper shortcomings or conflicts.

My father was well aware of the limitations of a musician's life, and knew from his own experience what the small career of orchestra player and teacher offers. No doubt he wished a better life for his son and, spurred perhaps too by his own lack of proper schooling, he was adamant in insisting that I take my "Doctor's degree" before embarking on a musical career – though what kind of "Doctor" I became, he didn't mind. But while he thus made it as difficult for me as he could to become a musician, in a subconscious way he led me towards that life, and I was easily led.

Initiative, memory, a feeling for form, a sense of the combination of sound and fantasy; these, and the underlying qualities to back them up – impatience, will-power and tenacity – I have inherited from my father but in greater measure, I think, than he possessed them himself.

My fine musical ear is an inheritance from my mother, but hers was more perfect. Her auditive and manual equipment was in the category of genius, and had she had energy and fantasy as well, she could have been one of the exceptional musicians of all times. As it was, she was my wonderfully talented "Mami", very beautiful in her younger years, serene and wise in her old age, transfigured in her last years. She lived to be ninety-one.

Her family was of mixed Austrian and German blood, and some French. It was her grandfather who moved from Vienna to Hungary. He owned a brick factory in the vicinity of Budapest, a booming, important business in a country just about to be built. It was a family of considerable wealth which was lost, speculated away to the last penny, by one of my mother's uncles. My grandfather, Antal Kunwald, after whom I was named, married a very beautiful German lady, who also brought the French connection into the family. He was an employee of the Hungarian railways, but that was only his means of earning a living. His vocation was the violin, of which he was a true master. He was forbidden by his father to take up violin playing as a profession because "such things are not done in good circles", and he was weak enough to obey this paternal command. And perhaps this was for the best, because with his kind of disposition he would probably have been unable to withstand the brutality of a free and open profession. But he kept his violin playing in fine shape throughout the years, and his home was one of the centres of Budapest's musical life. It was there that Joseph Joachim played string quartets with him whenever he was in town; and the cellist of the "house-quartet" was the famous David Popper.

My mother, Margit, was the youngest of four surviving children, all of whom had interesting lives and were far above average worth. The oldest of them my uncle Caesar, became a distinguished painter of his time and circle, and the most famous of the Budapest Kunwalds.

My mother was her father's favourite child; their relationship – as I knew from her – was a rare, fine, exquisite one. She lived cocooned by love in the secure atmosphere of a well established bourgeois family in the "Kaiserlich and Königlich" Empire around the turn of the century. She had no musical schooling to speak of, which was a pity, but it was easy for her parents to be misled into thinking that she did not need tuition, for she read music and played the piano, the violin and the viola, all skilfully, without having had any lessons at all. I heard her often on all three instruments, and played chamber music with her in several instrumental combinations throughout my childhood years, so I know her playing very well. Her best instrument was the piano, which she played with a fine touch and great facility. Her piano-playing was always clean, very natural and fresh, like new grass. The string instruments she played with a rather pale but sweet tone – perhaps in submission to my father? – but most reliably.

She played anything at any speed, in any key, as desired, and executed everything neatly and effortlessly. She could play string quartets on the piano, with all the four parts correct, without ever having read the scores.

Her marriage to my father, the young, unremarkable violinist, was in some ways a step down from her sheltered life in her slightly snobbish family. She started working to augment my father's income and gave piano and violin lessons. She also collected together a group of small children and made them sing children's songs and folksongs; this was her idea of making the young aware of music. My little sister, perhaps four at that time, and I, aged six, helped to keep the choir together, singing with them lustily.

It was my mother who gave me my first piano lessons. But it soon became evident that this could not be done within the family and another teacher was found. This was an acquaintance of my parents, a lady called Paula Brown, who had just launched a new method of piano-playing. She was stern and forbidding and I hated her method, which twisted my small hands. But I only played her way when she was present. Whenever I was alone – which was often – I forgot it and stretched my fingers comfortably over the keys. I also forgot about the lessons and exercises and played whatever came to my mind. Improvisation had its dangers, too; also its moments of anguish, as when, for instance, during a very dramatic fantasy about Richard III, I was pounding away with full force for several minutes at one of the bass keys of the piano (the piece was constructed solidly upon a C minor chord in the bass) and one of the strings broke under the strain. The sound seemed apocalyptic and the piano to be wrecked for ever. The hours of waiting for my parents to come home and hear me confess to having ruined the piano with Richard III, were humiliating. To my utter amazement my father took it quite calmly, disengaging the string from the instrument and even more calmly calling the tuner to put in another one.

It was our destiny never to be roused at the same time.

My mother's musical tastes were even more conservative than my father's and she had little patience with styles and sounds unknown to her. What one could learn from her was the clear-

34

water approach to Mozart, Schubert, Haydn – and somehow, through her presence rather than through her playing, the intrinsic beauty of the sound of the string quartet.

By the time I was about thirteen years of age, we were able to play chamber music at home in various combinations. I had, by then, learned to play the 'cello at my father's behest.

"Tóni," he told me, "you should really be able to help at the chamber music lessons. Every time I engage a 'cellist colleague of mine to come round, it costs a lot of money. Couldn't you learn to play the 'cello for us?"

I said I would try, and I did. Mr. Novacek, another colleague of my father, gave me lessons, and it was astonishingly easy, at first. Within about one year I was already of use to my father, and for some years more I continued to make progress. Although I never became a good 'cellist, the experience of actually being a string player was of enormous advantage to me as a conductor.

Meanwhile, my 'cello playing was not only serving to help my family professionally, it also provided great fun, for our family string quartet began to flourish. My father played first violin; my mother, viola; I was the 'cellist. Forcibly recruited as second violin was my painter-uncle Caesar, who played rather woodenly but very reliably, with an extremely worried expression on his face. He introduced every string quartet session by an elaborate ceremony of cutting his fingernails, even if we played on successive days.

Our music library, the bulk of it inherited from my grandfather, consisted mostly of chamber-music material. In it, amongst other things, there were four fat, violet-coloured volumes, which I still have and cherish, and in which were contained the complete string quartets of Joseph Haydn. We played some of these frequently and with great enjoyment. But we always returned to the same dozen or so and one day I ventured to propose, shyly, that we play them all. We did so. It took us the best part of a year. We arranged special Haydn sessions and played three or four quartets during each, as time allowed. As there were eighty-three quartets in all, it is easy to calculate the approximate number of sessions we needed to play the complete œuvre.

(In the time of my youth there were eighty-three. Now there are seventy-seven, because it has been proved that the six quartets of Op. 2 are not by Haydn. I have to confess that we did not notice the difference; we found Op. 2 as delightful as the rest.)

35

How much that experience did for me became evident only many decades later.

The fourth member of our family, my sister, two years younger than I, also played an important part in my early musical life. It must be said straightaway that Gizi – short for Gisella – blonde, blue-eyed and very beautiful, has a very great musical talent. I don't think she started to play the piano at a younger age than I did, but she played as well or better by the time I was about nine and she seven. It was then that we started to play Beethoven symphonies with four hands. This developed into a passion, and lasted for some years – in secret. We had this private paradise of ours away from everyone, because it represented stolen time. Both of us had to do schoolwork and our piano practice, and it was these labours that we cut short in favour of our four-handed playing. Our parents were both out from morning to evening almost every day. No wonder, then, that after some time we were very proficient with our four-handed Beethoven and knew quite a few of the symphonies by heart. But the better we remembered them, the more passionately we loved them, and the more we loved them the more we played them – to the detriment of other studies.

Until one day when we forgot to watch the clock and our parents, coming home late and together, found us in the middle of the "Pastoral", oblivious of the world around us.

The scandal was much less than we feared. Our father and mother were in fact rather pleased with what they heard, regarding it, to our surprise, as something of an achievement. But the stolen hours were over. We had to go back to serious work and relegate this pleasure to the background.

The other, most important, realm that I explored with my sister was that of the so-called *Lieder*.

It is interesting that the English language has not developed a word for the German *Lied* – song obviously won't do, or it would be in use. It shows sense and perception to have retained the original word, but it also shows that the art form itself has not become rooted in the Anglo-Saxon world. Nor has it in the Gallic or Latin. Neither *chanson* nor *canzone* means or is the same as the *Lied*.

I have already mentioned before that at a very early age our mother made us sing in a group with other small children, so singing to piano accompaniment was nothing strange to us.

Soon we discovered, rummaging in our parents' library, volumes of songs by Mozart, Schubert, Schumann, Brahms, Franz, Wolf, and others, and immediately started performing them for ourselves, my sister being the singer and I the accompanist. Although both of us still had children's voices, and I could just as well have sung and she played, we never reversed this distribution of roles.

The voice of my sister was high and sweet to hear. Later she developed a beautiful adult singing voice, with a quite unique facility for coloratura, and indeed she embarked on a singing career which began promisingly, but which ended as a casualty of the tensions of the Thirties and the war in Europe. My sister lived through all that time in Hungary and Germany, undergoing great stress and hardship. She came out of it unscathed, or almost so, but the price she had to pay was the loss of her singing voice.

But in those happy times when we were children, her voice was like a little carillon, and of course she could read and sing anything from sight.

Thus began a new passion, and with it an opening up of a new music world. It is impossible to tell how many *Lieder* we played and sang; very possibly we performed every song by Mozart, Schubert, Schumann and Brahms, and continued with Wolf, Strauss and more. First, we went over and over many times everything we found in our library. Then we saved from our pocket money and bought as many other volumes, secondhand, as we could.

This activity we did not intend to hide – it seemed more legitimate to us than the four-hand piano playing (very sound musical judgment indeed), yet it was a long time before anyone heard our "song recitals". Again we were discovered by our parents accidentally. As they told us later, they came home and heard a curious noise; a peepsing voice and rather heavy piano playing which they could not make out, beyond knowing that it was emanating from their children. They stopped behind the door, unseen by us, trying to make out what was happening. Finally it dawned on them that what they heard was nothing else but the "Four Serious Songs" ("*Vier Ernste Gesänge*") by Brahms, written for bass voice and piano. No wonder they could not immediately recognise the vocal line high up in the descant. But as for my sister and I, we "heard" the music as it was composed.

Our music-making, like our physical nearness, stopped with the end of our childhood, though in mind and affection we are closer now than ever. And all in all I cannot think of that period of our lives without being deeply moved and thankful for all the riches it gave at least to one of us for an entire lifetime.

5

Naming all those who influenced my musical life would make a very long list. But of those who had great, decisive, formative influence on it, there are only three more still to talk about. Two of them were my teachers, Leo Weiner and Zoltán Kodály.

Weiner was my teacher twice. First he taught me harmony, privately, before my years in the Academy, and later, at the Academy, chamber music.

He was a musician's musician if ever there was one. And a musician-maker *par excellence*. A bachelor and a loner, with only music in his heart and mind, he was to be seen daily, taking the fifteen-minute walk from his flat to the Academy, thence to the Artists' Club and back home. He had a somewhat shuffling gait, always leaned slightly forward, was short, and a bit stoutish. He had a curved nose, a protruding lower lip, and sharp eyes, which looked nowhere.

In his youth he was very successful with his compositions, winning prize after prize, but already in his forties became an honoured but neglected monument of just one short period in the fast-moving, telescoped history of the new Hungarian music. He was called the Hungarian Bizet, not without some reason, for his music does have the same exquisite, delicate craftsmanship as Bizet's. Had they been contemporaries, their international importance might have been comparable. Alas, Weiner was born about three-quarters of a century too late for his creative gifts to flourish as they deserved. His real importance was in another field, that of education.

It is difficult to describe what he taught and impossible to convey how he taught it. Only in his younger years did he teach counterpoint or harmony (he taught it to me for one year). Later he only taught chamber music, which was a compulsory subject for every instrumental student at the Academy. But his classes were always filled, and not only with his own pupils but with spectators, guests, students of composition, theory, singing, musicology, ecclesiastic music, and even non-musicians.

39

What he did was what every chamber-music teacher does: he took a chamber-music work, had it played by a group, and showed them how to perform it. That was all at first glance: but through and with this he was teaching infinitely more. All instrumentalists could learn in the course of his lessons the innermost secrets of their instrument. Groups could discover what the interplay of instruments means, what "ensemble" means. Composers could learn how to write really well for each instrument or combination of instruments, how to conceive and realise performable, living music. Singers could learn how to breathe. In short, everybody learned from him – but what? "Taste", "quality", how to demand the utmost from oneself, and almost as much from others, in the supreme service of music.

The beauty of his teaching was above all the utter simplicity of his aim as well as his methods. His explanations were short and to the point. He preferred to show us rather than to tell us how to do it.

But how show us?

He did not play any instrument. He poked around on the piano helplessly. A violin, a 'cello, he could not even hold. And with this arsenal of physical inability he confronted us, the pupils of advanced classes of the Academy where everyone aimed to be a wizard on his or her instrument and was a little wizard already.

This is not hearsay; I was there. I know how proficient we were. I was one of the weakest pianists, and I was pretty good then. And I know, too, how much we learned from him and how easily he transformed us. We were so many pieces of blotting paper absorbing him, through his few words and silly-looking demonstrations.

When he pushed away the brilliant young pianist from her seat and showed her, with not a single right note in it, a passage which she had just played "perfectly" but not to his taste – she understood. To violinists he demonstrated the Kreutzer Sonata with two pencils, one held under his chin as violin, the other in his right hand as bow. After such a showing the phrase came from the real violins played with real bows like a being newly born.

One of his many revolutionary ideas was that a French horn can produce a soft sound. I do not know what the standard of horn-playing was in the early Twenties outside Hungary (from what I read in Richard Strauss's writings, I must assume that it was not very different), but I heard the first soft sound of a horn after about two years of Leo Weiner's stubborn insistence, pursued in the face of a general outcry in which even professors of the instrument itself joined.

He was not given to flattery. The highest praise we ever heard from him – and very rarely – was: "You will be a good musician one day." Those upon whom this verbal medal was bestowed could not be spoken to for weeks.

There are no two ways about it, he transformed the taste and prowess of an entire music generation in Hungary.

It is difficult to conceive how this small, funny man could bring about such a change. For he was really a type belonging in a cartoon-series, or a book of funny stories.

We heard for instance – and it is absolutely believable – that when the Nazi occupation of Hungary was imminent, during the Second World War, Weiner, who was Jewish, was urged by his friends to leave the country. All was prepared for him, including a position in a music school in England. But he refused to go.

His reason: "When I go to my usual restaurant here and tell George to bring me a cutlet, he knows exactly what I want, and I know exactly what I am going to get. Who would do that for me in England?"

He stayed, had a nightmarish time, and barely survived. But at least he knew what sort of cutlet he would get, if the day ever came when he could order one again.

He was well over sixty when all that happened. His fiftieth birthday – still in the "good old times" before 1939 – was to be celebrated in great style. This was decided by his many friends, who caused him no little chagrin with their plans for a gala dinner to be given in his honour by a very prominent family – one of "the 400" – in its stately old mansion. More than one hundred guests were invited, and all the pomp and circumstance of the great feudal past was displayed. Liveried footmen, splendid butlers, maîtres d'hôtel, the finest silver, cutlery and precious china, gorgeous, opulent food, the best wines, not to speak of the extravagant elegance of the guests as it was only to be seen in those "faux Paris" of Eastern Europe.

Leo Weiner sat at the right of the dowager hostess. No sooner had he made himself comfortable in his chair than he lifted his spoon and gave it a vigorous cleaning with his white damask

41

napkin, as he was accustomed to do in the none-too-clean bistros he frequented.

The hostess paled, gave a grave look at the maître d'hôtel, who in turn gave a stern look at the head waiter, who in turn gave an annihilating look at the under waiter, who in turn snarled at the footman, who bustled up with another spoon.

As soon as he saw the new spoon, Professor Leo picked it up and started cleaning it with his napkin.

From hostess to footman, the same scene was repeated, with more urgency than before.

When the cleaning of the third spoon started, the same pantomime achieved hysterical dimensions.

As the fourth spoon arrived, Leo turned to the footman, and addressed him sunnily: "What do you think, my boy, shall I clean your whole bloody set of silver?"

Funny, serious, forgotten, remembered Leo Weiner: none of us Hungarian musicians, born within the first two decades of this century, would have become what we were and are without you.

The next direct providential influence upon my musicianship came from a giant: Zoltán Kodály.

He was my teacher at the Academy.

And not by accident.

I chose him.

When I went to him to become his pupil, Kodály was already a living legend in Hungary. Contrary to the false impression that somehow got round about him, he was not a hermit type. He was seen everywhere, always busy with something or other, preoccupied, immersed in his thoughts. Not only musicians but the people in the street knew his rather exotic figure well.

If I were to paint a word-portrait of my teacher, I should start it with the cry of the street-urchins:

"Christ on skates!" they yelled, as they beheld the serious, bearded man in breeches, carefully and slowly cutting figures on the ice during the severe Budapest winters.

Kodály loved skating and spent at least one hour a day at the rink during the season. He loved hiking, too, and he was a great swimmer. It was he who later proposed to make swimming an obligatory course for all pupils of the Academy of Music. *"Mens sana in corpore sano."*

When I first went to see him, after having enrolled in his class, he was a young man of thirty-eight. But I was fourteen and very much afraid of him. Our first meeting was not promising. The master was austere. No smile came from behind the reddish beard. No encouraging word was spoken. A few halting, murmured instructions, giving the time and place of the class – that was all.

At that time the Academy, founded by and named after Franz Liszt, was experimenting with a new system: one teacher took one composition class and kept it through the full four years of the course, teaching all subjects of the curriculum. The class which included me was the first to be taught in this manner. And so our group of young people was closeted with Zoltán Kodály for four years in three to six hour-long sessions four days a week. We and our master knew each other very well by the end. Or rather, he knew his pupils. The pupils knew as much about him as they could make out. He was not readily self-revealing and gave no help to others in making personal contact with him. Throughout the four years he spoke very little. The uncomfortable feeling of awe, rather depressing at the start, soon vanished, however. The pupils felt free and easy. Yet the distance remained until the last day of the course.

I was by far the youngest, the Benjamin of the group. The others – we were fifteen altogether, all men – were much older. Anywhere from eighteen to twenty-eight or thirty. For a boy who still spoke with a child's voice, it was quite strange to sit next to a classmate who calmly announced the birth of his second child one morning. This kind of thing on our side of the benches and the great red beard on the other was rather a lot to take at the start.

My being accepted into this class at my age was due to the ruling custom of the school at that time. There was no age limitation for attending classes. Anyone who could pass the stiff pre-examination musically was accepted. But in order to receive a diploma, one had to produce a certificate called "Matura", which was given after the obligatory and very severe exams at the end of the year corresponding to one's last year in an English school's sixth form or one's senior year in American high school. I passed the musical tests without difficulty. There were no others to determine that I was a rather childish fourteen-year-old. This put me under a considerable strain for the best part of two years.

43

There was nothing I could not do that was required of me. But there was little I really understood, at the time, of what I was doing.

I can say that I was Kodály's disciple twice: first when he taught me and the second time when I understood what I had learned.

There were other difficulties. My home was a deeply musical one, but very conservative, and steeped in the German school. And Kodály was then the revolutionary and keenly nationalistic leader of the new Hungarian music. So who was correct? My father – an excellent musician in his own right – or my teacher?

The picture I have so far presented is decidedly negative: an austere, outwardly uncommunicative teacher; a boy bewildered and too young for his class; a Montague-Capulet situation between teacher and parents.

It is to the everlasting credit of Kodály that out of this situation resulted the undisturbed progress of the pupil, with enough storage of information to last the better part of a lifetime; a steadfast friendship between teacher and pupil which lasted until the end of the teacher's life and, as far as the pupil is concerned, still continues; and, finally, a gradually achieved and necessary freedom from parental influence, without any ill-effects.

How did Kodály do this?

No method comes to mind. He did not push, did not bully, always spoke very little, very matter-of-factly, and always very softly. He was strict, but one expected that from him. In fact, his pupils wanted him to be strict. He planted this wish into them. He influenced his pupils greatly, but not directly, either by action or word.

His learning was profound, his talent very great, his general education, the wealth of his information, staggering. Yet his greatest quality as a teacher was, perhaps, his presence. A gift very rare in men. It is mostly women who reach their fullest achievement not through what they *do*, but through what they *are*. Kodály possessed this gift. It was a strong, radiating force which is felt, I am sure, even now, after his death.

The class was a good one, hard-working, talented, enthusiastic. The nationalistic tendency caught on very soon. Only in a few cases – as in mine – did it meet obstacles created by other traditions. But it reached everyone sooner or later. This new "Hungarianism", however, did not lower the academic level. Neither did the use, not merely tolerated but indeed gently encouraged, of contemporary musical language. Oscar Wilde said that the only trouble with innovations is that they become old-fashioned so quickly. Thus it happened with the advanced school of 1920-24 and has continued to happen to other schools since. But one thing is true: no matter how new and revolutionary that musical language was for its time, it was a *musical* language and was well and firmly rooted in the music we knew as music and in its nature. Then it may have seemed revolutionary music. Now we know that the process was evolution, not revolution.

Kodály gave us other values as well. A thorough knowledge of the craft of music writing. I have said before that he taught everything: harmony, form, counterpoint, orchestration, aesthetics. And it can be added that whatever his pupils wrote, be it jazz, pop music, symphonic music, none of them wrote, ever, a sloppy bar.

The pupils dispersed far and wide after their school years ended. Most of them kept in contact with their master. Not all became composers, although it was composing that Kodály taught. The knowledge of composition is the basis of all musical learning. It is mandatory in any branch of musical activity. According to their special inclinations, the members of the class took up a variety of musical professions. They achieved various degrees of success. Not one of the 1920-24 class was a failure, as far as I know.

The classes were not without humour, either. In his dry way, Kodály could be quite funny. One day I appeared in class with my arm in plaster.

"What happened to you?"

"I broke my arm."

"How?"

"I fell from a horse."

"Why did you get on it?"

I got irritated: "Professor, I cannot just sit all the time!"

"What else do you do on a horse?"

When composing for the human voice, we were instructed to pay the utmost attention to the nature of the voice we wrote for. Once I was particularly proud of having found a melody which I thought good for several kinds of voices. I wrote a note on my paper: "This piece is equally singable by high or low voice." When Kodály returned the paper the next day, I found a note written by him under mine: "That means: by neither."

Once a classmate of mine noticed that the Professor was looking at a piece of music just handed to him. It was upside-down. Respectfully he called attention to this unfortunate circumstance. Kodály did not move, but continued looking at the paper. At long last he said: "A good composition is good in every direction."

He criticised sharply but never discouragingly. Under his influence it was the criticism of the pupils themselves that grew more severe than his.

He had no easy time either with the more old-fashioned senior teachers around him. He was under constant pressure to be more conservative. To this his answer was: "I cannot teach yesterday."

For his pupils he stood up bravely, when he felt he should – in school and afterwards. In a difficult moment of my life, many years after I had left school, I received an unsolicited letter from Kodály, a very simple message, designed to give me courage. Mine grew a hundredfold from that friendly gesture, which I shall never forget.

When the last moment of the four-year course arrived, we pupils stood around his desk, waiting for him to sign our certificates. His pen gave out. We offered him our pens. I presented mine also – a great exception, for it was a very precious fountain pen which I had inherited from my grandfather. I had never before let anyone else use that pen. Holding it out for him, one pen amongst many, I thought: "If he takes it, we will be friends for life."

He took it.

My school time ended in 1924, and was immediately followed by my official entry into the musical profession, through my engagement as a coach at the Opera House.

During the four years I spent there the unparalleled triumph of the Hungarian musical theatre was achieved by Kodály's *Háry János*. He had already started writing it during my last year in class, and I was involved with it in many ways: as coach, as conductor of backstage music and choir, as proof-reader of orchestra parts and part-author of the hastily produced vocal score. This function as Jack-of-all-trades to Kodály brought a new dimension to our relationship.

After 1929, when I left Hungary, we met less frequently – although our contact continued until forcibly interrupted by the outbreak of the Second World War.

After the war our friendship was reasserted with increasing

warmth. We met in London, in the USA – where I invited him to conduct his works with my orchestra – in Salzburg, and, of course, in Budapest, during my infrequent visits to my home town.

The first of our postwar meetings took place at his hotel room in London's Gloucester Place. After the first emotional moments and some general conversation he enquired, did I still write music?

"Not still – again," I said.

"Show me something."

I had with me only the score of a Missa Brevis, which I had just completed for choir and percussive instruments.

A voice-man first and foremost, he was interested, and bade me bring it along next time. His study of the score was slow and meticulous, while I sat by in silence.

"Quite Byzantine," he mumbled at one point.

After he had finished, he put down the manuscript and said: "Thank God that you have found it expedient to use an E major chord for the word *pacem*!"

It was his way of showing approval. But the remark made me think.

Kodály, once the great revolutionary, had now become the conservative, who was glad to find one consonant chord in the writing of his formerly too conservative pupil.

Tempora mutantur
Et nos mutamur in illis.

Some years later, for Kodály's eightieth birthday, I planned a present from all his pupils – that is, from all his pupils who were active composers – a set of variations of a theme composed by himself. There are still many of us, five living outside Hungary, the rest (far more numerous) within. I contacted those whom I knew in the Western world and wrote to the Composers' Union in Hungary to invite everyone's co-operation. Only my four expatriate colleagues replied. They were Géza Frid from Amsterdam, Ödön Pártos from Tel Aviv, Tibor Serly from New York and Sándor Veress from Berne. We waited a long time for a reply from Hungary, but none came. The date of the birthday drew dangerously near, and we decided to go it alone. Accordingly, we wrote the "Variations on a Theme by Zoltán Kodály" which was finished in time and performed and broadcast first on December

47

1st, 1962 in Holland, under the direction of Jean Fournet. I conducted it two weeks later, on Kodály's birthday, in Israel.

No sooner had we completed the piece than our Hungarian colleagues replied. Yes, they would like to participate in the project. I answered sadly that it was too late, but proposed that another work of the same kind, with many more and much shorter variations, should be written. This was done. Twenty-three old pupils of Kodály participated in a piece called "Kodály Köszöntő" (best translated as "Toast to Kodály").

He was in astonishing form throughout all his later years, and his death shortly before his eighty-fifth birthday shocked all who knew him. More than that: one could not help, in a way, feeling angry with him – angry and cheated. For the first time, it seemed, he had been unfair to us. It was not a peaceful feeling of grief, but one of revolt, a refusal to accept the condition of mortality. It was, I thought later, the last thing he had taught us.

Looking back upon his person, his life, his achievements, it seems to me that of his compositions his many unaccompanied choruses are the most important, and amongst his other activities the pedagogic theories of his later years, notably the development of his educational system for young children.

The greatest teaching he imparted to us who were fortunate enough to be under his immediate care was to demand of ourselves total dedication. He put it very simply, in a phrase all his own: "Each must bring his brick to the building".

To my teacher's phrase I would add now, after half a century: "And let us not worry about the place where the brick is fitted into the wall."

The brick that is never seen is also essential to the building that it is helping to uphold.

Another paraphrase of this thought would be: "All flames are alike. The size of the fire depends upon what is burning."

6

THE NEXT MAN WHO HAD A DECISIVE INFLUENCE ON MY MUSICAL life – more indirectly than directly – was a beacon blazing to the sky. He is Béla Bartók. I did not include him among my teachers, although I learned a great deal through him – as much as I was capable of learning – for he never taught me at school, never gave me marks.

But he was present, in essence, throughout my life.

At first he was only a name, a name which I heard from my early childhood. A formidable name, which caused heated discussions between the grown-ups. A name that stood in the air, like a thunderstorm about to break, holding back nature's pulse for an instant. With pride I listened to my father as he defended it.

Then the name became music: a set of piano pieces which I was given to play, small easy studies, called "For Children". I was then six years of age, the pieces only four. They were very different from any music I had heard so far, yet, unlike the name of their composer, far from formidable. To my amazement and pleasure, I could master them – it was quite courageous of my teacher to assign them to me – and soon I knew fifteen or twenty out of the set of twenty-eight and would play them with great delight to anyone who was willing to listen.

Then came the man. One day I went to a concert with my father. On the steps of the concert hall he said to a passer-by: "Good day, Professor Bartók."

My heart missed a beat.

"Is this your son?"

"Yes. Tóni, say 'good day' to Professor Bartók."

I did so, bowed, mumbled, and took the Professor's outstretched hand.

"Is he a musical boy?"

"Yes, he is."

"Does he play the violin like you?"

"No, he studies the piano."

"Does he do well?"

49

"Rather. He plays your pieces too!"

"Hm. He must play for me some time."

"Certainly. Goodbye, Professor."

"Goodbye."

And there I was, with ears as red as traffic signals, flustered, mixed up.

Bartók was rather small, smaller than my father; very thin, pale, white-haired. (This is no mistake. Bartók had then, at thirty-four, white-grey hair.) He had thin lips, barely moving for a timid smile, and barely parting to allow softly-spoken words to be heard; a fine, straight nose; and eyes! – there never was such a pair of eyes! Large, burning, piercing – his looks had something of a branding iron – they seemed to mark everybody on whom they fixed.

From then on I began seeing him, from time to time, in the street, in a concert hall, greeting him when we passed with a bow, which he returned with a nod.

I never played his pieces for him, and he never spoke to me until much later, when I was enrolled in the Academy. There he did not teach me. He had a piano class but never taught composition and gave no explanation for his refusal. Recently I heard that he once told a younger composer, Sándor Veress, that he regarded composition, basically, as an instinctive function, guided by subconscious forces, and was afraid of damaging those sources by dragging them to the surface in the course of teaching.

There is no reason to doubt the truth of that statement. It would fit in well with the next-best guess, namely that he was no teacher at all, had no real innate gift or desire for teaching and only taught as much as he was obliged to do to make a living. From this point of view it was natural – and very honest – to choose to teach piano-playing. He was already recognised without dispute as a superb pianist, and he could concentrate on the problems of the instrument, without involving his own music. In fact he seldom gave instruction on his own piano music, and never "officially", in class.

He took his piano-teaching very seriously and made many first-rate educational editions of works by Bach, sonatas by Beethoven, and so on.

His rooms were just across the corridor from those of my teacher. His physical nearness was much felt, even through walls. At Academy concerts, examinations and other school occasions I

50

often heard the high, somewhat rasping voice; sometimes even in short conversations with me.

By that time I had heard more of his music. The first performance of his Second String Quartet, which I attended, was a cataclysmic experience. Awed as I was by it, I understood nothing of it at all. I was surprised that it ended in a very slow, sad movement and the giant middle movement, a scherzo, of demonic power, mowed me down like a hurricane.

This, like much other "adventurous" chamber music, I heard performed by the locally very famous and excellent Waldbauer Quartet. Imre Waldbauer, son of a friend of my grandfather, was a fine violinist and dedicated chamber-music player. He won everlasting merit by supplying the music-lovers of our city with the best and most important new, contemporary chamber music, as well as a steady diet of the classical and romantic quartet literature, for several decades. It was from this ensemble that I heard for the first time the string quartets of Debussy and Ravel, both quartets by Kodály, five string quartets by Bartók (the sixth I first heard in America played by the Kolisch Quartet), the quartets by Schönberg, Alban Berg, the string trios by Dohnányi and Kodály, the duos by Ravel and Kodály, the violin-piano sonatas by Bartók and many more.

The figure of Bartók was much discussed throughout his lifetime. From his very early years he had a small group of ardent followers, but the large audiences remained closed, even hostile, to his music until the last years, perhaps months, of his life. It was heartbreaking to be witness to his happiness – he was already very ill – a happiness caused not only by the superlative performances he heard then of his works, but also by their spontaneous acclamation by a public suddenly awakened to the sounds, the force, of his music. True, his music had developed clarity and superiority by then which made its digestion by a greater multitude easier than that of his earlier works. This was not, as some critical voices announced, the start of senility, nor a conscious "playing down" to the masses – this Bartók could not even have conceived. After his death Kodály compared the life and work of his friend to the path of an arrow – a moving and true comparison.

By the time I lived across the corridor from him he had turned an important corner of his career: his only opera, *Prince Bluebeard's*

51

Castle, had been performed at the Opera House seven years after it was written. Interestingly enough, there was no Hungarian ready to conduct it. An Italian conductor, Egisto Tango, who was then regularly engaged at the Budapest Opera, became one of the first of Bartók's champions, by performing not only his opera, but also the first of his choreographic pieces (one cannot correctly call them ballets), *The Wooden Prince*. The home town première of his third stage work, *The Miraculous Mandarin*, did not take place until many years later, after much to-ing and fro-ing and many adventures.

At the time of the first *Bluebeard* performance (1918), my father thought I was too young to see it, that it would be too heavy for me. Perhaps he would have permitted me to hear it, had I confided my own first creative stammerings earlier.

But the waves of the event did not pass by me unnoticed. It was a mixed success. It provoked great enthusiasm and complete rejection, furious debates, deep divisions. The opera was kept in repertoire for some time (it was still performed in the early 1920s), but later it was inevitably dropped, not to reappear for good for another decade or so.

The piece, in one act, lasting barely an hour, was strong medicine at the time of its writing. One of the first modern psychological operas, it cuts deeply into the inner structure of man-woman relations, carefully searching the depths where their worlds meet and separate, where man and woman in their quest for each other hurt and get hurt and are in guilt towards each other. Béla Balázs's hauntingly beautiful text is raised to superhuman dimensions by Bartók's masterly, strong, poetic setting. It is not his most "perfect" work, but for many of us it is his most deeply inspired.

The Wooden Prince, a charming folktale, very difficult to realise satisfactorily on the stage, was – and is – a moderate but constant success. Its charming peasant style evokes the lyric fantasy of children's stories.

The problem of Bartók's third stage work, *The Miraculous Mandarin*, was its libretto. Menyhért Lengyel, a very successful playwright (his *Typhoon* was performed everywhere with gusto; his Hollywood film *Ninotchka* was also world famous), produced another of his eroto-philosophic pieces expounding the male point of view. Its message was similar to that of Wilde's *Salome*: "the mystery of love is stronger than the mystery of death".

In *Salome* this sentence is pronounced by the heroine of the play

52

as she achieves orgasm while contemplating and caressing the severed head of John the Baptist. The Lengyel-Bartók work demonstrates, without words, that a man – the "miraculous" mandarin – cannot die, no matter how often and in how many ways people try to kill him, before achieving the same fulfilment with the woman of his desire.

While in today's theatre this would be a mild, even old-fashioned, proposition, in the early Twenties it caused riots wherever the piece was performed, which occasions were few, because at most theatres it was prohibited.

In Budapest there was no thought of a performance until 1926, when the young director Miklós Radnai summoned up enough courage to propose it to his superior authority, the Ministry of Education.

At this stage, for an instant, destiny linked my own life with the vicissitudes of Bartók's *Mandarin* and brought me into a closer relationship with the composer. The opera director asked me to play the *Mandarin* music for the committee of "experts" on two pianos with Bartók himself.

It is impossible to convey how momentous this occasion was for me and how much I cherished that assignment. I practised with Professor Bartók for two or three days, and I think we gave about as impressive a performance as it was possible to give of a piece so completely orchestrally conceived.

The committee seemed very impressed. But the performance did not come to pass. The government refused its permission on "moral grounds".

Apart from "morals", the work was a great problem for the choreographer-producer. I saw and heard several performances in later years, and while many were excellent musically, all I have seen were scenically unsatisfactory, except those with the *mise-en-scène* of Aurel Miloss. It was one of those rare occasions when there was enough rehearsal time, a fine cast, a superb producer, and a splendid result.

By chance the librettist, M. Lengyel, was present – a very old man at that time. After the performance he scrambled backstage, hoping to get a curtain call as co-author. Nobody knew him, however. Nobody understood what that old man wanted on the stage, why he was getting under everyone's feet. He was about to be rudely thrown out, when I passed by and recognised him. (I

53

happened to be the conductor of the evening. It was in Florence in the early 1960s.) I was very touched to see him, ugly old soul that he was. He had had a rough time in his last few years and I understood only too well his craving for one more bow, perhaps the last in his life. I tried to explain the situation to the stage manager, but he vetoed the curtain call. No one, he said, would know who this "mandarin great-grandfather" was. The argument went on and on but the applause did not, so the debate became pointless.

Another early contact with Bartók was through folklore. It is well known that he and Kodály brought the giant task of collecting, analysing and cataloguing Hungarian folksongs to fulfilment. The movement itself had started much earlier, but they introduced system into hitherto sporadic efforts and brought the great labour of love to fruition.

Behind that gigantic undertaking was their belief that the roots of the musical arts are in the music of the people, that is, the peasantry of each country. The beautiful simile of a tree suggests itself, which is universal through its fruits, through its shade, through the rest and nourishment which it gives to all who want them, but which, in its roots and trunk, in the life-giving juices it sucks in, is inseparably bound to the soil, to the spot where it grows.

The connection between folklore and learned music should be natural and continuous as it was in Italy, France, Germany and many other countries until fairly recent times, when the creative musical force of these peoples became extinct. There are no more new folksongs surfacing in Western Europe.

In the Carpathian region – where today's Hungary and most of its neighbouring countries are located – indigenous musical development was severely interrupted by the Tartar invasions, a long occupation by the Turks and an even longer rule by the Germans.

While folk-art pursued its own course, sometimes openly, sometimes underground, learned art was imposed by those who occupied and dominated these territories. The strongest of those influences in Hungary were German, and they were not always willingly accepted.

Those who became aware of the existence and vitality of

Hungarian folklore were automatically also political "rebels". Bartók's early years were his very active "down with the Habsburgs" period, as can be seen in his letters, in his articles for periodicals, and also in his music. In his early "Kossuth" Symphony the musical themes associated with the hero and other Hungarian melodies are contrasted with a caricature-version of the Austrian hymn "*Gott erhalte . . .*", which Haydn composed in pure delight and enthusiasm and which in this piece is cruelly and jubilantly annihilated.

In Hungary the folk-music situation was especially complicated by a thin surface layer of gipsy music, which, in fact, is embellished and instrumentally adapted peasant material, though it was for some time regarded, even by musicians of the stature of Franz Liszt, as the original music of the Hungarian people.

Once the folk music of Hungary had been "excavated", upon those very old and very primitive bases, a brand-new "modern" music sprung up, perhaps the most forward-looking of its time at the beginning of the 1900s.

Its international importance was due to the emergence of those Hungarian giants, Bartók and Kodály, who were without parallel elsewhere.

Their presence at that place and at that moment was an incredible coincidence, unique in musical history. It also made life very difficult for the next generations of creative musicians, many of them very gifted, but none of them of the stature of the two "grand old men". They tend to react by leaving the folklore basis and conforming to the international trends of serialism, post-serialism and other devices, often regrettably.

It is interesting to note that while Bartók's music became widely known and welcomed, he himself as a man and musician was never understood, and probably still isn't. Even Stravinsky, whose own background might have led him to appreciate Bartók's mentality, has misunderstood him, belittled his connection with folklore, and condescendingly writes of his "profound religiosity". The shoe was on the other foot: Bartók was an avowed atheist, and it was Stravinsky who was religious, fervently, to his bones. Stravinsky's early compositions were also deeply connected with folk music. He then abandoned it to embrace neo-classic and subsequently serial styles of writing. Bartók had only one arrow to shoot, and only one target. He hit it dead centre.

The collecting and cataloguing of Hungarian folklore was no small undertaking. The gathered material alone was staggering – well over 10,000 melodies. These were partly written down by collectors, partly preserved on cylindrical wax-tubes, the early, primitive method of recording. Bartók, Kodály and their friends first put these on paper, then prepared the material for musicological study by cataloguing it according to the system of Ilmari Krohn, the Finnish scientist.

During my school years that task was not fully completed and Kodály organised a working seminar, in the course of which his composition pupils could, if they wished, give some help. Participation in the seminar was voluntary, but all of us joined in eagerly, although it nearly doubled our hours at the Academy. (My own life was already heavily burdened as I had to pursue my piano studies, go to high school like all other boys of my age, help my father in his chamber-music classes and give – from my sixteenth year onwards – piano lessons to small children in order to earn some money.) Bartók also participated in the seminar, irregularly but quite frequently, and the presence of the "great duo" gave us students a wonderful stimulus.

Later I was to wonder just how necessary it was for the good of our own, new, music, and for that of our two masters, who could have spent their time more creatively, to catalogue and analyse such enormous quantities of material. But it was done through the perfectionism of the "two great ones" – and there it stands, a unique and monolithic example of diligence.

Bartók himself pursued his single-minded creative life. When I left Hungary, our contact was very slight for some years, until we met again in New York.

It is hard to imagine that Bartók, the most Hungarian Hungarian there ever was, could bring himself to leave his country for ever. This step cost him much; indeed it was a sort of suicide. I am convinced that his life was shortened by leaving his homeland and that he knew this and reckoned with it.

Why did he go?

It is simple: he valued individual human freedom above everything else.

He fled specifically from the increasing right-wing pressure but, essentially, he stood against tyranny of any kind. He left orders that no street was to be named after him in Hungary if there was a "Hitler Street" or one named after any other prominent Nazi. It was beyond the range of his imagination that there could ever be a "Stalin Street" in Hungary or he would, no doubt, have altered his message to meet that contingency as well.

His life in America was difficult. So was his life in Hungary, but the foreign atmosphere made it nearly insupportable to him.

He lived and died in poverty. His American poverty was not greater than what he knew at home, but more painful to bear, because it was poverty in a strange country. "How could we sing in a strange land?" asks King David's psalm. Bartók did sing; indeed, masterpieces came from his pen in that strange land. Only he knew how much suffering these cost him.

It is easy to accuse the world of neglecting him, but he was nearly impossible to help. University positions were offered to him which he refused to accept; there was practically no way of getting near him with any sort of helpful action. His pride – and stubbornness – surrounded him like a stone wall.

Yet he was a very "human" man, who enjoyed a quiet laugh, a little gossip, and sometimes, but not often, a drink. Once he not only surprised but scared me by drinking two Bloody Marys in quick succession in my flat. He was already unwell at that time. His long, progressive illness weakened him gradually. His eyes grew more and more enormous.

In one way his last American years brought him the greatest joy of his life: recognition of his music.

His attitude towards performances and performers of his works was appreciative, but demanding. "I imagined it a little quicker", he would say, very modestly, but he would go on saying it until he got what he wanted.

I was present when Menuhin, who had commissioned from Bartók his Solo Sonata for Violin, played it for him before its public première (which was a great and spontaneous success). It is a fiendishly difficult work, and Bartók, knowing this, accommodated Menuhin's requests for minor changes wherever he could – but was quite firm in refusing them when he felt the need.

He was, subsequently, very moved by Menuhin's incomparable performance.

His comment was (aside, in Hungarian): "Well, if all composers could hear such performances of their music . . ."

A time when helping him was possible was at the commissioning of his Concerto for Orchestra. The idea for this really came from Joseph Szigeti, who also was instrumental in arranging for Benny Goodman to commission Bartók to write his Contrasts for Piano, Violin and Clarinet. As I heard the story, Szigeti, meeting Serge Koussevitsky by chance in New York, told him that Bartók was ill in hospital and that something should be done for him. It is to the great credit of Koussevitsky that he acted immediately, and all the more so as he felt no great personal affinity either for Bartók or his music. He went to visit Bartók right away.

The meeting of the elegant man of the world and the emaciated, giant-eyed Bartók in his hospital bed must have been an extraordinary sight. Koussevitsky made his gesture at the outset of their conversation, offering the composer a commission for an orchestral work of his choosing.

"But look at me, Mr. Koussevitsky, I am hardly myself any longer – how could I write a new piece for you in this condition?"

"Never mind, Mr. Bartók," said Koussevitsky in his famous Russian-English. "You write piece when you feeling better!"

Bartók, with a sigh, said that he would gladly do so.

"It is all settled, then," said Koussevitsky, and took out his bank-book to write a cheque for the fee.

"Oh no," Bartók raised a pale, skinny hand, "you can pay me only after I have completed the piece."

Whereupon Koussevitsky, with a quick look at Bartók and an even quicker flash of thought, answered: "I am sorry, Mr. Bartók, conditions commission oblige write cheque for half commission fee when commission is made."

Bartók had no rejoinder to this. He asked for music paper and pencil to be brought to the hospital, and wrote his Concerto for Orchestra in an incredibly short time. Working on it did him so much good that when it was completed he was able to leave hospital. That commission meant much more to him than the unexpected material help.

Just when the Concerto was completed – the ink was possibly still wet on the last page – Bartók and his publisher, Heinsheimer, then with Boosey and Hawkes, asked me to meet them. They showed me the new score and said that they both thought this piece would make a good ballet. I understood immediately that this was a brainchild of Heinsheimer, and I was there because of my connections in ballet circles (I was conductor for two ballet companies in my time). Obviously the publisher hoped that I would arrange for a ballet company to buy the rights of the piece and thus give Bartók some extra income.

I was not optimistic, and knew by experience that the ways of the ballet world are inscrutable. As it turned out, however, Heinsheimer's plan met with no obstacles.

The American Ballet Theatre bought an option for the staging of the work and, who knows, a choreographic masterpiece might have resulted, for the choreographer who wanted to produce it was none other than Anthony Tudor. (Why the plan was never carried out to the end, I never knew.) I played the score for him on the piano, and he was enchanted. He wanted to hear it again and again. I obliged to the extent of my time and more, but when he told me that he had to hear it not ten or twenty, but hundreds of times, I gave up as far as my own playing was concerned. However, I went to a private recording studio at Carnegie Hall and had acetate records made of my performance, and handed them to Tudor.

Koussevitsky, who was then studying the work for the première, heard of these records, and asked me for copies. He liked to hear everything he was to conduct, and often had new scores played for him on the piano by his "court-pianist" Jesus Maria Sanromá. I was glad to send him the records and, as he told me, he made "good use of them".

The Concerto for Orchestra was an immediate success; it went round the world at lightning speed and is still one of the most performed works composed in this century.

About the première many tales circulated. Members of the Boston Symphony Orchestra told me that when Bartók arrived for the last rehearsal, Koussevitsky told him: "Mr. Bartók, whenever you have a remark to make, please do not hesitate!"

Bartók thanked him.

Only four or five bars into the first movement he raised his hand and explained something to Koussy in whispered conference.

Ten bars later – another interruption.

Two more bars – a third.

And so on.

After about twenty minutes this became very tiresome and Koussevitsky said: "Mr. Bartók, perhaps you could take paper and pencil and make your notes as we go. At the end you then will tell me all you want."

This happened, and the orchestra members observed Bartók sitting in the stalls feverishly writing all the time. When the last movement ended, he went on scribbling for a while and then rose, armed with his notes, and, as my informant put it, "full of pep". The tired Koussy led him, with bent back and dragging step, to the conductor's dressing room, where they disappeared.

The intermission lasted an unusually long time. When they finally reappeared, the sight was different: Koussevitsky led the way with easy, springy gait, Bartók shuffled behind him listlessly.

Koussevitsky then mounted the rostrum and announced: "Gentlemen, Mr. Bartók agrees with everything."

On the other hand, my friend George Kelemen, the distinguished otologist, then professor at Harvard University, who was present at the last rehearsal and the première of the work with Bartók, told me that after the concert Bartók said to him: "You know, every member of this orchestra is such a great artist. They all know how to play everything – at first sight – just right. Without any further instruction."

What Bartók himself said to me shortly afterwards was simply: "Nothing had to be changed."

Not much later he took me aside and asked: "Do you know what the interruption in the fourth movement is?"

(The fourth movement of the Concerto for Orchestra is called "*Intermezzo interrotto*", the "Interrupted intermezzo". It consists of a quiet, meandering melodic part, interrupted by a strain of vulgar band music, which dies away, and the haunting first part is heard again – changed in a most subtle way – to end the movement.)

"Oh yes, Professor!"

"Well, what is it?"

(It is obvious to all musicians that this vulgarity is a quote of some kind.)

"It is from Lehár's *Merry Widow!*"

To my surprise Bartók look puzzled and asked: "What is *that?*"

Could it be that he didn't know Lehár's, our countryman's, world-famous operetta?

No, he didn't know it.

I gave up.

He said with a twinkle in his eye: "I will tell you what it is, but you must not tell anybody else as long as I am alive."

I promised. (And I kept my word.)

"It is a parody of Shostakovich!"

And of course it was: very clearly audible, once one had been told, but I would never have spotted it.

Then Bartók told me of his dislike for Shostakovich.

He never said anything derogatory of anyone, especially not of another composer. This was a singular instance.

I record the incident here not to diminish Shostakovich but because the story is unique and very human. In my view, neither figure loses by the telling of it.

From what Bartók said it became clear that he had read and analysed Shostakovich's work, that he held it inferior to his own, and that he had almost a complex about the Russian's great success – he was very much *en vogue* at the time – which he did not think was fully merited.

"And thus I gave vent to my anger in the Concerto," he concluded.

His own, very touching description of that movement was:

"The melody goes its own quiet way, singing to itself – when suddenly it's interrupted by that brutality, at which the orchestra laughs and gives it a 'raspberry'. Then the melody is alone again and continues its walk, as before, only a little more sadly."

The connection between the quote and the Lehár and Shostakovich melodies is shown here (all transposed into the same key):

Lehár's *The Merry Widow*:

Heut' geh ich in's Ma – xim, Dort ist es so in – tim,

61

Shostakovich's Seventh Symphony:

Bartók's quote:

After the première of the Concerto, Koussevitsky's admiration for Bartók increased by leaps and bounds. After the first performance he told Bartók: "This is best piece written in last ten years!"

After the success in New York: "This is best piece written in last twenty years!"

A month later it became the best in the last thirty years.

When the praise reached the turn of the century, Bartók could contain himself no longer and softly asked: "Including Shostakovich?"

The last time I saw Bartók was on his last birthday, on March 25th, 1945, in New York. I went to see him in his two-room apartment, with some books as a present. I entered through the open door. He was not ready, and called to me from the bedroom, bidding me sit down. He was alone in the place, his wife was absent. While waiting, I looked around and saw a small, yellow Eulenburg pocket-score. I found to my astonishment that it was the score of Grieg's Piano Concerto, the last piece of music I would have expected him to read.

When he came out, he found me smiling over that score.

"What amuses you so much?"

"Professor, how on earth do you come to read that score on your birthday?"

"My birthday has nothing to do with it. It is a very popular piece, and as it happens I have never played it or heard it, so I wanted to make up for it by at least reading it through. So much is said about it, good and bad!"

"And what do you think of it?"

"Oh, in its own way it is excellent, very professional, clean writing. And a very important piece, as was Grieg's entire output."

"How so?" We had looked upon Grieg as one of the peripheral late romantics, pleasant perhaps, but not important.

"Yes, very important. Don't forget that he was one of the first to dip into the folk music of his own country, casting off the German yoke!"

The circle closed there.

In August of the same year I was conducting in Havana when the news of his death came through. We knew that he was very ill and witnessed his gradual loss of strength, but we did not know that he had leukaemia, cancer of the blood – and were not prepared for his leaving us so soon.

Neither was he. On his deathbed he was working diligently – completing his Third Piano Concerto, which was his deeply moving legacy to his wife. He did indeed succeed in completing the score; only the last seventeen bars still had to be orchestrated from his short score. This was done by Tibor Serly, who later also undertook to write the full score of the posthumous Viola Concerto, commissioned by William Primrose. The part of the solo instrument was finished, but the orchestra accompaniment existed only in sketch form. To decipher it and to give it definite shape in Bartók's spirit was a formidable task. Serly's version was much criticised, to my mind unjustly. It is a fine example of music reconstruction, enabling us to hear one more work by Bartók in, I believe, very much the way Bartók himself would have presented it.

My grief in Havana was very great, and those days were dark and lonely. I was conducting Beethoven's "Eroica" Symphony, and in a few words I dedicated that evening and the performance to Bartók's memory. I had thought it a gesture that would affect only myself, making me feel a little better by reaching out to Bartók from that tropical nowhere, and I was deeply moved when at the end of the performance the audience, unbidden, rose and remained in absolute silence, until dismissed.

What I have written down about Bartók can scarcely describe

him, nor can it give a true picture of his importance in music history or of his influence on my musical life. Certainly his was a human as well as a musical influence. My memories of him are of an awesome natural phenomenon, and they strengthen me in times of stress.

7

As I HAVE SAID, MY FIRST PROFESSIONAL JOB WAS THAT OF COACH (*répétiteur*) at the Opera House, where my father was still a member of the orchestra. It was not, however, through this family connection that I was employed, but through the Academy.

It so happened that, at the time that I received my diplomas, one of the younger teachers was appointed director of the Opera House. His name was Miklós Radnai. He was not one of my instructors, but knew me as a good pupil with ambitions to become a conductor. So when one day he stopped me on the stairs of the Academy and said: "When I am Opera Director next autumn I will ask for you as co-repetitor. Will you come?", I said "Yes" without hesitation.

The way to become a conductor in those days was through the Opera House, and the first step was répétiteurship. So Radnai was offering me a perfectly normal beginning.

The appointment of Radnai created quite a stir in our local music circles. Until then the directors of the Opera House had generally been members of the aristocracy, mostly of little or no musical distinction, with only two exceptions. The first was Ferenc Erkel (1870-80), an interesting man and himself a composer of operas, who played an important and constructive role in the progress of the lyric theatre in Hungary. The second was young Gustav Mahler who was, for a short period (1894-98), a remarkable director of the Royal Opera in Budapest. It was during his régime that Brahms once said: "If you want to hear a good performance of Mozart's *Don Giovanni*, go to Budapest."

Radnai did well, and the years of his directorship marked a great step forward. The repertory expanded, the company gained in strength, the ensemble work improved, progress was made in every aspect, auditive and visual.

Many new operas were presented, and quite a number of these were assigned to me for rehearsing with the singers, whom, under a system now regrettably almost extinct, I had from the first reading to the première, and for "maintenance work" thereafter.

My modest work at the Opera began inauspiciously. At the very start I had to rehearse the new production of *Pelléas and Mélisande*. I fell head over heels in love with the work, and with Debussy's music altogether. By that time my Wagneritis was waning – the Wagner addiction in those times was a veritable disease of the young – and Debussy's style was the right antidote, liberating mind and heart for new impressions.

That kind of music was then very new indeed, and for some of the older people – including the conductor of our performance, a nice, reliable but very old-fashioned man – quite puzzling. At one of the piano rehearsals, an elderly baritone was struggling with the part of Golaud and the equally elderly conductor was beating the time as well as he could to what I was playing as well as I could, when I suddenly noticed that something was badly wrong. The singer's notes did not correspond with my accompaniment at all, and the conductor's beat did not correspond to either. My heart stopped, the world went dark before my eyes for a moment, then I knew what had happened: I had inadvertently turned over two pages. With a flip of a finger I turned back the page, found the phrase at which the singer had just arrived and was continuing on, outwardly calm, but inwardly totally crushed. For I was convinced that my so-far excellent career of one week was now completely ruined and that I would be instantly dismissed. However, at the end of the hour both the Mr. Kammersänger and the Mr. Conductor took their coats and left with not unfriendly nods. I decided that the conductor, out of the kindness of his heart, did not want to dismiss me in the presence of another person, and would do so first thing next morning. Nothing happened. I lived through two or three painful days and sleepless nights until it dawned on me that the crime had been unnoticed!

This and other similar events helped me to lose the excessive respect I had for practically everybody at the Opera House. That was a good thing, for I badly needed more self-confidence if I was to make headway in my chosen profession.

The four years I spent at "the theatre" (as the Opera House was affectionately called by its inhabitants) were magnificent. I was like a piece of blotting paper, learning from all experiences, good and bad. As well as great and portentous events a parallel row of absurd things happened to me. This delightful dual road it has been my happy lot to walk throughout my life.

One agreeable result of my new appointment was the amount of money I was suddenly able to earn. My piano-playing, though not good enough for a concert career – which did not interest me anyway – was unusually good for a *répétiteur*. Not only was I assigned the most interesting repertoire at the Opera, including all Richard Strauss's and other contemporary works, but the singers also engaged me for private coaching.

All my life I have been intent upon earning money. I had seen the difficult life of my parents, and how hard they had to work to make ends meet and give their children the superior education they did, and in consequence I regarded, and still regard, poverty as unnecessary, disagreeable and humiliating. But my impatience to be self-sufficient was not always beneficial. Only too often I was satisfied with the second-best, when the best was just around the corner. "A bird in the hand is worth two in the bush" is not the best proverb for those who wish to be "great".

All the same, it was wonderful for a boy of my age to work with great singers, for though their names may mean little now, Feinhals, Kemp, Schorr, Kiepura, Fleta, Chaliapin, Battistini, Jeritza, Journet, Wildbrunn, and many others were all artists of the highest quality.

A very special adventure was my meeting with Karl Burian, the remarkable Czech tenor, who died in that same year that my operatic work started. He drank himself to death, dying horribly of delirium tremens. His stage presence was magical. Imagine a short, ugly, middle-aged man, with sparse red-grey hair (sometimes covered by a wig), a ravaged face distorted by drink (which no make-up could hide), stooped shoulders and at best a lurching, somewhat insecure gait. And imagine this gnome-like figure side-by-side – or worse, embracing – one of the huge, over-bosomy Brünnhildes or Isoldes of those times. Grotesque – a Hoffnung cartoon come alive – and yet his audiences were completely enraptured, hearing and seeing the young Siegfried or Tristan. Such is the power of a great stage talent. And such was Burian's power. At rehearsals he was sleepy and absent-minded, if sober; or heartbreakingly funny when slightly drunk.

Every performance in which he appeared was like a huge game of roulette. Until he actually appeared on the scene, and sometimes not then, no one knew what state he would be in. One evening, singing Lohengrin, and even more unsteady than usual, he almost capsized the swan-boat. Then, stepping out of it with surprising assurance, he sang *"Nun sie bedankt, mein lieber Schwan"* with such ethereal beauty that our terror turned to delight. The anxious watchers backstage began congratulating each other, shaking hands, embracing. Thank God, all was well!

But – what was this? His song finished, Burian got up from his kneeling position, took a long, ominous look round the stage, and started a deliberate, pompous walk towards Elsa and King Heinrich. Arriving in front of them he took Elsa's hand, carried it to his lips, kissed it gallantly, clicked his heels like a lieutenant of Dragoons, and – rendering Richard Wagner's elaborate three-act effort completely superfluous – introduced himself loud and clear: "Lohengrin!"

For Herod in Strauss's *Salome*, he did not even have to make himself up, poor, sick creature that he was. His characterisation of the King of Judea was shattering, and one of his most famous parts. (He sang it at the world première in Dresden in 1905.)

One morning I was told by Radnai that Kammersänger Burian wished to have a piano rehearsal for his Herod (*Salome* was on the programme for the following evening), but wasn't well enough to come to the theatre. Would I therefore go to him? I went. He lived in the Hotel Royal, not far from the Opera House. Entering his room, I was choked by the awful stench, and shocked by the disorder and filth in which this man lived. The bed was unmade, the floor was littered with old newspapers, crumpled and dirty clothes, and remnants of several days' food and drink. The windows and shutters were closed. Burian himself was in a red velvet robe over a nightshirt. He was barefoot and unshaven, but apparently in good spirits.

"Ah, my young friend, here you are! Good! Let's start rehearsing!"

I looked around for a piano. In vain. There was none in the room.

"Very well, Mr. Burian. Where shall we go?"

"Go – why?"

"Hm – eh – "

"Oh, the piano! We won't need any!"

"???"

"Let me tell you how we will do it. You sit here and beat the time. I will remain sitting where I am, look at you and think over my part. When I make a mistake I will stop you and we will do that bit over again in the same way."

Never had I heard of such a manner of rehearsing. But I did as he wanted.

That dingy room must have presented an eerie spectacle: a young man, sitting with a big score on his lap, silently beating out varied tempi, while, two paces away from him, his glassy eyes fixed on the young man's moving hands, an elderly figure, looking like a king of tramps, sat slumped, immobile.

This strange pantomime went on for as long as it took to "rehearse" the entire part.

At the end Burian said: "I did not make any mistake."

What could I do but offer my congratulations?

Then, suddenly, he got up, grabbed the score, opened it, turned the pages, found a spot and pointed to it.

"Don't forget to tell Maestro Rékai [the conductor] that here" – he pointed again with his finger – "here I will make a great, long pause! Don't forget!"

This was utter nonsense. What he showed me was the middle of a word. No sane person would have made a pause there. It was simply impossible.

So I made up my mind to "forget" to tell the conductor.

When I left Burian at the end of our strange rehearsal, I was full of pity and felt determined to do him a good turn.

"Mr. Burian, wouldn't you like to have a piano in your room?"

"No, my boy. What for?"

"For instance, to rehearse better."

"Why? What was wrong just now?"

"But, Mr. Burian, if you want one, the Opera Director will be glad to send you one."

"But why? I don't play, I don't need it!"

"Well, wouldn't you like to try your voice sometimes?"

At this a sly, broad smile crossed his ruined face, he lifted a straight finger, and after a long, conspiratorial look, said: "My young friend, I like to be – agreeably surprised!"

The following night, he sang splendidly. All was in order, everything was going well, it was a great evening.

Until the spot arrived to which he had pointed with his finger. Sure enough, suddenly, in the mi----ddle of a word, he made a great pause. The conductor, not expecting it, plunged ahead and a terrible scramble ensued which took two or three minutes (on the stage two or three eternities) to straighten out. Only then, watching the proceedings with a very bad conscience, did I see the light: it made *theatrical* sense to tear apart that word, characterising the sick mind of Herod.

Perhaps the oldest singer I have worked with was Matteo Battistini. He was over seventy then, and his condition – vocal, mental, physical – was phenomenal. When I worked with him on Renato in *Ballo in Maschera* I could admire, probably for the first time in my life, the finest style of Verdi singing.

His second role during that brief and unequal collaboration (he was over seventy, while I was under twenty) was as a most urbane Scarpia in *Tosca*. He was as worldly and aristocratic as can be imagined. It was hard to believe that *that* Baron Scarpia really had to resort to tricks, not to speak of brutality, to obtain the favours of a beautiful woman. What a contrast when he arranged his own killing. He asked our Tosca to stab him in the neck, which she willingly did, using the customary rubber knife. He then grabbed the knife, holding it to his neck while he fell to the ground, and writhing in agony he smeared a tubeful of red make-up, which he held hidden in his hand, all over his face and chest. It was a gory spectacle the first time, ridiculous thereafter.

Third, he sang (in French) Mephisto in Gounod's *Faust* (which the composer called *Marguerite*). It was an object lesson in "*le style galant*", an unforgettable example of fine vocal production, expression, economy and discipline.

Mari Jeritza was then in her first years as Diva, and often came to Budapest as a guest. She was immensely popular and rightly so. We heard her in a great variety of parts. Some small phrases which she sang like no one else, before her or after, remain in my memory like diamonds. For instance:

"*Mein armer Bruder*"

in *Lohengrin*, or

"Heinrich! Heinrich! Was tatest Du mir an?" as Elizabeth in *Tannhäuser*.

She also sang Carmen (red haired), Salome (blonde), Turandot (she was the first great singer we had heard in that part), Tosca, and many more.

These splendid guests brought so much to impress the mind and heart of a young musician. Yet the continuous work with our home company was even more profitable. There were about fifty to sixty singers under permanent contract – who really stayed there – and they formed a fine, steady, sure-fire ensemble, for a repertoire that comprised never less than forty operas per season, lasting ten months each year.

The creation of that ensemble was the merit of Miklós Radnai. At that time – it was the middle Twenties – there were few opera companies, outside Vienna and Berlin, of this size and standard. For a small and peripheral place like Budapest it was no mean achievement.

But, of course, the conductors were my greatest sources of learning.

Italian opera posters call the conductor *"concertatore e direttore"*. This means something like "preparer and conductor", with *"concertare"* meaning "concerting" or "co-ordinating all efforts".

While on the symphonic platform the conductor is, obviously and always, also the "co-ordinator", at operatic performances this is not always the case. Most of the time a staff of *répétiteurs* has prepared the production. In the past, the person who was to conduct it would also have led the preparatory work. Nowadays, he appears later in the game, often too late to be the *"concertatore"* as well as the conductor. And when, in the course of the season, the operas are "taken over" by another conductor or even by several, they are clearly only conductors, and not the "concerters" of that performance.

This situation is regarded as unavoidable in every opera house. In my view it is deplorable, because a performance stands or falls at least as much by its "concertation" as by the way it is conducted (or sung). Since enjoyment is individual, I cannot prove my point of view. But for me – and, I know, for a great many others – a well thought-out, well-felt, well put-together, well rehearsed, well-prepared, well *"concertato"* performance is the only source of supreme pleasure, and indeed of supreme excitement in opera. The most brilliant voices or most masterly conducting are no substitute.

In the 1920s, the strength of our Opera House was the ensemble, the *"concertazione"*. The conductors were only senior *répétiteurs*, without that special, guiding force and spirit that are essentially required in a master conductor.

The senior conductor of Hungary at the time of my youth was a disciple and follower of Hans Richter, named István Kerner. During my early childhood he was already the "grand old man", chief conductor of both the Opera House and the Philharmonic Orchestra, and much revered. His name was much bandied about in the daily conversations of my parents and their circle. I saw him often in the street, a large, stout man, with a small felt hat perching rather comically on the top of a snow-white lion's mane, low-hanging walrus moustaches almost snow-white too but stained a little yellowish by tobacco, in a black overcoat with a black cane. He was the veritable caricature of the grand old man which he really was and which he played to perfection.

He had, as I later learned, a difficult and rather sad life. At that moment, when I entered into the service of the theatre, he was still the chief conductor, but very ill and feeble. He rehearsed and conducted a revival of Mozart's *Nozze di Figaro*, but had to quit after the second performance and never conducted again.

On my first day I was introduced to him and, as the Benjamin of the house (I was the only member of the music staff still in his teens) I was ordered to kiss his hand when he asked me to approach him. This thought disgusted me profoundly, and when I finally did bend over his benevolently outstretched hand, I very nearly vomited on it. As it was, I managed a "stage kiss", not touching him with my lips, and fled across the large room towards the door while he wished me well and admonished me to be "good and diligent".

This was the entry of Maestro Kerner into my life and his exit from "the theatre". His conducting manner was, visually, around for some while longer, one or two younger men having adopted his movements, which he inherited from Richter. It was an awkward, ungainly sight, like bears swimming. The upper arms were almost horizontally extended from the shoulders, other movements were executed from the elbow to the wrist, the latter held as stiff as the shoulders. If good conductors move like that, all is well; they can move how they like and still bring about the desired performance.

It must never be forgotten that an orchestra conductor's movements are never performed for the benefit of the listening or, unfortunately, onlooking public, but only for the singers or instrumentalists, and relate to what was agreed and understood by all at the rehearsals.

The same Hans Richter – who, as it is well known, was one of Wagner's chosen conductors at Bayreuth, a regular conductor in Vienna, and for many years conductor of the famous Hallé Orchestra in Manchester – held it as a maxim that "a conductor has to prove himself at rehearsal". At the performance he must restrict his activities to a minimum, merely reminding those whom he is leading of what was previously established.

If only the many of the young generation of would-be conductors who practise before a mirror to the sound of a gramophone record, learning nothing except clowning, would take this to heart!

I learnt much from the fine examples of guest conductors in Budapest. But though they could leave the special mark of their personalities they could not make great changes; they were working on the existing performance level established by dedicated rehearsing.

There was Franz Schalk from Vienna, very thin and frail, with a small beard and bearing a perilous resemblance to a goat, coughing all the time and behaving rather facetiously. He was a thorough and expert musician who was able to achieve great effects with very little visible effort. He held his baton like the bow of a violin.

Starting the tremendous tremolo of the overture of Wagner's *Flying Dutchman*, he would say, in a cracked, thin voice, between coughs: "Gentlemen – with the greatest vehemence, please!"

Whereupon he would raise his baton two inches high, and bring it down – half an inch.

And the orchestra played with shattering vehemence.

It was Schalk who once explained to me during a rehearsal of Mozart's *Entführung* how the pianist at a stage rehearsal must not "accompany" but play in such a way as to be leading the singers, not only in the absence but also in the presence of a time-beating conductor. I received this lesson during my first two weeks at "the theatre" and it radically changed my attitude at the piano there and then.

There was Bruno Walter, who first led me into the beauties of *Fidelio*, and from whom I first heard, in concert, symphonies by Mahler.

There was Erich Kleiber, ill-mannered, excitable and thoroughly splendid, who conducted *Rosenkavalier* (rather new then), *Carmen*, *Nozze di Figaro*, *Tristan and Isolde* and other operas as well as concerts.

A great personal disaster befell me when he was conducting Berlioz's "Symphonie Fantastique" at one of the Philharmonic concerts.

I was assigned to conduct the bells in the last movement. These bells were not played by chimes, as they are now, but, as in the score, by a pianoforte and a tam-tam, backstage. As the players of these instruments had no visual contact with the rest of the performers, they were conducted by someone who looked through a peep-hole at the conductor on his platform. That person also heard the music played by the orchestra, before his own music started, when the noise made by the piano bass and the tam-tam deafened him completely to other sounds. That someone was me. The rehearsals went well. Mine was a simple task; it did not require a genius.

The first public performance was not the concert, but a so-called "public dress rehearsal". These rehearsals took place, always before sold-out houses, on Sunday mornings at eleven o'clock.

On the Saturday evening before that fateful Sunday there was a great ball in Budapest, the first I was ever invited to. I had a wonderful time – so wonderful that I did not return home that night at all, but remained until about seven-thirty in the morning, leaving with the last, most resilient guests, but in a much inferior condition to those experienced people. I went with them to a bistro on the hillsides of Buda to eat sauerkraut soup; they told me that would put everything right. It didn't. Then they told me to go to the Turkish bath and have a hot steam plus cold shower treatment. I did that and it helped or at least I thought so.

By then I had to go to the concert to "ring the bells". I arrived in good time and in more than good spirits. I took my place at the peep-hole, gave the cue. All seemed well. But as I continued to look through the peep-hole I saw Kleiber's bald head getting first pink, then red, then claret-coloured, and his face showing unmistakable signs of ill-controlled fury. I wondered what had happened in the orchestra, but because of the noise of the instruments I was conducting, I could not hear anything. Only when my last bell sound had abated did I note that the music Kleiber was conducting was not what I was supposed to hear, although it was from the same symphony. A second later I realised what I had done: I had conducted those bells in double time!

Dies irae – ruination – apocalypse! What could I do?

I took my coat and ran. Before the symphony was over, I was out of the house.

The next concert was on the Monday evening, and in the meantime my friends in the orchestra concealed the identity of the culprit. Kleiber, I was told, raved and ranted and absolutely insisted on another man for the Monday concert. I was engaged again, and since there were no more festivities to go to, by then I was another man.

The bells, also, were quite different from the Sunday ringing, slow and sedate. Kleiber asked to see the bell-man and I was ushered – unwillingly – in to his dressing room.

He shook hands with me. "That was all right. The chap on Sunday was an idiot."

Twenty years or so later I met Erich Kleiber in Buenos Aires at an after-concert party. I asked him if he remembered that incident. He did – and he was still angry. I told him who the chap on that Sunday was. He said, "He was an idiot."

Kleiber was a remarkable musician and a remarkable conductor. Several of his performances remained models in my mind. Amongst others, that of Berlioz's Symphonie Fantastique.

Later I had one more reason to admire him. During the Second World War, when he had left Germany and gone to Latin America, he built a first-class symphony orchestra out of the very weak performing forces in Havana. Never before or after Kleiber was there a symphony orchestra on the island of Cuba of such calibre, as I know from experience, having conducted that orchestra twice, just before Kleiber came and just after he left.

That example showed me forcefully what one man's energy and talent can do.

Clemens Kraus, then a very young man, came to us, I think, from Vienna. For me his presence was personally momentous, because he was the first foreign authority to appreciate my compositions and to encourage me to go on with them. Kraus called me to his hotel. He had my unfinished Orchestra Suite in his hands, told me that he liked it, and that I should "write some music every day – every single day of my life".

I often wish I had followed his advice. But I had to make a wide circle before coming back, late in my life, to my first passion – the writing of music – without which I now know I cannot exist.

One day a youngish Englishman appeared in the pit, rehearsing *Tristan and Isolde*. He did so efficiently, with broad gestures, obviously savouring the music and the occasion to the hilt. He had a little black goatee and sparkling eyes. He talked a lot of English, which nobody in the house understood. That did not seem to bother him at all, and things went swimmingly.

Two stagehands, leaning against some scenery, eating their bacon and bread, looked down at him.

"What does he want here?" asked one, chewing.

"They won the war," replied the other.

An exchange which, had he heard it, Sir Thomas Beecham would have enjoyed – and would have loved to re-tell in his own inimitable way.

Richard Strauss came for two weeks, to conduct his *Salome* and *Rosenkavalier*. This was a great event, for me especially, because these two operas were among those entrusted to my care at "the theatre".

As we had made several cuts in our performances – most of them in *Rosenkavalier* – I was sent, as soon as he arrived, to see him about these, and to enquire if he had any other wishes. I did not get far with my mission.

Arriving at the Hungaria, the best, most elegant hotel in town, splendidly situated on the left bank of the Danube (never blue but greyish-green and dirtily majestic), I saw him, his tall frame slightly stooped, standing with two dachshunds under a tree. The dogs were busily snuffling about and shuffling the ground with their hind feet, which, apparently, was not all the master expected of them. He greeted me in a friendly way, but waved aside any discussion on *Salome* and *Rosenkavalier* and problems pertaining to them. Instead he invited me to share his preoccupation with the two dogs. We walked together for a good while on the embankment of the Danube, called the "Corso". About half an hour and many trees later the dogs did their duty and we returned, all four of us well pleased, to the hotel. There the dogs were taken upstairs by a porter and Strauss repaired with me to the restaurant where he treated me to a share of his coffee. He still did not want to hear anything about his operas.

"We shall see at rehearsal," he said.

This was the beginning of two exhilarating weeks.

To go through two of Strauss's major works with the composer himself, first at the piano rehearsals – he himself conducted for me with barely perceptible movements of his forefinger while I played – and then to watch him as he conducted the orchestra rehearsals, gave me a lasting understanding of his operas.

His approach to his own music was objective, cool, almost indifferent. But he knew his works inside out – I have met several very good composers who did not – and went about their performance as a fine conductor would.

With that professional nonchalance went a great natural authority, which was, of course, expected of him and thus became less awesome. His manner was friendly, matter of fact, his instructions short, clear, brought forth in the form of suggestions which it would have been unthinkable to refuse.

Speaking about the characters of his operas, he seemed to attach great importance to their youth. He repeatedly warned our Baron Ochs not to portray an old roué, but a rough and ready, not very intelligent country squire not more than thirty-five years old, who will within a couple of years after his misadventure with Miss Sophie Faninal tell of it gleefully, as one of his youthful pranks.

He also told the singer of the Marschallin to treat her melancholy monologue at the end of the first act as a fleeting cloud of sadness. She was far away from losing her beauty and charm. She had just turned twenty-four, twenty-five at the most; and her renouncing of Octavian and helping him to have his new love – which was very nice of her – is less of a sacrifice than it would seem at first.

77

Surely, if there was a fourth act to *Rosenkavalier* it could easily start in the same way as the first "with, perhaps, a tenorino".

Salome, he explained, was surely no older than sixteen. Only a very spoiled sixteen-year-old could have done what Salome did, an older woman would have done much better or much worse. "It's an operetta, with a deadly ending," he said.

He rehearsed the scene of the Jews several times over, although it went faultlessly the first time, because he was delighted to hear it in Hungarian. "It is much more Jewish this way," he said with a broad grin.

He took great pains to rehearse the small parts and spent more time on those than on the leads. Several small cuts we had made in just those scenes he asked us to restore.

As a conductor he was remarkable. Facing the orchestra he was as detached as in the rehearsal rooms, unimpressed by the splendour of his own orchestration. He sat in a chair while conducting. Even so he was so tall that he perched high above the orchestra.

He did not interrupt often. I sometimes wondered why not, when he left several glaring faults uncorrected. Later I noticed that most of those faults corrected themselves. It takes, however, a very practical mind to judge in an instant which are the self-curable ills and which are not. This is a quality of the true conductor and Strauss had it to the full.

His beat was clear and very large, without big movements of his hands or arms. He made his very long baton move, describing wide arcs in the air by small movements of his wrist, his hand held firm in front of his chest. Even a half-blind singer or player could not miss that beat.

His demeanour was unvarying, amiable but cool.

He was met on his arrival with deep respect, which grew with closer contact, but friendships and affection did not spring up.

Besides the operas, he also conducted two concerts. One consisted of his own works: Don Juan, Till Eulenspiegel and Heldenleben. This concert was marked by the same competence and the same detachment in performance as were the operas. I still use some bowings, and wish I could remember more he showed to our string players. His lack of haste, which allowed character, texture, form, balance to unfold and develop as a process of nature, will always remain in my mind.

The second concert was devoted to Mozart's Haffner Serenade and the last, C major ("The Jupiter"), Symphony.

It was a revelation! The stooped, tall figure, almost absent-minded before, now stood erect. His eyes were everywhere. He was like some giant panther ready to jump. Involved — and more than that, dedicated to, dissolved in the music — he awoke to life.

The more I think about it, the surer I am that I have never heard Mozart's orchestral music performed with such power and persuasion than at that occasion.

The memory of that performance shines with growing clarity in every detail. So does the memory of my own astounded enthusiasm for the mingling of the two great talents that filled my eyes, my ears and my mind, and my deep respect and tearful devotion to the genuis whose music I heard and to the man on the podium.

How could such moments be put into words?

Very timidly I said something to Strauss after that concert — we were already on such close terms that I carried his scores and his baton-case — about how wonderful it was.

We walked together.

He kept silent. He nodded as he walked.

Then he said: "*Ja, ja, das ist Musik* . . ." in a faraway voice.

Then suddenly, in quite another tone, as if he had decided to say something "worthwhile" to me he said: "You know, there is no such thing as temp*i*, there is just temp*o*."

He turned to me, while saying this, stopped for a moment, then resumed his walk, obviously tremendously pleased.

We walked further in silence, until we arrived at a nearby house where he was expected for an after-concert supper. At the doorway he shook my hand and thanked me. I was much moved, and could say nothing.

Stravinsky came at that time to play his Piano Concerto. I met him later quite often. This was but a short introduction.

The occasion was a concert of his works: "The Nightingale" (the symphonic poem made after the opera), the Piano Concerto, and *Petrushka*.

The conductor was Emil Telmányi, the eminent Hungarian violinist, by then living in Denmark.

He wanted to become a conductor and was helped by Radnai, the opera director, who engaged him to conduct *Il Trovatore* at the Opera House, and arranged the Stravinsky concert for him.

Both tasks proved beyond his power. *Il Trovatore* will test the skills of even the most experienced opera conductor and Stravinsky's music poses problems to its performers, even now. Then it was brand new, practically unknown.

Stravinsky was patently unhappy; at one rehearsal he exclaimed: "*Sie zerbrechen mich!*" ("You break me to pieces!")

The orchestra was not very pleased either. I was part of it, playing the piano in the two orchestral works, and was very bewildered, for that kind of a spectacle I had never witnessed before.

Telmányi's conducting career came to a halt, but his fame as a violinist did not suffer from that setback. I heard many beautiful performances by him and later had the pleasure of conducting Carl Nielsen's Violin Concerto with him as the outstanding soloist.

The slim, very elegant, red-necked figure of the young Hans Knappartsbusch – later the famous old "Kna" of Munich and Bayreuth – made fleeting appearances. Ferdinand Loewe, the small man with the longest baton, came from Vienna a few times. The elegant *grand seigneur* type, Weingartner, Strauss's *bête noire*, appeared not infrequently, as did Abendroth from Leipzig. Kajanus came from Finland to conduct Sibelius, whose music we had never heard before and disliked from then onwards; and from Italy a young conductor called Bernardino Molinari, splendid in his music, obscene in his language (he must have learned a few four-letter words in German, apart from which he spoke only Italian). Of Toscanini we heard from far away; the legend was already in the making but on my horizon he appeared later.

The guest conductor of that epoch whom I have left to the last, because he played the most important role in my young life, was Fritz Busch, music director of first the Stuttgart and then the Dresden Opera House, until 1933 – that is, until the end of Europe as we knew it.

He began visiting Budapest in the 1920s and came often. He was a great favourite of the music-loving public in my home town. He brought with him a very large, varied repertoire, and pleased us as much with his versatility as with the freshness and cleanliness of his performances.

He was – or so it seemed to me – the least German of the German conductors. In fact, as a conductor, I did not think of him as a German at all, in spite of his appearance and bearing which were, in contrast, typically Teutonic.

He was tall, heavy-set, blond, with a small face in a large head and sparkling blue eyes. He had a very Germanic style of speech, but an easy, humorous disposition; all in all he was a very winning personality.

One of his three brothers, Adolf, was a well-known violinist (father-in-law of Rudolf Serkin, the pianist); another, Hermann, was a 'cellist; the last, whom I never met, an actor.

Fritz was a refreshing, mercurial man, a splendid musician, an excellent conductor, a fine, upright person. Under his tense, nervy baton music-making flowed easily, with force and grace mingled in an intriguing, personal style which was remarkably faithful not only to the written page, but to the spirit behind the page.

He, with Karl Ebert, the stage director, was responsible for a stimulating Verdi renaissance in the German opera houses. It was he who introduced Strauss's *Intermezzo*, *Die Aegyptische Helena* and *Arabella*. As head of the Staatskapelle in Dresden he greatly enriched the horizon of that orchestra, and of its public. In 1933, when Hitler came to power, he was sent away – one could really say thrown out – from his post in Dresden.

He then went to Scandinavia, where he first put the Copenhagen Radio Orchestra on the map, then headed the Stockholm Philharmonic for some years. He was also the musical head of the Glyndebourne Festival, organised by John Christie in Sussex in 1934, at first exclusively for the performance of Mozart's operas. There Busch, again together with Ebert, achieved a remarkably high standard of fine performances in the best ensemble-style. During the Second World War he worked mostly in South America, and also in the USA, where our paths crossed again. After the war he returned to Glyndebourne, which was expanding with a larger repertoire. He conducted to the end of his life, and was much in demand everywhere.

It was at "the theatre" that I met Fritz Busch personally. I do not remember which operas I was rehearsing for and with him, but our friendship grew from a working relationship, in spite of the great difference of age and professional standing.

During one of his visits, he made the remark that altered the course of my life. It was a very casual invitation, or mention, that, should I be travelling in that direction, I must stop off in Dresden, hear some performances at the Opera there, visit him, and possibly stay there as one of the music staff.

By that time – this must have been in the 1926-27 season – I began to be restless at "the theatre". There were many reasons for this.

I had quickly gained experience and assurance as a *répétiteur*. Conducting assignments had started successfully and it seemed quite possible that one day I would be the music director of the theatre. But I had a growing feeling of discontent with what I knew, with the scope of my experience.

The outside world became for me a magic land where "real" music was made, where I could hear and see and learn all that I couldn't at home.

To that must be added the worsening political climate: the rise of fascism in Italy; the turn to the right in Hungary itself, after a short-lived Communist régime; and the emergence of anti-semitism. I suddenly discovered – with vague foreboding rather than accurate knowledge, for my political notions were of the sketchiest – that I was in "the Jewish camp" and that this might prove to be a handicap. That aura of happy mental freedom I had known since childhood was gone.

The fact that I belonged to a family of mixed but mostly of Jewish blood was, of course, no news to me. But any implications of that were completely disregarded by my parents, their friends and, indeed, our entire society, which basked in the brief sunlight of that short period of enlightened liberalism which existed during the early part of the century. People elsewhere may have been less fortunate, but the atmosphere and surroundings of my early life were as I have described. The shock to my sensibilities on awakening from that dream existence was, in consequence, traumatic.

These then were the most important reasons which, during the years from 1925 to 1928, made me more and more determined to break out of the narrowing cage that my homeland was now

82

becoming for me. There was also the very genuine "Wanderlust" with which I was born.

I had had some glimpses of the world before; when I started to earn my own living, at sixteen, I soon began to make foreign trips. The first of these led me to Italy. I travelled alone, and visited Venice, Florence, Ravenna and Rimini.

In Venice I found a room in a pensione in the Orologio, the building across from St. Mark's Cathedral, where the Mercerie begin their winding way. On the top of that building the big clock shows the time to the entire city – very much in vain, for nobody in Venice wants to know how late it is. Above the giant dial, the two familiar bronze figures strike, with their immense hammers, the huge bronze bell between them every thirty minutes.

It was exactly under that bell that I had my small room. It was the cheapest lodging in town, because the longest sleep to be had there in one stretch lasted exactly twenty-eight minutes, from the end of the reverberations of the half hour that had passed to the preparatory rattle of the huge, rough mechanism before the next.

To make it worse, I fell ill from falling asleep while sunbathing on the Lido. There I lay, for four or five days, burnt like a piece of overdone steak and racked with a high fever, under the cruel hammering of the two bronze torturers. A strong young body sheds these ills fast. But I could never again look at the Orologio without feeling the hammers on my skin.

Nevertheless, Venice was enchanting for me, as it is for everyone.

Florence was an even greater surprise and joy. When I went with my bag from the railway station into town in search of lodgings, and came to the River Arno with the Ponte Vecchio on my left and the green hills of the other side of the river in front of me, under a dark blue, sun-drenched sky, it was so beautiful – what could I do? I put my valise on the pavement, stretched my arms to embrace all that magnificence – and sang, loud and happy.

I found lodgings in a charming small pensione on the Lungarno Acciaioli. It was not very cheap but I could just manage to afford it because during my sunburn in Venice I did not eat for four days. This may have weakened me physically, but it bolstered my economy.

The pensione was run by a delightful young lady. She was Swiss and – well, delightful. Some years my senior – as practically everybody was then – she accepted my shy courtship charmingly and with exquisite taste and grace.

Thus I learned to know Florence in the best possible way and the nicest possible company. It was a hot summer, with little relief in the evenings, but I was enchanted; the air was light and fragrant with the loveliest soft winds of spring.

She showed me and I looked.

She taught me and I learned.

We walked and talked. We had our own dreams. They were very different. Her dream was to own her own pensione in Settignano. Mine was to know the world and fill it with music.

Her plans, I must say, were far more advanced in their way than mine.

As parting gifts we gave each other the same book, which both of us knew: *Fiorenza* by Thomas Mann.

I wrote a few timid letters, but had no reply. Some years later, I went to the same house in the Lungarno Acciaioli. The pensione was no more. I tried to find the one she had planned to own in Settignano, but could not.

My trip continued after this beautiful intermezzo. I went through Bologna with its old churches and leaning tower (it is not only Pisa that has one!), through Ferrara, a severe town of faded greatness, to Ravenna, bare and yellow, a strange unfitting frame for the enormous and gripping Byzantine mosaics, and to Rimini with its splendid beach and its eerie medieval castle, still echoing the sighs of Francesca, the fights of the Malatesta and the murder of Paolo.

The beach was full of holiday-makers, and I joined its outdoor life for a week. I only vaguely remember that I got in with a rather international group of young people, led and master-minded by a Polish countess who was probably neither a countess nor Polish. She chided me with "being always angry".

I was not, but may have looked it, for looking angry and frowning is a peculiarity of my face. At times this has been useful, at others harmful, but in any case I have never been able to control this facial expression, of which I am completely unconscious. Now it is too late. But I should have worn a badge saying: "Don't mind my looks, I love you and trust you." This would have been true. I did and do love and trust people, sometimes too much.

My other early contact with the world outside Hungary – apart

84

from my momentous childhood voyage to Denmark – had been through visits to my relatives in Berlin.

My mother, my sister and myself visited another mother, son and daughter: my Aunt Elsa, my mother's elder sister, and her two children, Hans and Grete von Dohnányi.

Their father was Ernö (Ernest) von Dohnányi, a world-renowned pianist of his time, a very gifted composer, and for some decades the leading force in the musical life of Budapest.

I did not include him with the group of people who had the greatest influence upon my musical development because we had little if any personal contact during my formative years, after the age of eight or so. But he put his stamp upon the music-making and music-listening tastes and habits of the city of Budapest and of all Hungary.

His talent was enormous. His sphere of activity encompassed all facets of music-making. He composed piano pieces, chamber music, symphonic works, three operas and one pantomime. He played the pianoforte with a very special, personal mastery. His programmes ranged from matinées for children, with the two-part inventions by Bach, the "easy" sonatas by Mozart and Haydn, the Bagatelles by Beethoven, the children's pieces by Bartók and so on, to cycles of the complete Beethoven sonatas, which, thanks to his numerous and masterly performances, the music-loving public of the city knew almost by heart. He participated in many chamber-music concerts, with our beloved Waldbauer Quartet and other ensembles.

His sonata recitals with the violinist Emil Telmányi were always sold out. He held the chair of master piano classes at the Academy for a long time, and was director of it for a period. Moreover, he was for two decades or so the enlightened musical director and chief conductor of the Budapest Philharmonic Orchestra. His conducting was perhaps his least remarkable achievement, but his leadership was intelligent and stimulating. There was not much new and interesting orchestral music written in those days which we did not hear while it was "red hot".

This remarkable and most amiable, handsome man came to Budapest from his native Pozsony (today Bratislava) when he was eighteen. He was a pupil at the Academy at the same time as my father, who arrived with his much more modest package of talent from the other end of the country. Both of them found their way to the Kunwald house, which was a fine home of music, where the head of the family was an excellent amateur violinist, where Joachim and others visited and played quartets and other chamber music. Both were welcomed in that circle and, not very long after, each boy married one of the daughters of the house. The elder daughter was my Aunt Elsa.

Until about the outbreak of the First World War, the family ties were close. Uncle Ernest – Ernö – often sat at the piano in our apartment and played for hours on end.

He is directly responsible for my never having acquired the habit of smoking. He would storm into our place, throw his hat and coat in a corner, go straight to the piano and start to play magnificently, a cigarette hanging nonchalantly from the corner of his mouth.

I was terribly impressed, both by his playing and his cigarette. No sooner had the grown-ups departed than I lit a cigarette, placed it carefully in the corner of my mouth, and began to improvise on the piano.

That is – I would have begun to improvise, had I not choked from the smoke I inadvertently swallowed.

After I had recovered from the dreadful cough and nausea, I realised that I wasn't Uncle Ernest's equal. I had to give up either the piano or the cigarettes. I decided in favour of the former and finished smoking for good.

The Dohnányis left Hungary around 1912, when my uncle was appointed professor of the State Conservatory in Berlin. Shortly afterwards he divorced my aunt and married Elsa Galafrès, a German dancer who, in turn, divorced Bronislav Hubermann, the Polish violinist, to marry him. The family ties broke up and Dohnányi vanished for many years from my personal horizon.

The mutual hostility between the families was enduring and sometimes grotesque. Much later, when I started to be noted as a modest but not untalented newcomer on the music scene, and some journalist unearthed the one-time family link with Ernest von Dohnányi, he deemed it worthwhile to issue a statement, which was published under the headline: NO RELATION!

Dohnányi himself came back to Hungary when the First World War broke out. My Aunt Elsa and her two children remained in Berlin, and became completely "Germanised".

After the war we went several times to Berlin during our summer holidays, and the four of us children became very close friends. This friendship has continued between the three of us who are still alive.

Hans, the oldest of the cousins, met a tragic death during the Second World War. He was a brilliant boy who married Christel Bonhoeffer, daughter of a well-known psychologist. As a lawyer he entered service in the government. When Hitler came to power, he continued his work, although he disliked the régime. But later, during the war, he became a member of the group around Admiral Canaris, which plotted Hitler's death, and was captured after the abortive July 20th coup in 1944. With his brothers-in-law Klaus and Dietrich Bonhoeffer, he was hanged.

But from the ruins of that family a splendid new generation grew: the two sons of Hans have brilliant careers; Klaus, the elder, is in government; Christoph, the younger, is one of the prominent orchestral conductors of the new generation.

"Uncle" Ernest, the father of the family, remained in Hungary until the end of the Second World War, when he was accused of having been a supporter of the Nazi régime, basically a groundless accusation.

After the war he had to leave Hungary and finally found a haven at the University of Tallahassee, Florida. He was head of the piano department at that university's music faculty, and lived there until his death in 1960.

We met again in his last years. For some time I did not wish to see him, because I disliked his Nazi reputation. One day a letter from his grandson, my nephew Christoph, changed my mind. Then about twenty years of age, he was with his grandfather in Florida, and wrote asking if I could help him in his career as conductor. He complained that his name, Dohnányi, was a great handicap for him because the wrongdoings of his grandfather overshadowed the martyrs' death of his father. What could he do?

I told him that while I could have him to spend a year or two with me, I thought that the USA was not, then, a good place for a budding European conductor. Concerning his other problem I said that time would certainly ease the situation but that the real solution of it would be to make his name respected because it was *his*. He is now in the process of achieving that handsomely.

This correspondence made me think about the old man, and realise that whatever his faults might have been, he had now paid for them.

The moment of reconciliation came one evening when I was on tour with the Minneapolis Symphony Orchestra, of which I was then musical director, and was conducting a concert in Tallahassee. I had prepared a short piece by Dohnányi to be played as an encore and had requested that he be present at the concert. After the programme was over, I told the audience that there was a remarkable musician in their midst, who now was responsible for a University music class in their city, and once had the same responsibility, many decades ago, for an entire country. Then we performed his music and I invited him on the stage to thank the cheering public.

We embraced and were friends. I asked him to come for a visit to Minneapolis where we gave the USA première of his Second Symphony. At the same concert he played a Mozart piano concerto remarkably – improvising his own cadenza, as he always did – and revived old memories with a recital of Beethoven sonatas.

I saw him last at the Barbizon Plaza Hotel in New York, in bed with 'flu; he got a cold while he was recording some piano music of his, and his heart did not stand the strain. He died a few days later.

To go back to my twentieth year: I was getting restless in Budapest, and beginning to feel insecure; my composing was drying-up; it seemed impossible to perfect myself further in the art of conducting at home; my foreign trips enchanted me; the closeness to my Dohnányi cousins was exciting. Hans impressed with his brilliant mind and studious nature, Grete with her beauty, wit and talent (she showed great promise as a sculptress). Between the two of us a warm, loving relationship sprang up, amounting to more than cousinly friendship.

All the good things of life seemed to be abroad.

My wish to leave Hungary actually ripened, although it was anything but a realistic project.

I was earning quite a good salary, but had no savings, no means whatever which could set me up in a new career in a foreign land.

This could not hold me back, however. I embarked on the outlandish plan of applying for a state subsidy. Today, when subsidies and grants abound in great quantities, this is nothing out of the ordinary, but then it was unheard of. The few confidants I told about what I had in mind ridiculed me.

"Forget it," they said. "You will never succeed in getting one."

But they were wrong. I did succeed. I managed to arrange an interview with the Secretary for Cultural Affairs, a certain Mr. Robert K. Kertész, who, to everybody's surprise, perhaps even his own, granted me a stipend in short order.

After the period of delirious happiness occasioned by this triumph was over, I began thinking in earnest about what to do and where to go.

The direction was West.

Naturally.

8

THE OUTSTANDING MUSIC CENTRE OF THAT ERA WAS GERMANY, AND in terms of operatic conducting, the greatest city was Berlin. There the State Opera Unter den Linden had Erich Kleiber as music director. The Charlottenburg Opera under the directorship of Bruno Walter had started up. The Kroll Opera, directed by Otto Klemperer, was about to open; and the Philharmonic Orchestra, with the young Wilhelm Furtwängler, offered an unparalleled musical experience.

Next to Berlin came Dresden, with its very fine State Opera House, under the music direction of Fritz Busch, who also directed the famous Staatskapelle. Though more modest than Berlin as a musical centre it was not inferior in quality, and was the place favoured by Richard Strauss for the premières of his new operas.

There were other cities, such as Leipzig or Munich, but it was Berlin and Dresden which tempted me most. First, I decided, I should go and have a look at both. So, on my next summer holiday, I went.

My visit to the Unter den Linden Opera left me awed by its professional competence. Performances like that of *La Forza del Destino*, conducted by Leo Blech, were almost over-disciplined musically and all too grand scenically; I could hardly bear such clockwork performances. It was also, for me, disastrous in the human aspect. From Kleiber, the top man, down to the doorman, everyone to whom I tried to speak showed the same morose haughtiness. The heap of self-inflated people had a nauseating effect, and I did not feel brave enough to penetrate that fortress of vanity, no matter how rewarding it might have been professionally.

Dresden, however, captivated me at once. The city – alas, it does not exist any longer as I knew it then, having been devastated during the war and only partially rebuilt – was sedate and charming, one cannot say old fashioned, but with a way of its own, withstanding the changes of time. It was a beautiful, peaceful (very un-Germanic) enclave on the banks of the River Elbe with the

Royal Palace, the famous Brühl Terrace, the Opera House and the Drama Theatre all as impressive as they were inviting.

The Opera House – today a gutted, empty shell – dominated a large square with easy-going majesty; an impression that continued as one entered the building.

There was a fine harmony between the house and what went on in it, a quietly competent, sprightly and vital presentation of the *"dramma lirico"* (the word "opera" does not suggest itself here). The large horseshoe theatre was painted silver and blue instead of the customary and more pompous gold and red.

Fritz Busch, to whom I presented myself, received me in a most friendly manner and gave me a ticket for that night's performance of *Khovanshchina*, as well as an invitation to come and see him briefly before his rehearsal the following morning.

It was a splendid evening. The producer was the Russian, Issai Dobrowen, who had also conducted the earlier performances, but not the one I heard. The excellent cast was headed by the towering figure and overwhelming voice of Ivar Andriessen, whom I later came to know well. A small tenor part was sung by Max Lorenz, a minor baritone part by Paul Schoeffler, both star singers of the next few decades. The sounds from the orchestra-pit were of a quality that I had never heard before.

Yet when, next morning, Busch asked me for my impressions, I proceeded impishly not only to praise but to appraise, enumerating virtues and failings of the performance as they came to mind. My good memory helped me in quoting correctly, and bolstered my courage.

Busch's reaction was astonishing: "Well – I'll tell you something," he said. "If by any chance you want to leave the Budapest Opera, you can come here as my assistant. You won't earn much, because I shall be adding you to an already full quota of staff, but you won't starve."

And that was that.

The doors of the "world" had opened. It was hard to believe; and it is hard to express what I felt. Not gladness or happiness, but awe; fright, yet also great confidence. I did not know exactly what I would be expected to do, or what I expected of myself, except some general excellence.

I also had a keen sense that it was at that moment that I left home – by which I mean not only the place of my upbringing, but

91

also the place where I had begun to fit into a system. It went through my mind that I was turning my back on a possibly comfortable future. But my decision to leave that behind and to embrace a new kind of life, with far wider horizons but also far greater uncertainties, was made in full consciousness and with a great and confident joy.

That feeling has proved to be the basic mood of my life.

Things did not go as smoothly as I expected. It turned out that I was to receive the study-stipendium from the Government of Hungary in the form of a paid six months' vacation from "the theatre" but that I was, at the end of it, to return for an indeterminate period to let my "alma mater", as it were, profit from the result of my studies.

When I wrote to explain this to Busch, he agreed to grant me a leave of absence after six months for a similarly unspecified interval. Thus the problem of my double service was solved.

A way was also found of enabling me to be of specific service to the Budapest Opera House as a result of my foreign experiences. Director Radnai planned a production of Verdi's *La Forza del Destino*, never before performed in Budapest, and I offered to bring home the complete data of the Berlin and Dresden productions of that work, the former conducted by Leo Blech, the latter by Fritz Busch.

But when I did so I was profoundly shocked and disgusted by the ignorance of that fine opera displayed by all concerned at "the theatre" and the nonchalance with which they approached what could and should have been a great adventure. This experience, in a melancholy way, confirmed me in my belief that I had taken the right path.

So the moment for leaving my parents' home arrived. I tried to make it easier by saying that I would only be away for a time, and would be back after six months. But my father would have none of that. He regarded my leaving as final, and any later returns as visits.

He declared this in harsh tones, biting his greying-blond moustache to hide his emotion. My mother busied herself with looking after my luggage. I had the impression that for her the separation in space had little meaning, and indeed, in later years, I had ample proof of her transfigured approach to life. My sister was at home, very young and very beautiful and seemingly lighthearted, but I knew little about her in those days. Our adolescent years took us away from each other after our very close childhood, and before the greater closeness of our more mature age.

When my modest luggage was all packed, there still remained some time to spare before I had to leave for the railway station. We had said all we could say. The clock seemed to have stood still.

What could we do?

I went to the piano and began to play, I no longer remember what. Perhaps some improvisation of my own, or music remembered, anything that came under my fingers.

This both loosened and tightened the pressure of the moment.

My father paced up and down and barked: "That's right! Whenever there is nothing more to say, one should make music!"

We didn't speak much more. Our eyes were moist. I had a lump in my throat. And then the time was up.

It was as my father said. I left "for ever". I returned several times, but never again to live at home, in my parents' house or in my city.

9

IN DRESDEN, I SOON FOUND A ROOM FOR A VERY LOW RENT AS A sub-tenant in an old-fashioned but comfortable apartment. Breakfast was included in the arrangement; for the other meals I did as best I could. It was a thirty-minute walk to the Opera House – I used to walk the same distance at home – and my work started immediately.

It was an enviable position, to be the special assistant to the GMD, as the General Music Director is called, and I plunged into it with enthusiasm.

Busch's idea was to get me acclimatised as soon as possible, and he thought that the best way to go about this was for me to hear an opera performance every night as part of my duties. Before each performance he told me about the cast I was going to hear, extolling especially the virtues of the stars who were to appear and to whom he wished me to listen particularly carefully, for it was from these older, mature artists, he believed, that I could learn most about the art of the human voice. And indeed, in that way, I learned a great deal, though perhaps not exactly what Busch had thought I would learn.

The first of the great ones I was to hear and watch was the baritone Friedrich Plaschke, a famous name in those days. The first role I heard him sing was that of Telramund in *Lohengrin*.

Busch conducted.

The production was beautiful, the singers, chorus, orchestra excellent; I drank it all in with the joy of a gourmet. But when Telramund stepped forward to sing his first line, "*Dank, König dir, dass du zu richten kamst!*" ("Thank you, O King, for having come to judge"), my blood stopped in my veins.

An old, faded, tremulous voice came from the throat of that grand old man, the words crisp, clear and delivered with great authority but with more than questionable intonation. The impression was rather pitiful. A perpendicularly raised thumb from his tightly closed right fist, a standard gesture that hardly ever changed, was supposed to add dramatic force to his characterisation. I did not dare to laugh and was not sad enough to cry; I simply watched in bewilderment. The impression he made on me remained the same throughout the three acts, though towards the end the surprise effect had gone, to be supplanted by a tired feeling, like eating stale salad. Yet the audience roared its approval whenever he appeared before the curtain.

Afterwards I went, as agreed, to see Busch, who was sweating and beaming.

"Well?"

I told him how much I admired the orchestra, the chorus, the tenor, the soprano. I also congratulated him – but with some difficulty, for I have never been good at bestowing effusive praise face to face. I expatiated on the fine preparation and so forth.

"And Plaschke?" asked Busch, with shining eyes.

What could I say?

I was too intimidated to blurt out my opinion, and not dishonest enough to lie. So I stammered something to the effect that perhaps the best days of this singer were over, or maybe he was indisposed . . .

"He, indisposed? He, supcrannuated? He never had a better night! That poise! That delivery! That accuracy! That strength! Ah? you did not understand anything! You have a lot to learn! You must listen to him again!"

I did.

The next time he was King Philip in *Don Carlos*, then Hans Sachs in *Meistersinger*, then Barak in *Frau ohne Schatten*.

And, then slowly, I *did* understand. What I was witnessing was a beautiful, touching union between an artist and his public – to which group his colleagues and his conductors also belonged – who heard and re-lived in his singing an entire lifetime of pleasure, enjoyment, guidance received from him, *their* singer, who was indeed a very great artist, because he could make the public – which was *his* public – remember his art and love it through his mere presence, which spiritually remained intact, withstanding all physical ravages the years could bring.

This was a tremendous lesson to learn.

How many artists have such lasting union with their audience today, when the public is merely "window-shopping" in the foyers of art?

One or two, perhaps – or none.

95

Work at the Dresden Opera House went on at a steady, intense pace. As in all repertory houses of that epoch the main emphasis was on ensembles and daily rehearsals. About ninety-five per cent of the company was present all the time, and besides the very careful study of new productions, much loving attention was given to the current repertoire.

The effort was centralised: there was a chief of musical studies, under whose command all assistants belonged, not excluding myself as the music director's aide.

This man was a delightful fanatic. His name was Erich Engel, and he really was the *Engel*, or angel, of his department. Like all who knew their business he could appear in white clouds or with flaming sword, as the occasion warranted.

He supervised the rehearsing of the younger men under his command, and took care of the final shaping of all the most difficult ensembles himself.

He was a stocky, rather heavy-set man, with short, cropped black hair, somewhat greying at the edges, large eyes, deeply sunk under bushy brows, full lips, grotesquely pursed in the ecstasy of work, and a growling voice splitting into unexplainable guttural staccatos while he showed all those wonderful people with beautiful voices how to sing.

The operatic repertory he knew from Adam to Zandonai. His piano playing was rough but competent. As Fritz Busch proudly said, he was the best coach in the world. The secret of his greatness in his chosen métier was that he had no ambition to become a conductor himself. The desire to stand as soon as possible on our own feet as conductors ruined even the best and most conscientious amongst us fledgling-conductors for prolonged coaching activities.

The reason for Engel's lack of ambition was a physical failing. He was just a little hard of hearing – not much, but enough to have prevented him from coping successfully with the complex masses of sound by which an opera conductor is engulfed in the pit. Wisely and cheerfully, he adjusted himself to that disability, and chose a field where he could and did reach the top.

The music staff itself was an oddly assorted group.

Busch's two fellow conductors had been with the Dresden Opera House for ages; they were as much a part of its interior as the gargoyles are of the exterior of a Gothic cathedral.

The first was Kutschbach, an elderly Saxon of impregnable phlegm and about a half-century's experience of opera conducting, well meaning and friendly but without any trace of imagination or humour.

The second was Stiegler, a somewhat younger man, very gifted but of dubious character. He was lazy, yet useful because he could take over any performance at short notice, thanks not to his knowledge but to his enviably quick grasp, which enabled him to get away, in a superficial sense, with almost anything.

With him I had little contact, but from Kutschbach, who was a fatherly soul, I learned quite a lot. Indeed, from this dry Saxon I received a most useful piece of advice for approaching the music of Bruckner:

"You must think you are improvising it yourself, right there and then," he would say.

This impressed me considerably. For with my southern temperament, I had quite a problem with Bruckner, which I had been trying to overcome since childhood, and I found Kutschbach's approach very helpful. Later I also realised that this over-simplification, intelligently applied, throws a sharp light upon the dualistic nature of Bruckner's work; its formal and contrapuntal rigidity and its complete inner freedom, indestructibly combined.

Kutschbach was very proud of having met Richard Wagner personally. His account of that meeting was as follows:

The great man, then in his late sixties, was in his native city Dresden when Kutschbach was a young, budding *répétiteur* of about eighteen. It so happened that one day he got a call to appear at Wagner's dwelling to play the piano for a rehearsal of the master with the three Rhine Maidens.

"When I arrived there," Kutschbach related, without the slightest trace of a smile, "I found Wagner in the room with three naked women – who couldn't even sing!"

The operatic conductor-aspirants' mentality is – or should I say was? – a curious conglomerate of drive, ambition, frustration, self-indulgence, self-denigration, impatience and criticism. They know the routine of performance so well that, free from the immediate "danger" of being called up to perform, they feel in a way superior to their chiefs, the conductors, who go into the pit night after night, risking their necks and showing their mortal weaknesses – which the assistants, for the time being, can hide.

Indeed, the severest judge of any opera conductor is his *répétiteur*, who is more than ready to criticise him unmercifully if he commits the slightest error.

As I had already had battle-experience, I observed this armchair-conducting on the part of my colleagues with amazement and amusement.

Often I saw them, sitting side by side on the organ-loft (the elevated and isolated square space containing the backstage organ was the *répétiteurs'* citadel), their music stands with the scores of that evening's opera neatly spread out before them, batons in hand, eagerly prepared to "start off" the show. (Even at that early time in my life it seemed to me an utterly useless and stupid occupation to "conduct" in that way, and later, when I was teaching or working with young conductors, I warned them earnestly never practise conducting by beating time to the sounds of a gramophone record, or of a live performance on the air. Conducting is done inside the head and the movements of the body are of secondary importance. They are accessories of the mental process, so to say. If someone feels the need to practise his movements, he probably hasn't practised his *music* thoroughly enough. If he had, and still must overcome some physical awkwardness, these movements are best practised to the sounds of an instrument played by someone, a friend or colleague, who follows the movements of the would-be conductor and plays according to his indications.)

My friends in Dresden did not know this truth, and proceeded merrily with their conductorial guessing game, while I looked on angrily, with arms folded across my chest, in mute protest. They watched the stage manager sending the conductor of the evening down to the orchestra pit, heard the applause which greeted him, and set out to calculate how many minutes or seconds would pass before he got ready for the downbeat. This was an intricate calculation and they had studied the conductors of the house well. One, for instance, touched his cuff-links (2 seconds), another blew his nose (5 seconds), the third put on his glasses (3 seconds), and so on, before taking the baton in his hand. Then each had a personal way of looking around (1 to 10 seconds), each waited just so long for the audience to fall silent until, finally –

Down! went the batons on the organ-loft and the orchestra in the pit either started to play or it did not.

And when it didn't, they blamed the conductor, not themselves. "Phooey, Busch!" I often heard them say after such a "false start", as they called it, gnashing their teeth and looking very, very superior.

The singers were good, and easy to work with. The Wagnerian tenor, Kurt Taucher, at the end of his vocal career but with a lifetime of experience; Max Lorenz, then beginning; Plaschke, who became my father figure; Burg, the older baritone; and the young Schoeffler. Then the ladies: Elizabeth Rethberg of the golden voice; Maria Rajdl, beautiful and charming; Jarmila Novotna and many others, all Aladdin's treasures for a young musician.

Soon I was "one of the gang", had much to do, my work was appreciated, my opinions were listened to, and I began to make my own mistakes.

My gravest error of judgment concerned a young, charming singer, who just then joined the ensemble, fresh and brand new from nowhere in particular. Fritz Busch told me to work with her for a week and then tell him what I thought of her.

My report was negative. Voice – yes, but raw. Intelligence – yes, but –. And so on.

Busch said: "I don't know. I do have confidence in her. Go on, work hard with her for another week."

I did. My opinion remained the same, as it did after the third week too.

Then Busch told me: "Well, perhaps, I'll try teaching her myself. You sit in on the coaching sessions and watch."

Things went well. Busch, I realised, was a splendid coach, and I learned a great deal. But so did the young singer, who was none other than the soon-to-be-famous Maria Cebotari. Alas, she died very young, a mere fifteen or so years later, in her full glory as a singer.

That incident taught me an important lesson. I tried hard to emulate my master. I knew then, what I still know, that a good opera conductor must also be a good coach.

Those were the times of good, thorough, ample rehearsing. Where are they now?

In those days one was asked: "How much rehearsal do you need?"

Now: "How much can you get by with?"

The Dresden Opera House, as I have said, was at that time Richard Strauss's favourite place for having his operas premièred. Thus it had a strong and intense Strauss-tradition, quite different from other Strauss-centres, such as Vienna, Munich and Berlin, and perhaps more intimate, more personal. During my year there his *Aegyptische Helena* was the new work, and superb it was too, with Rethberg, Rajdl, Lorenz and Burg. Busch conducted. I was fortunate to play many rehearsals with this ensemble.

One of Strauss's great favourites was Maria Rajdl, a lyric soprano with a very fine, not too large voice, a dark, southern, almost Levantine beauty of infinite finesse and grace. He wanted her to sing *Salome* and indeed this would have been ideal, except for her light voice, which could never triumph over Strauss's heavy scoring. This was pointed out to him, but he would not be deterred: "I will change the orchestration, so she can come through," he declared.

And he did so in superb fashion, as only he could. It was not a reduction, it was a new approach to his own music, which remained the same but became, magically, more tolerant towards the voice. This was achieved with the simplest means.

The performance took place and Rajdl was an immense success, a Salome as never was heard or seen before. There was no question of the performance being repeated elsewhere, because it was bound to Dresden, and even more to the score which existed only there.

Rajdl soon disappeared from the stage – and it must be that the score adapted for her was destroyed in the holocaust of war, as it has not reappeared. Reduced orchestrations of *Salome* come up from time to time in small opera houses, but these are minor efforts, nothing like the stylistic miracle achieved by Strauss.

The other rare Strauss opera given regularly was *Intermezzo*, the only one for which he also wrote the libretto, an autobiographical piece. It received a racy, fine performance, and offered frothy, light, lyrical entertainment, like the fashionable plays of Somerset Maugham or Ferenc Molnár.

The year in Dresden yielded more for me than a purely musical education. It gave me a sharp insight into the structure of the world of the theatre as it then existed in Germany, probably the best organised, most efficient and most prodigiously maintained cultural establishment in the world at that time.

After the collapse of the Hohenzollern Empire at the end of the First World War, the Weimar Republic took over all the responsibilities of the Imperial Court, including cultural affairs, and the flowering of the performing arts under that régime, until 1933, was a unique phenomenon, never to be reborn.

Every theatre, opera house, and orchestra in the country was owned and operated by government at some level: those of greatest importance by the states which replaced the former principalities and kingdoms; those of smaller scope by municipalities.

The conglomeration of the Prussian State Theatres in Berlin was the largest organisation of its kind. Munich, Hamburg and Dresden were somewhat smaller, operating fewer houses, but certainly not inferior in quality.

The structure of these theatrical empires was vast and top-heavy, involving an over-elaborate bureaucracy. Nevertheless, it worked.

The overlord was the so-called "Generalintendant" (general director), often a figurehead, but just as often a crafty expert of theatre who was appointed by government. He was – at least for a nineteen-year-old répétiteur – a mythical figure, seen only on very special occasions and then only from very far away as a blurred and awesome outline. Under his command was a staff the size of the army of a Balkan country, which took care of the Opera House and the Drama Theatre, one or more of each, as the case might be.

The opera chiefs were the General Music Directors who were responsible only to the Generalintendant and also very lofty and unapproachable personages. The relationship that existed between Fritz Busch and myself was quite exceptional, as I later found out. It was made so, of course, by Busch's initiative, when he hand-picked and imported me to the Dresden Opera. I accepted his generous and friendly approach to me naively, as the normal situation which it was far from being, as the rank of répétiteur was the lowest on the artistic ladder.

The hierarchic system that existed on the whole was rather overbearing, stiff – indeed, very German – yet there were hidden veins in it through which warm human blood circulated. This was seldom allowed to show, but I remember one instance when it did.

101

Every year, on one, hopefully sunny, spring day, the entire personnel of the Dresden Opera House went on a day-long boat-trip on the River Elbe.

The boat was chartered by the Generalintendant and the trip was his present to the staff. He himself, of course, was absent, but everyone else was there, from Fritz Busch, who came with his large family, to stagehands and floor-cleaners.

It was an occasion to which everyone in the house looked forward, and the one excursion in which I participated lived up to every expectation. Food and drink were plentiful and good, the landscape was lovely, the air balmy and breezy; the company's mood ranged from spirited to bawdy, and the general atmosphere was as free and easy as German "Gemütlichkeit" would allow.

In the late afternoon, as the boat made its way homeward, I witnessed a rare scene. Herr König, the excellent but extremely portly principal oboist of the Staatskapelle (the orchestra for the Opera House) was being lifted off the ground by four of his colleagues, making as if to throw him over the ship's rail into the river. A sixth man was photographing the group, to the hilarity of the bystanders.

When I enquired about the reason for this unusual ritual, I was told that it was all a great joke, and of great importance, but something that I as a foreigner would not understand. I must just wait and see and meanwhile keep quiet about it.

This last request seemed a bit pointless to me since half the passengers had looked on anyway. But as lots of beer and wine had flowed, and Mr. König remained on board ship after all, I soon forgot about the incident.

Not for long, however, because the photograph was developed and clandestinely circulated among the orchestra members and the *répétiteurs'* group. It was inscribed at the bottom: "Throwing the King overboard."

That sentence was a standard expression in a then popular card-game called "Skat", which is played on stage in Strauss's *Intermezzo*, then in our repertoire. And the sentence, "Throwing the King (König) overboard" is actually sung by a member of the cast.

The plan was that the photo, so vividly illustrative of the phrase, should be pasted on the cover of the score of *Intermezzo* so that when GMD Busch conducted that opera next, he would see it when he mounted his stand, and . . .

What exactly was supposed to happen then I really do not know. No doubt Busch was expected to smile or be amazed or both. But at any rate all of us thought the idea was great and the job of pasting the picture on the front page of *Intermezzo* was given to our group, the *répétiteurs*.

We accepted the honour with pleasure.

But nothing happened, and one day, with serious faces, my colleagues informed me that in their opinion this pasting business was too daring a thing for us to do on our own. In their well-considered, unanimous view, the consent of none other than the Generalintendant must first be obtained.

And who was to obtain it?

I was.

From that moment on I was "the anointed one" of the group. I was treated with great respect and consideration, but also with pity and sympathy, like the "chosen youth" due to be sacrificed to the god Baal at the next feast day.

I, nothing daunted, though sensing the dark unknown, set out immediately to accomplish my mission.

I quickly learned that it would not be too easy a task. When I strolled over to the management building, haughtily called "Generalinterdanz", and announced to the first receptionist I passed that I wished to see the Generalintendant, I was met with a cold, unbelieving stare and was handed a small piece of paper on which the location of the *Anmelde-Raum*, meaning Application Room, was given.

On arriving there – it was Room No. YXX on the fourth floor – I was scrutinised by a sour-looking middle-aged man (he must have been at least thirty years old), with a lisp.

My name? (He didn't like it.)

Occupation? (He didn't seem to know what a *répétiteur* was.)

Whom did I wish to see? (Raised eyebrows when I mentioned the exalted name and office.)

The object of the proposed interview? (My first reply, "Personal", was not accepted, while my next, "Concerning a photograph", provoked further questions, and further suspicion when I appeared unwilling to answer them.)

Finally I had to answer the same questions in writing, on a

printed questionnaire, a large, orange-coloured sheet of paper, with my address, references (I put down Fritz Busch and Mr. König), and was told that I would be notified in the mail whether my request would be granted or not and when I had to present myself in case the reply was favourable.

By the time this grilling was over, several other sour-looking gentlemen had gathered around me, looking through me with half closed eyes, letting out such signs of *ennui* as cleaning their teeth with their tongues, shooting their cuffs, and adjusting their neckties, in silent but obvious demonstration of their disapproval and contempt.

I left the Generalintendanz less jauntily than I had come in and waited.

The days passed. I went about my business. But the unfinished affair of the interview weighed me down, and the photograph of Mr. König on my dressing table looked less and less funny each morning.

My colleagues, to whom I had faithfully reported my ordeal, asked for my news, first daily, then at successively longer intervals. At home in Hungary the matter would have been slowly forgotten. But not in Germany. There it remained hidden, like a growing tumour, causing a slowly increasing feeling of nausea.

Then the reply arrived, after three weeks or so, a postcard in the morning mail.

Mr. Doráti has to be present at Room ZXX, on the next Thursday, at 11.40 o'clock, when the Generalintendant Dr. Reucker will receive him.

My colleagues rejoiced; they thought this was a great victory. I didn't. The whole thing was the most terrible, embarrassing nonsense.

On the appointed day, having asked for leave of absence from the morning rehearsals (raised eyebrows from Erich Engel; and when I told him that the reason for my request was an interview with the Generalintendant, the eyebrows went up two inches more), I put on my best suit and went, with the König photo in my pocket, punctually to the place appointed.

I was received by a solemn, dark-suited, bespectacled secretary, who verified my "orders", took away the postcard and gave me another paper, with which he sent me to another room, where an even more solemn, more dark-suited, more bespectacled and evidently superior secretary verified that paper, exchanging it for a third, smaller one. With that I went further, to meet an incredibly over-superior secretary, where things began to get serious. He took away my small paper and ushered me, now paperless, into the next room, where a uniformed attendant took me in tow and guided me through various rooms and corridors to a large ante-chamber, with a lot of chairs and a few tables. On the walls were dozens of life-size portraits of former Generalintendants and there was an elegant desk, behind which was seated a very dignified white-haired lady who told me, without a smile, to sit down.

We remained alone in the large room, in dead silence, for about twenty minutes.

Finally, without any warning, the lady rose, beckoned me to approach, and opened the door behind her desk.

There I was in the inner sanctum. It was a vast hall, with a great number of terrace windows, very light, white-walled, and hung with old paintings of theatrical catastrophes (battle scenes, executions and the like), sparsely and splendidly furnished in the style of Louis whatever-the-number-was. Fifty steps or more away, in front of a tapestried wall, stood an over-large desk, quite out of keeping with the rest of the room; and behind that desk, out of keeping with everything else but very much in keeping with himself, sat the overlord, Generalintendant Dr. Reucker.

He motioned with a long, thin, pink hand, and I approached carefully, anxious not to slip on the wooden floor, which gleamed like a mirror and was laid out in fantastic, complicated symmetrical patterns.

At first I noticed only the Generalintendant's pince-nez, with its brightly glistening lenses which prevented me from seeing his face until my eyes got used to those two small spotlights. Then, gradually, I discerned red-grey hair, rather like that of a thoroughbred poodle; a long, thin nose, evidently worn down by the pincer pressure of the glasses; pink, somewhat freckled skin; and a very high, white, starched collar, which made him look as if he had to stretch to be able to look out over it. This collar had a very tightly knotted tie at its base, somewhat like the funnel of a steamer in tropical waters. Its owner wore a light grey, absolutely uncreased suit. He was distinctly skinny.

As I approached him, step by step, my curiosity about the man overrode my feeling of awe. I had never seen a real live General-intendant before, and this was, indeed, an interesting specimen.

The glasses gleamed, and the wide-set, small, light, blue-grey eyes, as they gradually became visible, certainly took everything in. It occurred to me later that it was probably also the first time that the Generalintendant had met a real live *répétiteur* face to face.

"Well, young man, what can I do for you?"

He spoke softly, slowly; the question sounded genuine, the voice agreeable.

As I heard him speak, suddenly the miserable, faded dullness of my mission struck me with crushing force. The old, by now pointless joke, and the pitiful role I had agreed to play in its sorry execution, made me a worthless idiot.

I fumbled in my pocket for the photograph, praying for the earth to open up and swallow me.

But it didn't.

I began to stutter:

"Herr Generalintendant . . . you see . . . it is this . . . that the King . . . that is . . . that Herr König . . . that he . . . is being thrown overboard . . ."

"Who is — what?" the astonished Generalintendant whispered.

"As you see . . . in this photograph . . ."

"Good God! What is this?"

Perspiration ran down my nose. It was a terrible moment.

"You see . . . Herr Generalintendant . . . this picture . . . the King thrown overboard . . . was taken on the Elbe excursion . . . and it was very funny . . ."

I nearly cried.

"And then . . . we thought . . . we must paste this on to the score . . . of Herr Generalmusikdirektor Busch . . . so he sees it when he next conducts *Intermezzo* . . . because . . . to throw the King overboard . . . this is sung . . . it occurs . . . verbatim . . . in the opera . . . and I was sent . . . to ask . . . to ask . . . your consent."

There it was. I had said it. The earth did not open to swallow me up and no other cataclysmic event occurred either.

Instead there was a long silence.

Dr. Reucker reached for the photograph, took it into his long fingers and looked at it seriously, attentively. Then he put it on his desk, bent over it, scrutinising it again, from all angles, this way and that.

Then he looked me over, from head to toe and back again, slowly.

Then he looked out into nowhere with a dreamy, yet precise expression on his face.

The pause was interminable and I became more and more miserable and ashamed of myself as the soundless minutes passed.

Then he slowly turned to me, very deliberately picked up the photograph and gave it back to me.

I held it, stupidly, and heard him say, softly and crisply:

"No, young man, on no account must you paste this photograph on the front page of the score. You shall paste it" – a long, dreamy look into his own youth, perhaps – "you shall paste it on the page where – the sentence occurs."

The thin, pink hand offered itself for a wordless goodbye.

I returned to my colleagues in a one-man triumphal cortège. Thenceforth I was definitely in a higher echelon of humanity than they.

The pasting was not my job. Our group, no doubt, did what was necessary and did it well.

But I never heard anything about the success or otherwise of the joke. Probably it fizzled out.

From Busch I learned as much about conducting as one man can learn from another. To teach conducting is impossible. It is a thoroughly practical activity, which has to be adapted to its environment at each attempt, like mountain-climbing or sailing. The ground rules exist, and they are simple to impart and to understand, but to know them means practically nothing. The only way to learn more is to watch another conductor – with luck it will be a good one, but any kind will do – and, if he is good, to work under his leadership for a limited time. From then on it is up to oneself entirely.

With Busch, who was a very good conductor, I had the chance to do both. I played under his baton several times, in his orchestra, but more often than that I played the piano when he conducted ensemble rehearsals with singers. These were the most instructive occasions. What I learned from him essentially can be simply stated:

I learned *what is expected of me, while I am conducting, by those for whom I conduct.*

I learned that and more in Dresden. I learned discipline, and perhaps pride. I learned not to compromise. Busch's smile was a mile wide when, after about three months, I said to him about something or other, "That is not up to *our* standard!"

Grateful and happy as I was, I was impatient to continue on my way. I felt I was ready to have a conductor's post of my own. So I set out from Dresden to look for one in one of the smaller opera houses in Germany. It is always very difficult for a young man to find such a post, and it was much more so then than it is now, for at that time previous experience was valued more highly than it is today. And at not quite twenty-three years old, I had very little of it. But my determination won, and in a matter of a few months I had found a post for the coming season.

My search for independence was not mainly artistic. A conductorial contract was the condition I had set for myself in order to do what I most wanted to do at that moment – to get married.

10

WHEN I BEGAN TO WRITE THESE NOTES, I MADE TWO VOWS. FIRST, that there would be no foreword, no epilogue and, above all, no asterisks or footnotes. Second, that of the three great subjects of life, "Wine, Women and Song", they would concentrate on the third, as befits the notes of a musician.

It was easy to omit the first subject, for, although I love and relish a good wine, I can take it or leave it.

But it is different with the second theme; women are an intrinsic part of my life and have enriched it infinitely. I could not, and would not, banish them from my thoughts. To deprive my pen of the joy of writing their praise is difficult.

Yet, I do so. There will be scarcely a mention of them throughout this book. When there is, it will be more between the lines than on them.

But let there be one exception.

The chronology of my narrative is interrupted anyway, so here I will tell one little story about women or, rather, about one woman. If it were not to be the only one in this book, it would be the first. It is about a kiss, also the first.

In the summer of 1917 my family went for a holiday, not to Lake Balaton, as usual, but to the Lower Carpathian Mountains in the north-east of Hungary.

It was a slightly spooky summer. There was the background of the war, strangely muted although we were not all that far from the Russian front. Things went badly, for both sides.

The landscape of ragged mountains and immense pine trees, was ominous too, and vaguely uncomfortable. For us children it was all new – new and full of mystery.

There were diversions, however: long walks in the forests, mushrooming (we soon became experts), and restaurants. It was the first time we had ever eaten regularly in a restaurant – we did so throughout the entire summer, in fact – and the process of getting dressed for it, walking to it in a group, ordering the food – all this was unusual and strange.

An old gipsy fiddler played in the place every day. He must have been at least a hundred. His face was incredibly wrinkled, like one of those plastic raincoats, not then invented, of course, which come out of a tiny envelope and can never be put back again. And his wrinkles, amazingly, continued below his face and down towards his shirt, which must once have been white, and his dinner-jacket, which must once have been black. (The Hungarian gipsies always wear dinner-jackets for work, never those flamboyant peasant dresses they sport when abroad. And generally one dinner-jacket lasts a gipsy his entire life, and is absolutely never cleaned.) This gipsy played with passion, but poorly, with dried-out fingers, and his instrument was a mere caricature of a violin, a veritable stringed cigar-box.

One day my father suddenly turned to me: "Tóni, run to the hotel and bring my violin."

I did.

My father took the fine instrument out of its case, went up to the gipsy and offered it to him: "Hey, *Bácsi*, try this one for a change!"

The gipsy took the violin hesitantly, tucked it under his chin and began to play. The sound that came out was surprisingly different from what we had heard before; it was really quite nice.

The old man's face changed and became transfigured; and as he played on with mounting fervour, tears streamed from his eyes. Silently and copiously crying, he played tune after tune, as if in a trance, never wanting to stop. His tears went all over the strings, the violin, the floor, disgusting and yet so deeply moving.

How my father got his violin back, I don't know. Perhaps the old man surrendered it willingly, after having had his triumph.

And triumph it was, perhaps the first and the last of his life. All the guests in the crowded restaurant were on their feet, clapping, cheering. It was a standing ovation.

That restaurant was the only eating and meeting place in the small village. Everybody used it for every meal, and often between meals.

Among the guests, at the same table every day, sat a solitary lady, beautiful, well dressed, and always in light colours, white, cream or beige. Tall, dark blonde, and with a splendid, wind-blown, outdoor skin, she kept strictly to herself, speaking little. In fact, I never heard or saw her utter a word, or address anybody. Even the waiters who served her seemed to know what she wanted, and brought her food and poured her wine silently, without a word being exchanged.

She sat at a small table near a window. The dark green bushes outside made a shining background to her light figure. The window was always open, and from time to time the breeze played delectably with a small strand of her hair.

When, straight of gait and erect of posture, she walked across the room to her table and later out again, conversation died down and many eyes followed her movements. Amongst them were the eyes of one eleven-year-old boy: myself.

Soon the lithe, enchanting figure of the "countess", as the villagers called her, held my fancy completely, and I began to live a secret, private life of the imagination. I told myself innumerable stories involving us both, all very adventurous, gallant – and innocent. Every book I had ever read until then was transformed to fit "us": we were involved in adventures in the prairies of America (*The Last of the Mohicans*), on a large ship (*The Children of Captain Grant*), on a desert island (*Robinson Crusoe*). and so on. She was always in dire peril, and I always arrived in the nick of time to save her.

We were, of course, close friends by then, as befitted a gallant rescuer and his much-rescued lady. Close friends in my stories, that is. In reality – for which I cared not a jot – I had not even caught sight of her, except far away at mealtimes.

Until one day, I went into the forest to "collect wood". This was a polite expression to cover my real activity, which was cutting down and stealing young saplings from which my sister, my cousins and I carved fancy walking sticks. This work was very much for our own private satisfaction, for cutting down the saplings was strictly forbidden, so we could not even display our masterworks for fear of being found out. In collecting the forbidden material, I often wandered in the forest, armed with a small saw, taking one or other of the many intricate paths that I had come to know well.

The afternoon in question was particularly enchanting. It had rained earlier, so that the leaves and grass were still glistening with rain drops. The air was fragrant and so clear that one could think it would break when hit by the soft wind.

111

I came out into a clearing. At the same moment, at the far side of it, the foliage parted to reveal a white and gold figure: the "countess".

She came towards me on the same narrow path. I moved forward, inevitably, against my will, in a trance, looking at her and through her, beyond her, above her, my heart beating in my throat.

Where I did not look, unfortunately, was at the path in front of me. I stumbled on a root and fell headlong on the muddy ground. It was the end. There was the gallant knight, at the feet of the beloved whom he had saved from so many dangers. But he was not on one knee, visor lifted, sword in one hand, rose in the other. Oh no! Flat on his face, muddy, dirty, with nothing in his hands (for I had dropped even the saw), he felt shame and humiliation.

The white wonder came nearer and nearer until she stopped where I was lying. She stretched out her hands, helped me to get up, and took from somewhere a handkerchief. With this she cleaned me – first my face, then my clothes – with great skill, seriously, efficiently.

Then she looked at me, without a smile, put the soiled handkerchief away, took my head into her two hands and kissed me on the mouth. Long, warm, strong (as years later I could verify), this was no motherly or sisterly kiss. It was a true kiss.

She continued past me, on her way into the forest. I stood there, kissed, confused – and probably changed for life.

The "countess" attended the restaurant as before. So did I, with my family, every day for the rest of the holiday. But, oh, not as before at all.

11

By the spring of 1929, after a mere month or so of intensive and determined search for a conductorial position, I found one, and I was ready to leave Dresden to become my own master.

When I told Busch, he congratulated me heartily. But when I added that the real reason for my hurry to get out from under his wing was my wish to marry, he was less enchanted. He thought I was far too young. So did my father, who opposed my plan with his usual violence. In vain, of course; he soon understood that my determination could not be shaken, and his turn-about was complete; he was, as soon as he had given in, on the best of terms with my future bride. Her father merely cautioned us to wait until I was in a position to raise a family. My interpretation of this condition was that I had to be on my own in my profession, and I fulfilled it at once.

Klári was eighteen – I had just turned a very immature twenty-three – and I was very much in love with her. She was very beautiful. We met in the house of mutual friends where I was giving a lecture course on opera for young ladies. Her parents welcomed me warmly, although I could hardly have been the answer to their dreams as their only daughter's future husband.

Sándor Kórody, Klári's father, was a banker and businessman. They were well-to-do, which embarrassed me considerably. But love won out, and I was absolutely determined to become their equal and a good bread-winner, as in due time I did.

So, at the end of the Dresden season, I returned home, married Klári, and, after a brief honeymoon in Italy, went with my young bride to Münster, the capital of Westphalia in Western Germany, where I had been appointed conductor of opera at the Municipal Theatre.

It was a charming-looking old town, with splendid churches – one of them, the Church of St. Laurentius, still had on its belfry the cages where the Protestant heretics were put, to die slowly of exposure in the name of God. It had an old, fine university, narrow, old, cobblestoned streets, and a very Catholic, very provincial population.

The theatre was a decrepit, disastrous building, fashioned out of the stables of a nearby castle. In it a large group of actors and singers offered a mixed diet of drama, operetta and opera, on a surprisingly high level of talent and accomplishment, it must be said. The municipal orchestra – which also played a full concert season – was not very large, but it was highly competent, as was the chorus.

My job was to take care of the opera department, and it proved a tough one at the start, due to my youthful years and still more youthful looks.

The first obstacle I had to surmount was actually getting into the theatre, for the doorman, when I said that I was the new opera conductor, eyed me from head to toe and laughed out loud.

"*Das kann ein jeder sagen*" ("Anyone can say that"), he replied.

He barred my way. I had to summon the help of the Intendant, who finally appeared and vouched for me.

In the theatre itself, I was met with general distrust. And though in due course I was able to win the confidence of the entire company, there remained one exception: the doorman. This worthy never lost his conviction that I was an impostor, and did not fail to let me feel his antagonism and contempt every time I passed his booth, which was at least twice, and often four or six times a day for three years. At first I minded this; later I made a joke of it and invited my colleagues to join in; the doorman, a bitter man, suffered more and more from his own hatred.

The Intendant, a curious, intelligent fellow, was an addict of the theatre, one of those by now almost extinct specimens of the type which ran the old troupes of strolling players. His name was Alfred Bernau. He hailed, like Hitler, from the German-Austrian border region, and sported the same kind of brush moustache. There the likeness ended, however. Bernau was decent, kind, rather soft-hearted; an amateur, as it were, although of great professional skill in his own field, which was the theatre of the spoken word. He was also a remarkable actor. Whenever, which was rarely, he took over a part, his performance was never less than outstanding. I never saw a more impressive King Philip in Schiller's *Don Carlos*. In the lyric theatre he was less expert. But this benefited me, because he left me to my own devices for months, checking only to see whether my enterprises were a success. As most of my productions luckily pleased our public, he soon trusted me blindly and gave me a free hand within our modest budgetary limits.

The beginning of my time at Münster was not without surprises and problems. Since Bernau did not know me he had, before my arrival, arranged almost everything for the greater part of the season, from repertoire to casting, according to his own tastes, which were, in the field of opera, questionable.

Thus it happened that, although I came to Münster prepared to the teeth, and secure in the knowledge of a repertoire of some seventy operas, the first one I had to conduct was a work I had never even heard of. It was Eugene d'Albert's *The Dead Eyes (Die toten Augen)*. Not as powerful as his famous *Tiefland*, which was at that time part of the standard repertoire and is even now performed here and there, *The Dead Eyes* is a short, compact opera, with a biblical story, the healing of the blind. Well constructed for the stage, and leading up to but omitting the appearance of Christ in person, it is not without its attractions. When I saw that there was no way out, I plunged into the score and learned it within a few days. And I learned it well. As I write this, forty-eight years later, almost the entire opera springs up in my mind. There they are, the melodies and harmonies, right "in my ten fingers".

Besides myself, the opera team at Münster consisted of the producer, Ruzicka, and the designer, Fritsche, the former a Czech, the latter a German, both very gifted, and both still in their twenties, although older than myself. Unlike me, both of them were rather leisurely, so I had occasion to trespass into their fields and dabble in my two great hobbies, stage-directing and designing, which I did under their names.

Our singers were also young and talented; a small house like ours had either gifted beginners or older mediocritics. Obviously, I preferred the former, and "went to town" with them with great gusto.

Instead of plunging head over heels into a new repertoire, I concentrated on giving first-rate performances of standard works, meticulously rehearsed and stylishly produced. We had no money for lavish scenery and costumes, but we tried to make up for this with intelligence and imagination.

In *Rigoletto* our production was based on a remark in one of

Verdi's letters: "I am writing the tragedy of an ugly man." To the staging we brought an expressionistic quality by the simple device of building the four sets, in turn, on the same, split-levelled ground plan. Thus, throughout the highly contrasting moods and designs of the four acts, the entrances, exits and groupings remained identical, creating an attractive Renaissance effect. For the staging of our *Carmen* we showed squalid, unkempt factory suburbs and mountain hide-outs and our Escamillo entered the bistro in "mufti". In the mountain scenes we tried to make the human bodies melt into the landscape as flora rather than fauna, as it were. We gave *Fidelio* the look of Goya's late paintings. In Puccini's *Il Tabarro* we made the river the hero or monster of the piece, and in *Gianni Schicchi* the towers of Florence grew and grew to dominate the stage at the end of the opera. Above all, we rehearsed day and night with our dedicated young company. It is quite astonishing what a difference it makes to an opera production if all the singers really know their way about on the stage, understand not only every word but every inflection of their text, and are constantly stimulated to project it; and when each member of a chorus is taught individually how to move and what to do.

Nor did we miss out on contemporary works. We gave Stravinsky's *Nightingale* and *Oedipus Rex*, Hindemith's *Cardillac*, the in those times inevitable *Schwanda the Bagpiper* by Weinberger, Bartók's *Bluebeard's Castle*, Ravel's *L'heure Espagnol* and other new operas.

We made many youthful mistakes, but I believe that in our modest way our productions were interesting and enjoyable. That kind of lyric theatre was perhaps only possible with a young team in a small provincial town, unharassed and away from the main highways of competition.

Life in the small city was in other respects dull. Our theatre was in fact the salt and pepper of the place, and only those of us who were able to submerge ourselves completely in our profession had a fully satisfactory life.

I was one of them. Less fortunate was my young wife, who had many lonely hours to fill while her equally young husband was busy at work.

At first we lived in a grand, rather nouveau-riche apartment

116

which proved ruinous to our very modest finances. So we moved for the rest of my term of duty in Münster into a small flat in the old city, renting two tiny rooms in the house of a taxidermist and sharing the place with innumerable stuffed animals from elk to fox. Our kind landlady treated us to curious and gruesome dishes like squirrel soup, badger pâté, ragout of stork and the like, which we tried, not always successfully, to refuse without giving offence.

It took only about fifteen minutes to walk comfortably from our flat to the theatre through the old city's narrow, winding streets. It was my custom to arrive very early each night, before the start of the performance. One Christmas Eve I had left specially early and strolled specially slowly to the temple of the Muses. But I stopped dead in my tracks at the stage door, where my enemy, the doorman, sat in his booth, smirking as my incredulous ears heard the strains of the overture to the opera of that night, evidently conducted by – myself. Rushing down to the orchestra pit, I arrived exactly as the final chords of the overture sounded, just in time to take the place of the ashen-faced producer, who had taken my place and somehow got through the piece – he was fortunately very musical – but was appalled at the thought that he would have to continue if I didn't arrive in time.

I had forgotten that the Christmas performance started thirty minutes earlier than on other nights. During my stroll through the city I had been lost to the world, and my colleagues decided to punish me by starting on time. As my replacement told me, he had never been so glad to see me.

It was only a week later than another disaster occurred. It was New Year's Day, when the theatre traditionally had an afternoon operetta performance. The night before, as was the custom in many theatres, we gave a traditional New Year's Eve performance of Johann Strauss's *Fledermaus*, which I conducted. That performance was distinguished by containing additional touches: impromptus in the dialogue, extra verses relating to New Year's Eve in the "*Chacun à son goût*" couplets and, last but not least, there was real champagne, served to the cast during the second act finale. That guaranteed a very lively third act, and raised promising possibilities for the festivities to follow, which in fact lasted well into the first seven or eight hours of the incoming year. No one was

117

very sober on January 1st, but most of us had a chance to sleep until the evening, when we had to be ready for the next opera.

Thus I was sleeping the sleep of the just when my telephone rang. It was the Intendant's office telling me that Mr. Wollmer, the operetta conductor, was in no fit condition to preside at that afternoon's show, and all the other conductors were unavailable for the same reason. I was the only hope and the performance was at three p.m.

"How late is it now?" I asked.

"One-thirty," was the reply. "We have been trying to raise you since eleven-thirty."

"What's on this afternoon?"

"*Frederika*." I had a vague idea that this Lehár operetta was about Goethe and one of his love affairs, but I had never seen or heard it.

"I can't do it. I don't know it."

"Oh, but you must. Please. There's no one else capable of standing on his feet."

"But I've never conducted this kind of operetta in my life."

The Intendant came on the line. He begged me, cajoled me; and finally, out of sheer weariness, I gave in.

I got dressed, went to the theatre, looked for the singers whom I had asked to come in early for a sort of "information rehearsal", but not a soul was in sight. All of them were in a bad way.

A thin, very sketchy vocal score, with no indication of the instrumentation, was the only one available. Apparently Mr. Wollmer conducted the whole work from memory.

But by then I was resigned to the worst that might happen, and descended, with shaking knees into the pit.

I held out bravely and we proceeded without catastrophe.

But suddenly my blood froze. Here we were: *delirium tremens* had got me at last.

Looking up on the stage – there, in the centre – I saw it.

No, it cannot be.

I looked again.

There it was – large as life, looking back at me, chewing, calmly, stupidly.

A big, woolly sheep.

Surely no one else had seen it, because no one seemed to mind. Everyone carried on in the most natural, normal way.

Shaken to death, I turned my eyes away from the stage and held on for dear life until I somehow finished the first act.

But after it was over, I refused to continue. I explained to the actors what I had seen. The white sheep was bad enough in the first act. I didn't want to see pink elephants in the second.

From the howling, hilarious reaction to the tremulous description it began slowly, very slowly, to dawn on me that my ruminant apparition was part of the *mise-en-scène*. ‾

We were a dedicated crew. Our fooling around was no more than the exuberance of youth. Professionally it was an ideal time for a young man. Recognition was not lacking either. Our fame spread, our small, dreadful-looking theatre prospered. We even had a regular subscription night every week for a special audience from nearby Holland, brought to Münster by train and taken back over the border after the opera. At the same time, offers for guest engagements were beginning to come in, of which I accepted as many as I could, and I found myself conducting *Tannhäuser* in Brno, *Lohengrin* in Frankfurt, *Ballo in Maschera* in Dessau, and so forth.

So much so that after my third season in Münster I had the courage to break away and try to live on guest conducting only.

We moved to Berlin, where my aunt and my cousins still lived, and rented a studio in a pleasant neighbourhood from a painter who was away in Italy. I formed a chamber orchestra with which I intended to give a series of concerts of contemporary music, and began my new career on what seemed an auspicious note.

I did not get far.

It was, then, the autumn of 1932.

One day I unintentionally opened a cupboard in our apartment and found a brown SS uniform facing me.

So, our painter-landlord, away in Positano, was a Nazi. As were so many.

Hitler and his men were on their way to power.

Curiously, and in contrast to my attitude of four years before, when one of my reasons for leaving Hungary was the uncomfortable and erroneous feeling of belonging to a Jewish minority which was being discriminated against, now, in Berlin, in the eye of the hurricane, as it were, I had no fear or thought of being personally threatened in any way at all. Perhaps my sensitivities

119

had undergone a change. In 1928 I was fresh out of school, a snail without a house, very vulnerable indeed. In 1933 I had four years of professional experience behind me (I did not know then how little that is), I was a musician, I thought a good one; and I bothered with little else except becoming a better one.

At all events, I took no notice of the ominous changes in the world outside. Not even the sudden downturn in guest engagements caused me alarm. I took it as a run of bad luck and went on with the organising of my chamber orchestra, for which I recruited a group of brilliant artists, all my age or younger, and began rehearsing with them, building a contemporary repertoire with which I shortly meant to astonish the world.

Meanwhile we had less and less to eat from week to week and I had to look for work outside my conducting profession to earn my living. I did whatever I could, took occasional engagements to play the piano, coached singers, and once even sang in the chorus for a movie.

On the set of that film I met the Hungarian operetta composer, Paul Ábrahám, who knew who I was and straightway engaged me to conduct his forthcoming show *Ball at the Savoy*.

This was my first and only contact with the world of the musical. (My brief encounter with *Frederika* and her white sheep was a one-day excursion into the realm of Viennese operetta, an altogether different form of stagecraft.)

At that time Ábrahám was a highly successful composer of musicals. His first success was *Victoria and her Hussar*. The second, *The Flower of Hawaii*. Both of these brought enormous incomes for all concerned, not least himself. Now ensconced in the glory of his sombrely sumptuous house in Berlin's fashionable Fasanen Strasse, he was preparing for his third great triumph.

The theatre rented was no less a place than the Grosse Schauspielhaus in Berlin, a huge barn with about 6,000 seats. The prima donna was Gitta Alpár, then at the peak of her career. As the male lead, or *bonvivant*, a certain de Kova, also a well-known singing actor of his time, was engaged. The *buffo* couple were to be the famous Hungarian team, Rózsi Bársony and Oszkár Dénes. Producer, designers, cast, all were waiting – for the music to be composed.

This was done in great conviviality at the "House of Abraham".

120

As the conductor to be (the composer intended to conduct the first few performances himself) I was invited to all these "composing sessions" and went to quite a number. They were remarkable occasions. In the course of them I drank more champagne than I have ever drunk in my life before or since; ate a great amount of oysters, lobsters, pâté de foie gras, pineapple, mango and what have you; participated – a little – in animated discussions concerning the still non-existent but slowly emerging masterpiece, and watched the entire procedure with bewildered amusement, or amused bewilderment, according to my mood of the moment.

There was great coming and going. Always present were Bársony and Dénes, who had the most fertile imagination of the group, very often Alpár and the two producers, anxious about their already very sizeable investment, and a number of hangers-on, ranging from a half to two full dozen. But the most important person was a small, thin, very ugly German musician, whose job was to take down the master's ideas and develop them into music numbers.

Not that Ábrahám could not do this himself. His musical background and training were quite thorough, and I am sure that, when he was less famous he did write his music alone. But success wrought havoc upon his poor mind. What started as laziness and spleen gradually became complete disintegration.

Things would go something like this:

" . . . Here, Oszkár, you remain alone on the stage, you are very, very desperate. You say . . ."

Silence.

Oszkár speaks up: "I say . . . I say . . . I want to go on a trip!"

Ábrahám joins in: "Splendid, splendid . . . a trip, that is excellent. That is always very good."

Long silence.

"Where do you want to go?"

Several suggestions are offered, everybody joining in.

"Poland!"

"Norway!"

"Greece!"

"Brazil!"

Oszkár turns up his nose at them all.

Suddenly Rózsi, who has not said a word but has been lying on a sofa, listlessly turning the pages of an illustrated weekly, speaks up.

121

Without stirring, she interjects her high-pitched voice cleverly into a moment's silence and pronounces: "Beludshistan."

Oszkár is electrified.

Ábrahám beams, shows his few decayed teeth, and whistles through his cigarette holder.

Oszkár begins moving his hands rhythmically, then his feet in dance steps – he is still sitting – and chants: "Beludshistan, Afghanistan, and Pakistan, Whatsisistan . . ."

Ábrahám pokes his finger at the upright piano. Two or three incoherent short notes emerge, reluctantly, from the ill-tuned instrument.

The ugly scribe begins to scribble, feverishly, on a large sheet of music paper. God only knows what.

Rózsi is back to her magazine. She has lost interest.

After a while the scribe gets up, takes his music sheet to the piano and begins to play something. No sooner has he started than both Ábrahám and Oszkár begin to yell vehemently: "No, no! Not that way! Stop! Slower! Faster! . . . You don't know anything!"

The poor little gnome is the only one who has so far produced a note.

Ábrahám again pokes his finger at the piano. Oszkár now walks, dances up and down the room, improvising a sort of text:

> "I'm going to Beludshistan
> but I stop first in Pakistan,
> not to speak of Afghanistan . . ."

and so forth.

Slowly, with everybody in the room singing, humming, tapping, a quickening dance rhythm, in the manner of the American jazz tunes then current, develops.

Ábrahám gets up, taps the scribe on his shoulder to tell him to move from the piano, sits down himself and plays, quite well, an eight-bar phrase in the rhythm of "Afghanistan, Beludshistan". The scribe takes it down.

Ábrahám stops playing and gives him peremptory directions: "Now this bit comes in again, up a fifth, then four bars to get back, then you know what to do."

The gnome-like scribe nods. He knows. He improvises it on the piano. Ábrahám stops him. "That's enough now. We do it later."

A round of champagne is poured. Everybody drinks. Congratulations are in order.

"Ho-ho, this will be a good one."

"Just wait until Oszkár does the 'Beludshistan', it will be terrific!"

A hit-tune was on its way to be born.

As it turned out, it wasn't the best tune in the show, but it was quite good. Both Oszkár and Rózsi sang it and danced it successfully many times.

And so, in this manner, the entire show got composed.

Even when it came to the orchestra rehearsals, Ábrahám changed his music by shouting to the players what to play instead of the notes that they had in their parts. When someone suggested that they might write down the changes just agreed upon in this manner, one of the producers, who was listening in the stalls, rebuked the pedantic intruder, "Shut up! Here we orchestrate by acclamation."

My glimpse into this astonishing, repellent world lasted only a few weeks. After a very successful première the show was slated for a long run. I took over the conducting from the composer after the first ten days or so. It was an easy and dull job. My financial worries were over. I earned a very satisfactory salary, and as only my evenings were occupied – rehearsing was over for good – I had plenty of free time on my hands, most of which I devoted to my budding, very hopeful, very fine chamber orchestra.

Meanwhile life outside went on. The senile Hindenburg was President of the German Republic. Hitler became Chancellor. The Reichstag burned.

Through all this, like many others, I moved strangely untouched, unknowing, unafraid. I saw the first official anti-Jewish posters, witnessed the visible remnants of Berlin's first – and no doubt, in comparison with what was to come, rather mild – pogrom. I was witness to diverse, grotesque transitions in human relations. The prompter of the theatre, so far an unnoticed little dumpy man, suddenly emerged as the thundering Nazi leader of German actors. Paul Ábrahám's ugly little scribe – who looked, by the way, much more Jewish than his truly semitic boss – suddenly revealed himself to be a savage Nazi despot, wearing all sorts of badges and terrorising poor, soft-hearted Ábrahám, who had fed him and taken care of him, and the other Jews in his entourage.

123

My disgust mounted, but I still did not feel personally threatened, and in fact I never was.

But . . . One day my chamber orchestra asked me to finish a rehearsal somewhat sooner than planned. Upon asking why, I was informed that they all had to go to a meeting. I went along with my friends: there were some questions I wanted to ask the officials myself. I had lately been receiving some curious communications recommending the dismissal of one or another member of my group as "not belonging", and I wanted to know what was meant by that phrase and who "belonged" to my orchestra and who did not.

That meeting changed the course of my life in less than thirty minutes. I looked and listened, and was sick unto death. The baseness, cruelty, vileness, criminality, inhumanity that was expressed in the conversations and behaviour I witnessed was beyond my comprehension and imagination.

Nothing deadly was arranged in that room. But everything that happened later, up to the concentration camps and ultimate genocide, could be felt there in a capsule, so to speak. Instant hatred was served up like Nescafé.

It was an appalling awakening. This was the Germany where I had been living for four years, being "useful"; this was the Germany of splendid literature and wonderful music that I revered and loved. All was but a mask then, and behind it was naked bestiality. "This is not *my* country" – was my first defensive thought. It flashed through my mind that if I saw this in Hungary, I would shout, shoot, fight, do anything, dare everything to stop it. But here in Berlin? This was not my place. I had nothing in common with these people. Off and away. Leave them behind. This was not the world I was seeking. This was prison. Filth. I must go. Now.

My reaction was as sudden and as violent as was the shock I had been subjected to.

I left the meeting, and walked back to our apartment. On the way I checked at the railway station – Banhof Zoo – the time of the next train to Paris. It left at eight p.m. I arrived at the flat (even now I cannot bring myself to write down the word "home", the word I cheerfully used until that hour), and announced to Klári that we had to pack fast and were leaving in four hours. She thought I had gone mad. But when I explained to her what I had seen, she understood. We packed our belongings in a frenzy. There was some hectic telephoning to our parents in Budapest. Mine just said quietly: *"Servus"* – and "write sometimes". Hers raised a great fuss; it was madness to plunge off into the vast unknown when things were going so well for me in Berlin. And if I absolutely must go, I should come home, where I had a name and a reputation. Why Paris, where I did not know a single soul?

We left at eight p.m.

Early next morning we were in Paris.

12

WHY PARIS?

It was the natural logic of youth. I had set out into the world, or into what I naively imagined was the world; and the world, as had been instilled in me since my childhood, was westward from my native land.

Its first station had been Germany. The next must be France, only a few hours away by rail westward. And so for that unknown, unknowing, unconnected young man, who was willing to start again from scratch, the natural goal was Paris, the city of dreams.

And particularly the city of dreams that did and do not come true. Its lure was always great and continues to be. Those who were drawn into its circle of light often remained there as foreigners, never acclimatised, never accepted, in a world of their own – a special purgatory from which there was no release promised or sought. To make one's way, to hold one's ground in Paris, was hard, was tough on a stranger. To get lost, to drown, to be down and out was easier and more comfortable than elsewhere.

When approaching Paris on that train from Berlin, I did not follow a lure, I did not have a wish to settle in Paris. What was important for me at that moment was not the arrival; it was the departure from where I had come.

Some acquaintance in Germany had told us about a small hotel in the Latin Quarter, with a grandiose name. We remembered it and soon we were installed in the Hôtel des Grands Hommes in the Place du Panthéon.

The "great men" referred to in the name of the hotel were, of course, those buried in the Panthéon, grandly spread out in the centre of the square. A short-cut for future "great men" was perhaps suggested by the funeral parlour occupying the street level front of our hotel. It did not worry us; and we did not intend to take up the offer – there was a time for everything, we felt.

There were no great problems: we had enough money to last two or three weeks, with appropriately tightened belts. Julien's restaurant was around the corner. There we could get meals on a subscription basis. If we bought twelve meal coupons, we had twelve meals for five and a half francs each, wine included; a very cheap price even for those, semi-golden times. Or maybe it was the other way round, we had twelve bottles of wine with some food added. Whichever way it was, it was satisfactory and life-sustaining. Occasionally there were unwelcome extras like a fat, green caterpillar undulating its way out of a piece of lettuce, flies in the soup and some hair in the vegetables. There were three cooks, one blond, one dark and one older one going grey, as we had occasion to deduce. But all that was part of the package.

I immediately set about looking for work and found some within a matter of days. I was back where I started in 1924, when I finished my studies at the Academy of Budapest. I was coaching singers, but much better than nine years ago; and I was doing it again with energy and interest.

That ever-present pleasure in "unimportant" things and tasks, while it has made my life more enjoyable, was, I now see, hindering me in what is called "making a career". What is "important"? To many people some great assignment, outward advancement, financial or other, recognition, decorations and the like. To some – as for instance, to me – it is to achieve a legato phrasing, to fashion a well-balanced bar, to do well what destiny has called us to do, wherever and whenever that may be.

I never could, nor would I have tried to, change my natural inclination, which has given me a profoundly happy and solid base upon which to build and live my musical life. My only regret is that life is so short. Given the rather slow tempo of my maturing, I could envisage that at the age of 150 years or so . . .

Meanwhile, that disposition enabled me to re-start in Paris, go back to my professional beginnings, without the least feeling of self-pity.

By chance, a few days after my arrival in Paris, I met a Hungarian couple, Henry Major and his wife. He was a well-known and accomplished caricaturist. His sketches were fashionable and appeared frequently in the French press. Few people knew that he also was an exceptionally gifted painter – potentially as great as all but the best of his contemporaries. It was tragic that he allowed his minor talent as a witty cartoonist to overshadow so completely his Rembrandtian genius with the brush. His nickname was Sicu (pronounced sheetsoo), and he looked as if he had modelled his own caricature into flesh. His wife, a severe-looking, stout lady, kept the reins of the household energetically and, I believe, well in hand, while exercising that rather spurious profession of singing teacher.

Few jobs are more open to the suspicion of dilettantism and charlatanism than that of voice teacher, with the possible exception of that of psychoanalyst – and perhaps, especially lately, that of orchestra conductor. Of course, there are a number of people in all those three callings who are above doubt, but inasmuch as the essence of these professions is deeply personal, unteachable and unlearnable except by experience, their ranks are dangerously inundated by the incompetent.

With the above I intend no reflection upon Mrs. Major's value and valour. I am, to begin with, not qualified to judge singing teachers. And further, I have no reason to think other than kindly and gratefully about her, for it was through her that I acquired my first coaching pupils in Paris.

Thereafter, I found I had no reason to complain. Word seemed to go around fast and soon I was fully occupied coaching. We could now advance from Julien's to restaurants several degrees its superior, and even an occasional taxi-ride was within sight. We kept our lodgings at the Hôtel des Grands Hommes for the time being, although for a while it looked as if we would have to move: the landlady had serious reservations about our much too frequent use of the communal bathroom. In vain we remonstrated that we were paying for our baths, and further that we didn't seem to be in the way of any other tenant, because no matter at what hour we wished to use the bath it was always free – she said that it was dangerous for our health to have a bath that often, and she did not want to be responsible for the death by *refroidissement* of two such nice young people.

We finally convinced her that we were sturdy enough to cope with that danger, and we were able to stay on. Luckily for us, because I do not think we could have found cheaper lodgings in Paris.

Not that the modest improvement of our way of living would have made me complacent. My main aim was to re-establish myself as a conductor. This was not easy for a completely unknown, young, non-French musician. Nationalistic feelings, as I soon noticed, were running high, but even Frenchmen had a

Margit Doráti with
Antal and Gizi in
1915.
The author and his
parents, Margit and
Sándor Doráti.

Sándor and Margit Doráti, *above*, and *below*, Gizi and the author, *right*, aged seventeen, all drawn by his uncle, Caesar Kunwald.

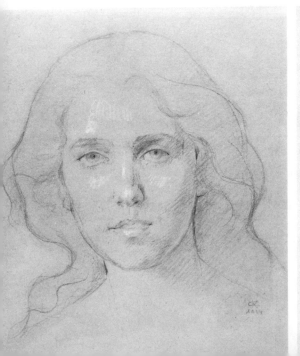

Sketches by Caesar Kunwald: self-portrait *below right*, Zoltán Kodály *top left*, Béla Bartók *top right*, and Leo Weiner *below left*.

Sketches by the author: *right*, the
Millenial Monument in Budapest.
Below left, Zoltán Kodály skating.
Below right, the Opera House in
Budapest.

Top, the author with daughter Tonina. *Above*, the author with his friend, the baritone Imre Palló. *Left*, Klári Kórody.

Tatiana Riabouchinska.

Tamara Toumanova.

Alexandra Danilova and Leonide
Massine.

Irina Baronova.

Richard Strauss.

Igor Stravinsky.

Arturo Toscanini.

Fritz Busch.

Ilse von Alpenheim.
Antal Doráti.

difficult time in attempting to make headway in the musical life of France.

But again I was lucky. Through some of the singers I coached I made acquaintances at the new state radio station, the PTT (Post, Telegraph, Telephone), forerunner of today's powerful Radio France but then operating on a very small scale and with, curiously, no proper music department as yet.

When I suggested broadcasting some orchestral music, the directors were all for it. They wanted to start right away. They only stipulated that the works chosen should not have been broadcast in France before, and that the programmes should be inexpensive.

It was not difficult to discover that the PTT station had never before broadcast an opera. My proposal to do so was therefore accepted with a rush of excited comments. It was more difficult to keep within the microscopic budget allotted to me. However, a suitable double bill was decided upon: Mozart's *Der Schauspiel-direktor* (*The Impresario*) and Gluck's *L'Ivrogne corrigé* (*The Reformed Drunkard*). I already knew a great number of singers and could get hold of more, so that it was not difficult to assemble a very capable cast for low salaries. A small orchestra of fine potential was also found without trouble. French instrumentalists are amazingly clever, resourceful, and competent – as long as they play alone. The problems begin when they have to play in groups. But for that performance, I succeeded in keeping their interest alive, and the rehearsals went beautifully.

At the last minute an unexpected difficulty came up: objections were raised in certain quarters to a foreigner being entrusted with the leadership of such an important event. The event was certainly very important to me, and the other participants, and to some extent perhaps also to the PTT directors. But no one else, it must be said, had ever heard about it, until the objectors raised their hue and cry – it was prepared in almost conspiratorial secrecy. As nobody could be found to replace me, a curious solution was reached. Another young conductor, French this time, was appointed, but not to take over from me. He was to sit in the studio watching and take my place if I suddenly fell ill.

I had no intention of doing him this favour. The performance was very successful, inasmuch as it served to provide the stimulus needed to get a permanent music department organised within the

PTT. The *ad hoc* orchestra was also transformed into a steadily employed group. All this happened within a few weeks of our broadcast, and the orchestra became the nucleus of the famous Orchestre National.

It was also discreetly suggested that my services should be retained on some permanent or semi-permanent basis – the directors of the station, by then my friends and well-wishers, would cope with the nationality problem. But destiny intervened again, and my life took another turn. Whether it was that the discrimination against me as a foreigner was a discouraging factor, or whether my abrupt departure from Berlin had made me temporarily footloose, I do not know. Neither do I know whether or not it was good for me to leave Paris so soon after my arrival. I did not ask myself (or others) that question. I followed my star. And so it was that the two small operas which I conducted on that summer evening in Paris were in fact my goodbye to opera, for although I later conducted quite frequently for the lyric theatre, I then ceased to be what I had been until then: a full-time opera-conductor.

13

As a consequence I was able, for the next few decades, to be an armchair–observer of the changes that occurred in the realm of opera, without being involved personally.

The greatest operatic event of our century, it seems to me, is the advent of the English-speaking world into the realm of the lyric theatre.

It came in seven-league boots.

During the earlier part of this century, well within my own memory, in England as well as in America, opera was an imported luxury, but not a part of "live", indigenous music culture. In London and England generally the Carl Rosa company and other touring groups existed. Sir Thomas Beecham began organising important but short opera seasons, lasting a few weeks each year, at the Royal Opera House. In America opera was also an upper-class pastime. The Metropolitan Opera House in New York was firmly established, employed the best artists available at enormous cost, and had sizeable yearly seasons. It dominated the national scene, but conspicuously failed to transplant the art form of opera into the soil of American music.

This phenomenon had deeper causes than the lack of government subsidies. That lack was and is a symptom rather than a reason.

At all events the English-speaking world lagged far behind the Latin and German countries in creating and performing opera.

The change in this century – a sudden and dramatic one – can be attributed virtually to the life-work of a single man: Benjamin Britten. He, almost alone, brought opera back to the English language for the first time since Purcell; or if one prefers to put it the other way round, brought the English language back to opera. This achievement is truly unique, and, notwithstanding the high esteem in which the image and music of Britten are held in his own country, still underrated and not fully understood.

But the same process that brought the English-speaking people back to opera introduced the new problem of the language in which it should be sung. This problem, now hotly debated, is seldom considered in context.

To begin with, we should recognise the fact that wherever an indigenous operatic culture exists – that is, wherever opera is part of the *living* theatre of its country – all operas are sung in the vernacular of that country. Naturally so, because a theatre not understood by its public is no theatre.

Those lands which had no opera culture of their own, and had to import one, brought them, very rightly, from their places of origin; that is, German opera from Germany, Italian opera from Italy, and so on, all performed in the original tongue as set by their composers.

This was also the case in England and America when the new wind suddenly started to blow, and the lyric theatre became, almost overnight, a more organic part of the indigenous theatre than heretofore. There was a sudden new interest in opera, a new demand for all operas to be precisely understood – in short, for hearing them in English.

But the "foreign" opera performances, that is, those sung in the original languages, were already present, almost traditional. And they also had something to say for themselves.

Word and melody melt in incomparable harmony when both are rooted together in the imagination of the composer. Translations always lose flavour in the trade for comprehension. This loss is accepted without dispute in the spoken theatre, as it was in the opera houses of Germany, Italy, France and Russia, where indigenous opera traditions existed: translations were used without further questioning. It was with the arrival of the English opera culture that the confusion started: suddenly the foreign tongue – the imported "original" language – was no longer enough. the public wanted to know about the goings-on on the stage, and it began to be downright pathetic to watch an audience seeing an opera which it did not understand.

One evening in the 1930s I was Fritz Busch's guest at Glyndebourne. Having been at work myself at the Royal Opera House that afternoon, I arrived only minutes before the start of the performance. Indeed, the house lights had already been put out, and I barely had time to grope my way to my seat before the overture of *The Marriage of Figaro* began. The house was full; the audience as smart as usual. The white ties and evening gowns gleamed in the semi-dark. The silence itself was elegant. It was also, I soon began to feel, rather painful. The starchy atmosphere was spreading like fog, stiffening all reactions that could be provoked from the stage by the spirited, pacy performance. It was regrettably and dismayingly evident that the Italian text was falling on deaf ears; no one knew what was going on, but everybody behaved impeccably.

Except one person.

Two rows in front of me, slightly to my right, the silhouette of a man's head, rising above the others around him, was moving. The head shook, nodded, widened with the stretch of a smile. In addition small noises, grunts and snorts of pleasure, issued from the tall head, whose owner was obviously having the time of his life. The contrast to the stillness of the rest of the audience was so startling that I could not help observing the one "black sheep" who dared to enjoy himself so unashamedly. His little private signs of amusement were all legitimate, coming forth at exactly the right moments. My curiosity was aroused, I wanted to know who he was. It was my plan to have a good look at him when the lights went up and then make discreet enquiries from one of my friends in the house as to who he might be. When the interval came I discovered that my plan was unnecessary: it was George Bernard Shaw.

Whether Shaw spoke Italian or not, I do not know. But he certainly knew the libretto of *The Marriage of Figaro*, line by line.

And that is the salient point: to value and enjoy the original language in an operatic performance it is not really necessary – though obviously it is helpful – to know that language. What is necessary, is to know the opera.

Therefore the true solution of the problem of language in opera is to create a situation in which operatic works become well known in the language of the public, who should then be given a chance – when they are ready for that great pleasure – of hearing them in the language in which they were composed.

In only one city in the world does this situation exist. London. There one can hear much the same repertoire in English at the Coliseum and in the original languages at the Royal Opera House, Covent Garden. This is a great boon and a great advance in the level of the capital's operatic activities and culture.

In the United States the operatic fortress of the Met was for too long the only dispenser of serious operatic art. What one might call broader participation came from elsewhere; San Francisco, for instance, with its well-established and valuable season; or Chicago, where the once-proud enterprise of Insull sadly crumbled leaving behind only the opera house itself, but was happily replaced by a new organisation, now flourishing and growing. The new strength of opera in the United States must be looked for in these institutions, and in the smaller but active and interesting organisations in Boston, Seattle, Houston, New Orleans, Washington, DC, Dallas, San Antonio and elsewhere, not forgetting New York City's second opera company (which performs many operas of the international repertoire in English). These opera companies spring up like mushrooms, so that any attempt to make a complete list of them would be futile. Every one of them performs a valuable cultural service. And as they grow, their standards will rise in proportion, until the roots of the lyric theatre sink deeper and deeper into the American soil, to its great enrichment and benefit.

As a by-product, this development will put an end to today's star system. The indispensable quality of "stardom" is its rarity. But, on the one hand, the difference between a star and a non-star performance will not be tolerated much longer by a growingly knowledgeable public. On the other, the stars themselves will fade. Even now, their strength is being progressively dissipated by the incredible fatigue of their enforced nomadic life, and in the end they will be unable to deliver what is expected of them.

The true future of opera lies in the ensemble principle, by which I mean well-matched ensembles of fine singers working together and staying together. This mode of organisation has never completely disappeared. A few, very few, theatres have always maintained it, and elsewhere, now and then, at the insistence of a maestro, a performance reflecting it turns up. So the ensemble principle will not need to be re-discovered. Even the public knows about it. And once the public starts asking for it, sooner or later it will get it.

But it is our task – that of the performers and presenters – to give the public a lead.

Opera is a conglomerate art form – the Germans have coined the awful but apt name *Gesamtkunstwerk* (meaning nearly what it should, namely "total-artwork"), and its performances go through a number of styles and trends.

In the early years of our century we had the "singer's opera", in which the vocal qualities of the singers dominated the performances. The music was distorted, the text neglected, the acting regarded as not even a necessary evil, and so forth.

Then came the period of the "conductor's opera". The music was restored to conform to the written score, and even when this was done pedantically or incorrectly, what emerged was preferable to the waywardness of the previous epoch.

Next came the trend with which we are still living today – the "producer's (or "stage director's" or "*régisseur's*") opera". To begin with this corrected, to very good effect, the shortcomings of the acting. It set store by proper casting, instead of casting for vocal reasons only. But it led to other excesses, principal of which was the restless search for novel dramatic interpretation. This all too often deprives our present-day productions of the sense and meaning intended by the composer, and leaves the producer open to the suspicion of being insufficiently prepared, insufficiently familiar with the material with which he is working, and – most important of all – insufficiently sensitive to the one essential component of music drama, namely the music. Artificial originality smells worse than stinking fish.

The next epoch will, I fervently pray, be one of full co-operation between musicians, stage director, and scenic artists, all equally responsible, all greatly concerned. I hope that is not wishful thinking.

At a recent meeting of musicians, musicologists and music journalists, called to discuss the "crisis" of opera as an art form, one attender stood up and announced that he would read out a list of viable contemporary operas. He then produced a very small piece of paper, from which he read his "list". It consisted of a single name: *Wozzeck*. This may exaggerate the dearth of new opera, but not by much.

Alban Berg's *Wozzeck* was at the time of its first performance in Berlin under Kleiber's direction – which I happened to witness – a very experimental piece. But so was *Tristan and Isolde*, so was

Salome, so was *Fidelio*, and so was *Pelléas and Mélisande*. It is the inherent strength of these works which have made them survive, which have made the enormous difficulties of their performance worthwhile.

There are enough creative treasures in existence to keep opera alive for a long time even if new masterpieces are in short supply at the moment.

And creative forces are always at work, unnoticed perhaps, and when the force is strong enough they will erupt like a volcano.

And quite possibly a new tributary to the mainstream of the singing stage is already flowing, unimpeded. I think of the most important contribution so far made by the New World to the stream of Western music: the American musical. This is a basically new, very vital art form, with a fresh approach to singing drama, and already what it has produced has been quite remarkable. It needs only (!) the miracle of a supreme talent, a twentieth-century Mozart (or a twenty-first century Mozart – we can afford to be patient), to fill this new form with the values we call "eternal": by which we mean lasting, or valid for a long time. Centuries? Millennia? Who knows?

Eternity exists. It is a lacework of moments, without beginning, without end, yet not a circle; "an unending lace of love", as a recent cantata has it.

Long enough for those who can feel the "ever" in the "now".

Eternity is here to stay.

14

PARIS 1933.

Trying to find my bearings in building a new life in a strange world, I saw and spoke with many people. Amongst them were two elderly ladies, the owners of a small theatrical agency, which was brought to my attention by a singer whom I coached. The two lady agents were flying about in identical grey pelerines like two huge bats, chattering disconcertingly in French, which they could hardly speak: one was Russian; the other Hungarian. These two ladies came to me one day, with the surprising suggestion that I should go over to England and conduct three performances of the Ballets Russes de Monte Carlo.

I had heard, vaguely, of that company, and accepted. At that moment I would have accepted anything; unwisely as I later came to recognise. Certainly I could do very adequate justice to whatever I might be required to conduct. And anyway three days were not much. I soon would be back from that adventure, with my purse a little less empty, ready to follow up my small but encouraging success with the French radio.

A period of strange preparatory manoeuvres started. A British visa had to be obtained, which proved more difficult than expected. Several middle-aged Russian gentlemen came to see me, in order to give me no doubt pertinent but certainly mysterious advice: I was not to mention to the immigration officers at Newhaven that I had come over to conduct the Ballets Russes de Monte Carlo. I should say that I was visiting someone.

"Whom?"

"Don't you know anyone in England?"

"No."

"Well, tell them you are going to meet – let's see – ah – Dr. Zbaworsky."

I memorised the name of the doctor, and promised to say that I was going to see him.

Further, I was asked to take a smallish, soft package with me and give it to a Colonel de Basil, the director of the company, whom I would meet in England. To the Customs people I was to say that it was a present for a friend.

My destination would be Bournemouth, which meant taking the train from Newhaven to Victoria Station in London, then changing stations and continuing by another train.

All this seemed easy enough, in spite of the fact that I spoke no English. My introduction to England however turned out to be complicated.

Because of the language barrier, communicating with Immigration was difficult, and my story that I had come to visit Dr. Zbaworsky, especially as I did not know what kind of doctor he was, nor where he lived, proved to be less than impressive. But, after long, tedious but always polite questioning, I was allowed to enter the realm.

For the Customs I had to open up my valise. On top was the soft package I was entrusted with.

"What's in this, please?"

"A present."

"For whom?"

"For a friend."

"What friend?"

I was lost. I had no friend in England. But, here we go:

"Dr. Zbaworsky."

"Ah, indeed."

The Customs man carefully undid the package. A strange object came to light, the like of which I had never seen at close quarters before. At first I noticed only that it was very, very pink. That already augured badly for a present to a doctor. When the article in the hands of the Customs officer was unfolded, it looked like a pair of very long, pink stockings or panties; at any rate, ladies' underwear of some sort. The things were ballet-tights, of course, half a dozen or so pairs of them – but neither the Customs officers at Newhaven nor I could identify them. First they tried to get some information out of me, but I had given up by then. I just shook my head and said nothing. Then they went into a long, hushed conference, at the end of which, evidently, they also gave up, because they motioned me, languidly, to close my valise and go away.

By then it was four in the morning (we had made a night crossing), but the light of dawn brought me no cheer. I had missed the boat-train, made my way to Victoria by a later one, took a cab – my first ride in one of those unique and friendly London monsters – to Waterloo, got into a train for Bournemouth and fell asleep. At times, with a jerk of the train, I woke up and looked out of the window to catch the name of the station. To my bleary surprise the train was evidently standing still, although I could have sworn that we had been moving while I was asleep. Yet, whenever I looked, we were always at the same station: BOVRIL. No wonder that, ignorant of that famous English beverage, I remained in the train until Plymouth, and had to make my way back to Bournemouth by yet another train.

There was no one to meet me, since I had arrived so late, and it took me some time to locate the Ballets Russes. They turned out to be a bunch of excited people all chattering at once in Russian or Russian-accented French. It was difficult to understand what they said, but I did at the end.

I had missed the rehearsal with the orchestra, and had to make do with very confused and confusing explanations as to how I was to conduct the performance that evening, and even what I was to conduct.

As it finally transpired, the programme began with a, to me, completely unknown ballet *Les Sylphides*, consisting of orchestrated piano pieces by Chopin, a nocturne, a prelude, a few mazurkas and waltzes. It ended with a medley of Johann Strauss's music, called *Le Beau Danube* (not the blue, but the beautiful), consisting of well-known and lesser-known waltzes and polkas, and between these two numbers came something named *Choreartium*. When I looked at the score of this, I was amazed to find it was the Fourth, E minor, Symphony by Brahms. Altogether, a bewildering and dismaying prospect.

Before descending to the orchestra pit, I was again given a great number of instructions, this time by a great number of dancers, choreographers, *régisseurs* – I could not make out who they all were. I was to wait here, to go faster there, to slow up at another point, and so forth. As I did not understand any of it, I smiled, nodded and dismissed the requests from my mind – a method of treating them which soon became my standard practice, and which proved infallible.

The orchestra, the Bournemouth Symphony, was surprisingly good, not a first-class body by any means, but much better than I had expected, efficient, on the ball, and often producing very agreeable sounds.

The ballets gave me a mixed impression.

Les Sylphides, danced by an array of girls in the white ballet-skirts called "tutu", and one boy, was composed of beautiful movements and groupings.

Le Beau Danube I liked better; it was a timeless and placeless fantasy in the Viennese manner, a sketchy story told in movement of a Hussar and his girls, with acrobats and other figures making up the background, delicate in the vein of a Saint-Aubin drawing, entertaining and brilliant, if slight.

But what can I say to describe that monstrosity, that gratuitous scenic travesty of a Brahms symphony, that seemed like a poor joke? Before a meaningless backdrop dancers appeared, alone and in groups, in a variety of costumes, performing movements connected in an arbitrary way with the mood of the music in the moment of their appearance. But exactly this arbitrariness made the entire effort futile.

The very essence of music is freedom of fantasy. Certainly it channels the listener's imagination. But it does not lead it towards exact, precise pictures, actions or thoughts. On the contrary, the fantasy of each listener remains individual. This is music's innermost secret and its incomparable magic.

What I see in the Sistine Chapel is prescribed to me by Michelangelo, I can see *it* and nothing else. But Beethoven bids me walk and breathe and live in freedom in the realm of his infinite paradise while listening to his music.

Every infringement of that freedom of thought and feeling which only music can give is not only a negation of the core of the art of music, it is also regimentation, a sort of spiritual dictatorship.

My painter-uncle Caesar, a very sensitive man, once said in a conversation about operatic *mise-en-scène*: "For the production of a Wagner opera a negative Reinhard would be necessary." A fine remark in a wider sense than intended.

Whoever, whenever, touches music with "extra-musical fingers" should be doubly careful: first, to establish whether such touching is necessary and beneficial; and secondly, if it is – and it sometimes can be – then to let that touch be guided by music and not be of the violating kind.

As it was, to my mind, in the case of *Choreartium*. It might have been a fine choreographic poem set to other music, but to be obliged to look at the rust-coloured cowls of a row of undulatingly marching nuns at the start of the second movement of Brahms's Fourth Symphony, or accept the jumps of tall boys wearing pink hats and sporting bunches of carrots pinned to their chests in the scherzo, was like a slight case of rape.

Thus, while admiring the efforts of an evidently very brilliant dance group, such as I had never seen before, I could not find myself in agreement with what they were presenting.

I consoled myself with the reflection that after two more evenings this interlude would be over.

How nice it would be if I could report here that my initial revulsion notwithstanding, I stayed on with the Ballets Russes de Monte Carlo because I fell deeply in love with one of the lovely ballerinas.

But I did not. And I will never know whether or not it was a mistake to linger in the world of ballet for as long as I did. I certainly profited from the association. Not only did it keep me alive (and living increasingly well) during a very difficult time, but musically also it gave me useful insights into many facets of my two callings, composing and conducting.

Still, perhaps it was a mistake.

At any rate, at the end of three days, I was offered a permanent position with the company.

It was a tempting invitation. Within two months or so the company would go on its first tour to the United States, and upon its return there would be lengthy seasons each year at Covent Garden. Furthermore there would be annual seasons in Monte Carlo (the company's nominal base), tours in Spain, and so on. I would also be allowed to accept other engagements.

There were two drawbacks: my earnings would be small, ridiculously so to start with, and as conductor I would be junior to an older man, Efrem Kurtz, who had been with the company for some time. But these were minor worries and the prospect of travel won, especially the lure of visiting the United States. But while I intended to use the job as a mere stepping stone in my career, I was determined, while I had it, to take it with proper seriousness.

This I did, from the start, and in more ways than one. I began to

141

improve the musical material, to correct sloppy instrumentations, to re-orchestrate such pieces in the repertoire as needed it. And as soon as my regular work as conductor started, I tried to persuade the dancers to respect the music to which they danced and not to distort it – something to which they had evidently given little thought.

15

THE PLACE WHERE I FORMALLY JOINED THE MONTE CARLO BALLET was Plymouth, where it performed for a week before sailing for New York.

That was in December 1933.

We embarked on the French liner S.S. *Lafayette*. It was to be a short tour, so apart from the famous "mamas" of the youthful prima donnas, no husbands, wives, or other relatives came along. Leave-taking on the pier was tearful. Klári waved for a long time before turning to take the train to London, from where she would go to stay with her parents in Budapest.

The Atlantic was smooth and the crossing was like a dream. It was also bitterly cold, so except for a few bracing strolls around the deck, the eight days were spent below.

This gave plenty of scope for getting to know the company.

They were a strange group if there ever was one.

At the head of the hierarchy was Colonel W. de Basil, himself. A remarkable man. I think that of his whole title only the "W." was genuine. It stood for Wassily. His claim to the rank of colonel was more than doubtful, and as his patent of nobility was also questionable, the *particule* "de" was probably unwarranted. His real surname, I heard, was Waskressensky.

No matter.

How he came to take over the heritage of Serge Diaghilev – for it was the remains of Diaghilev's great company and a good number of his wonderful ballets that were the basis of the new troupe's repertoire – I never learned.

The heritage that fell to him was indeed formidable. Diaghilev, who died in Venice in 1929, just four years before the time I am speaking of, was truly the creator of modern ballet, without whom the developments of the present day would be unimaginable. After his sudden death – he was in full vigour, when a sepsis following furunculosis took him away – there was no competent successor at hand. There were quite a few incompetent would-be successors, though. Amongst them de Basil emerged as the strongest and took over.

His chief gift was to be continuously lucky.

At no time did I ever detect in him any knowledge of music, dance, painting or stage design, yet he succeeded – by sheer luck, I think – in surrounding himself with people who really knew about all these things, and although he did not have Diaghilev's flair for co-ordinating the talents he brought together, those involved somehow managed to co-ordinate themselves.

As a businessman he was hopeless. Everything was neglected, late, forgotten or left incomplete. Yet always, at the last moment, he managed to avoid catastrophe – again, by luck.

He had a nose, if not for quality, at any rate for success. And he followed his nose, without hesitation.

As a negotiator he was extraordinary. Anyone who went to him asking for a rise in salary would undoubtedly end up giving him his last ten pounds.

He granted requests as seldom as he was refused one.

His style in argument was inimitable. Once he tried to persuade me to write the music to a ballet about Niobe, for which de Chirico had already designed the sets. I could not see a ballet ending with fourteen corpses or coffins on the stage. De Basil tried to entice me with glowing descriptions of the various scenes. He ended thus: " . . . And the third act! Why, that will be magnificent! Very solemn, a little mournful, but still terribly gay!"

It did not work. Niobe did not reach the stage, de Chirico notwithstanding.

His physical endurance was phenomenal. He cared nothing for pain. Once, travelling in an old-fashioned lift, he tried to stop it by reaching out of it and holding on to an iron bar. The lift continued upwards. De Basil broke his arm. He got out of the lift one floor higher than he wished, went down the stairs, entered the apartment where he was invited to a party, ate and drank, then went to hospital to have his dangling arm put into a plaster cast.

When he slammed the heavy door of an automobile on his hand, he quietly re-opened the door, looked at the mangled hand with amused astonishment, and went about his business. When his partners turned pale and felt ill from looking at the mess, he had his hand bandaged, out of charity.

His *sang froid* was no less remarkable. Nothing could disturb him, nothing bothered him. I heard that when once, in Czechoslovakia, he ran over and killed a man while driving his car, he first took out his movie camera and recorded the event, then made his hired factotum agree to take the blame. After that he waited calmly for the police to arrive, looked on when his man was taken to jail, and continued on his way as if nothing had happened.

Though possibly apocryphal, this story is completely in character.

He was also very clever at playing off one person against another, thus assuring his own position. His monetary dealings were always just – but only just – on the right side of shady.

All this does not add up to a picture of either a nice, or a worthy, man. Yet, curiously enough, he really was rather nice and if not exactly worthy he was certainly "acceptable". For those with strong nerves he was also very amusing.

The USA tour proved to be an overwhelming success – an epochal event, in fact, which opened the United States to the art of the dance, where it developed and flourished in an unexpected degree and reached an extraordinary level of perfection.

But we are still on board the *Lafayette*, meeting the company.

Next to be introduced are Serge Grigorieff, the *régisseur-général*, and his wife Lubov Chernicheva. Grigorieff was in charge of all scenic matters, from the productions themselves to rehearsals, matters of personnel, and so on. It was his responsibility to have the dancers, sets and costumes in the right places at the right times, the lighting organised and, above all, the repertory properly rehearsed and kept in shape. For new works the choreographers were at hand, but everything that was presented from the stock repertoire was rehearsed and put on by him.

He was a stalwart of the original Diaghilev company, where he had first been a dancer, then *régisseur* as he was with de Basil. He had a fabulous memory, remembering every step, every movement, of every dance in all the productions at which he had been present. As he was now approaching sixty, that meant a great many ballets carried around in his head.

He was a kindly man; his very Russian French was always friendly.

His wife, Lubov Chernicheva, was a stately, handsome lady,

145

who had also been a dancer with the Diaghilev group, and in her day high up in, although not at the very top of, the complicated balletic hierarchical ladder. Of apparently unquenchable ambition, she still danced a few parts – I remember four of them – all with admirable authority and power which, however, could not fully replace the magic of youth. She was, by the way, not the only dancer who continued to perform to the utmost limit set by age, and it must be said that all who did had much to offer, contributing in particular to the growing perfection of their juniors.

Madame Chernicheva was, I think, the absolute boss in her family, which included Vova, short for Vsevolod Grigorieff, their son, who was about my age and befriended me from the start. He did secretarial work for de Basil, which must have been quite an ordeal. His job was wearing him down, and he often returned to the very comfortable stateroom he shared with me – it was ordinarily reserved for the *agents des postes*, an agency I have never again seen mentioned on a ship – announcing with a sigh that yet another *catastrophe inévitable* had occurred.

There were four prima ballerinas. Alexandra Danilova, a mature artist and a sprightly, sharp, very intelligent woman, also came from the Diaghilev company. She was a virtuoso-type (I use this word reluctantly and seldom, for want of a better one: its colloquial meaning falls sadly short of what it is meant to signify), very interesting to watch on stage, and good company off it.

The other three were very young girls, no more than about fifteen at that time, infant prodigies of the dance. They were a sheer delight in the dance theatre, and I am quoting world opinion when I say that never before was there such a group of talent and grace assembled in any one ballet company. They were very different.

Tatiana Riabouchinska was frail and very blonde, softly, lyrically graceful, like a feather – a soft quill writing a poem into the air. I was told that she was the daughter of a well-to-do and well-known jeweller in Russia. Her father had died some time before, and she travelled with her mother, an emaciated-looking lady whom I often saw but whose voice I never heard.

Tamara Toumanova, a raven-haired, classic beauty, of breathtaking appearance and technique, was as different from Tatiana as night from day. Her movements were sharp and brilliant like a Toledo blade, her bearing somewhere between a black panther and a dragonfly. She travelled with both her parents:

146

"Mamicshka", a good-looking, rather plump, very gregarious and voluble lady; and Papa, who appeared more seldom, a dark–grey-haired, moustached man, never without a book or newspaper and never saying as much as a word to anyone.

Irina Baronova, who also travelled accompanied by both parents, was quite different again. Medium tall – she was the tallest of the three baby prima donnas, and I think also the youngest – had a round face, large eyes, a full, sensual mouth which precluded the otherwise possible epithet of "angel-face", dark blonde hair and a slender but solid figure. She danced with as much bravura as her star *colleginas*, but, at least for my eyes, had a far wider range of talent, and ability to convey, with the same technique, the same means as the others, a much greater range of characterisations, and an ability to penetrate more deeply into her roles than most other dancers I have seen, then and since. She seemed to me a more complete little human being than the other two young girls. Whether this made her life easier or more difficult, I wonder. The latter, probably.

Her parents were both working within the company, her mother with the costumes, her father with the scenery.

The male dancers were as remarkable as the girls.

The chief choreographer as well as principal male dancer was Leonide Massine, also of Diaghilev fame. He was, by then, a very accomplished and renowned choreographer, with a great number of fine productions to his credit, of which my great favourite was and remained *The Three-cornered Hat* to the music of de Falla. During the succeeding years we were to collaborate quite closely, but at that moment I regarded him with deep suspicion, for he was the author of *Choreartium* and another "symphonic ballet", *Les Présages*, which I did not yet know but detested even the thought of. Massine was then married to a very good comic dancer, Delarova, whose bizarre performances I greatly enjoyed. Our contact on board ship was friendly but aloof.

A primo ballerino of great talent and even greater promise was the young and handsome David Lichine. He had just divorced his first wife, who was also a member of the company, a very pretty French girl, who had the russianised name of Lubov Rostova. He was very much and very noticeably in love with Tania Riabouchinska, whom he later married. A splendidly virile and impressive dancer, he also had great gifts as a choreographer, as was shown later. In 1933 he was just starting out.

Extremely fine dancers were Leon Woizikowsky, Youra Shabelevsky, Roman Jasinsky, Yura Lazowsky and others.

The entire company, as I have already said, displayed an exceptionally high level of talent. It was not without reason that it captivated the New World as completely as it did.

On arrival in New York, we met the American impresario who had brought us over. He was another Russian by birth, and a very interesting and intriguing man. His name was well known then, and increased in fame and importance until the end of his life in 1975. There was no one in the world of music who did not know about Sol Hurok. He was the "last of the Mohicans", the last of what we can truly call impresarios in the real sense of the word, before that profession changed into another one: management.

I had met Hurok briefly before, in Salzburg, which he probably did not remember, for I was small fry for him then.

When he came on board to greet de Basil and the company, dapper and incongruously elegant in his long, black fur-lined winter coat, with black cane and felt hat coyly askew on his large round, bald head, I was introduced to him, while de Basil made secret signs of raised finger and turned-up eyes to convey how good I was. These signs were noticed by me but not by Hurok, for whom they were intended. He could not be bothered with such details.

He was surrounded by the stars of the company and by the press – a good number of journalists had come aboard on the pilot's boat – and was the obvious king of the occasion, which he enjoyed to the hilt, as well he might, since the appearance in America of our distinguished company was on his initiative and at his risk.

Bringing over the Ballets Russes was not the first or the last of such ventures in his career. This is what makes the difference between the impresario and the manager. The former presents an artist or a group in which he believes, and takes full responsibility, moral and financial, for them. The latter merely manages them, acting as a go-between in matters of contracts, engagements and so on.

Hurok made his way in his profession from the bottom to the top, step by step. His knowledge of the arts and his education in

148

them was nil, absolutely zero. But his love for them was as great as his instinct for quality. Slowly, he developed into a real, if naive, connoisseur in his chosen fields.

His career was by no means without its ups and downs. It had more ups than downs, however, and at that time he had a fine-looking office in the brand-new Rockefeller Center, and was very much on top of the world.

For a short while, not more than two or three weeks, I was uncomfortable with him. His rather vulgar, Jewish-American accent disturbed me and I felt offended by the slipshod, high-handed way he treated not so much me personally, as what I stood for: music, and more important, good music.

For him, I felt, music was a necessary evil that had to be lived with in the ballet world. It seemed to me he would be happiest if ballets could be danced to rhythms beaten out with a ladle on the bottom of a pot.

Altogether it was my impression that that was, more or less, how everybody felt about music in ballet. It was the most neglected part of that holy trinity which made ballet the high art that it is: music, dance and the fine arts.

I had every reason to think as I did, for during that first American ballet season the orchestra was treated in a very careless manner indeed. No attention was paid by the management to its quality, and it fluctuated dangerously in numbers: at the first sign of a small box-office slump it was suddenly and peremptorily reduced.

One day, when I bitterly complained to Hurok about the surprise disappearance of my second oboist, he gave me this classic reply: "Have you ever heard of a second oboe filling the house?"

As it happened, I made my peace with Hurok very fast. It was not only that I stopped making violent scenes about second oboes and so on, which always ended with my complete defeat. I also began to understand him, and to be drawn to him. He responded warmly to my approach – or, perhaps he had wisely and cunningly provoked it? After all, it was a sort of comfort to have the young rebel on his side, and our personal relationship after three stormy weeks became smooth and friendly. Our links never broke, thereafter, until his death. In the middle Sixties, he became my professional manager. As I "grew up", our friendship, though never very close – indeed I wonder if he had any very close

149

friendships at all – was on an even-footed basis of warm respect and understanding.

From that vantage point I can say that he was not an easy person. For his collaborators – and his entourage was always large – "life with Hurok" must have been very unsatisfactory indeed, because his ego obliterated any individual recognition in a wide circle around him. He always remained a rather primitive, uneducated man, relying entirely on his instincts and living on them and from them very well indeed. His vanity was enormous, which I do not say disparagingly. Vanity is an important source and nourishment of every human achievement, even the loftiest. This is not often admitted. In print, I have seen it stated by only one person, Sartre, who, with this statement, rose to very great heights in my esteem. Hurok had a great deal of vanity and ego and he did not hesitate to indulge in both. There was not an inch of space on his office walls which was not covered by photographs of himself in the company of kings, potentates and celebrities of every kind; himself in academic garb, receiving medals, honours; a large display of diplomas and prizes – there were very few he did not receive. He had one or two films made of his life, which were not without entertainment value; as one film critic put it, rather acidly, "Mr. Hurok's life consisted, apparently, of one heartwarming episode after another." He had his autobiography written, which I did not read, but which, with the material available, would have been impossible to make dull. And on top of all that, the stories he told about his life, especially his early life, were delightful.

The noise, confusion and bedlam of a disembarkation in New York must be lived through to be believed. Just to endure it was bad enough. To make things worse, some mysterious characters appeared from a mysterious nowhere, murmuring the words "Hurok office", and on the pretext of "helping me through Customs" relieved me of one of the very few five dollar bills I possessed before putting me into a taxi-cab to take me to my hotel. There I was given an unspeakably scruffy room, the only adornment of which was an old, broken telephone hanging on the wall.

"This is the New World," I thought, and went to bed. I was sleepy enough. My shoes I placed carefully and symmetrically outside my door. When I reached for them next morning, they were not there. I tried to raise someone to retrieve them, without success. No shoes.

I went downstairs in stockinged feet, bought another pair of shoes from my already dwindling funds and started to raise hell. About the shoes, about the room, about the theatre, about the orchestra, about the rehearsals, about life, about everything. I continued raising hell for some two or three weeks. By then I was acclimatised to America – or so I thought. At any rate, I calmed down and began to take things in my stride.

Hurok had rented the St. James' Theatre on 46th Street for us. It was in the Broadway district and was meant for plays, not ballet. The stage was restricted and somewhat slanting, the orchestra pit pitifully small, so that even our modest, "well trimmed" orchestra overflowed into the stalls and nearby boxes, the lighting facilities were insufficient, and so forth. These were severely counterproductive factors. The greater was the merit of the superb company in achieving the overwhelming success that it did.

Not in a day, either. The first programme included *La Concurrence*, with music by Georges Auric, a delightful, comic piece, about the rivalry of two tailors who keep shops on opposite street corners, its choreography one of Massine's small masterpieces. Then came the monstrous *Les Présages* danced – superfluously – to Tchaikovsky's Fifth Symphony, and *Le Beau Danube*, all three much acclaimed, as was practically everything the company presented. The sold-out notices did not appear on our posters at the start, but the success mounted steadily and soon the Monte Carlo Ballet had danced itself into the hearts of New Yorkers, as it did later into the heart of the entire continent.

The first New York season, planned for three weeks, was extended to six, and the tour that followed, taking the group through the north-eastern part of the country and including Boston, Philadelphia, and – as the most westerly point – Pittsburgh, was sufficient to confirm the success attained so far and presage further triumphs.

These did not fail to come. The American tours continued year after year, soon extending to the West Coast, and encompassing not only the entire USA, but Canada and Mexico as well.

The subsequent New York seasons, longer and more successful each year, were all held at the Metropolitan Opera House, where, with its adequate facilities, the company could show itself in its full glory.

In Chicago, where we always performed between Christmas and New Year to houses full to the rafters, the old Auditorium Theatre provided a creaky, but very adequate home.

In my quest for better music I had unexpected help from several American symphony orchestras which engaged the company to dance for a few performances. The initiator of this custom – for that is what it soon became – was a certain Arthur Gaines, then manager of the Symphony Orchestra in St. Louis with whom I later became closely associated. Others followed suit, and the company appeared regularly, with the orchestras of Philadelphia (where Stokowsky was the conductor at that time and undertook to conduct one or two ballets himself), Cincinnati (where Eugene Goossens, who had conducted for Diaghilev before, also gave expert performances of some of his old favourites), Minneapolis, Cleveland, Washington and San Francisco. These orchestras were sadly under-rehearsed for the unaccustomed repertoire, yet they were so many oases in the "music deserts" that these American tours in fact were.

The company's return to Europe from its first USA tour was delayed, and it was March 1934 when we reached Paris and proceeded on to Monte Carlo. There the director of the beautiful, small opera house was a Monsieur Ginsbourg, and the directorship of the ballet company was shared between de Basil and René Blum, brother of the politician Léon Blum, later a tragic victim of the Nazis.

There the respective families, wives, husbands, boyfriends and girlfriends, waited for the returning travellers.

Meeting Klári again was lovely, and somewhat strange. I had the feeling of things remaining unsaid. Yet it was an idyllic period, quiet, very old-world after the hustle and bustle of the new. Our hotel was the Mirabeau, now defunct, which, true to its name, did indeed look out on beautiful sights.

This was one of only two periods I had with the ballet in Monte Carlo. Although called after the city, the company's visits there became more and more sporadic.

The centre of its work became London. The yearly seasons, of several months' duration, were always at Covent Garden. At that time, the opera seasons were short affairs, arranged in grand style by Sir Thomas Beecham, very imposing, but not occupying more than a few weeks each year. The Opera House had no company of its own. The Royal Ballet was already in existence under another name but in its infancy, and not yet ready (this was 1934) to offer a substantial repertoire and commensurate performances. So there was a natural place for the Monte Carlo company to serve an already very ballet-conscious public, indeed at that time much more ballet-conscious than opera-minded.

This was an ideal, or almost ideal situation: a great theatre, with an atmosphere and patina of its own, fine rehearsing possibilities, an excellent orchestra in the London Philharmonic, founded by Sir Thomas Beecham a few years earlier. Sir Thomas was very much about, and now and then even conducted one of the ballets. Unfortunately, however, he lost interest in that activity when a newspaper accused him of having conducted uncomfortably for the dancers. He sued the paper and haughtily turned away from a thankless task. The papers accused me, not infrequently, of the same crime, but I neither took them to court nor did I quit my job – I needed it. Besides, I disapproved, as I disapprove now, of reacting in any way to newspaper or any public criticism. If I were to berate a reviewer for an unfavourable notice, I would have to thank him for a favourable one; both equally ridiculous.

The company was the toast of the town, riding high on the wave of an extraordinary success and its yearly seasons at Covent Garden grew longer and longer.

There were other visits: to Paris, where we performed at the popular, but very dirty, Théâtre des Champs Elysées; to Barcelona's old, noble Teatro del Liceo, where we were accompanied by the Casals Orchestra, founded and conducted by the great Pau, a legend even then. He received me a few times in his house, very graciously and warmly, not neglecting the very complicated social courtesies of Spain, which he could easily have dispensed with. At one time there was a Casals Exhibition, showing all sorts of souvenirs and memorabilia connected with his life. He offered to be our cicerone (just the two of us, my wife and I), and guided us through the collection with exquisite, naive charm. It was touching, and funny at the same time, to hear that serious, sometimes forbidding-looking man explain to us in dead earnest, "These shoes I wore when I was three years old."

The "workshop" of the company remained, of course, London. It was there that the repertoire was kept in shape and most of the many new creations were added to it.

Leonide Massine, as our chief choreographer, bore the brunt of the work, but he alone could not shoulder the whole task of providing the needed novelties, so other choreographers were regularly brought in. Michel Fokine re-established his classic *Petrushka* and the even earlier *Firebird* and *Shéhérazade*, from the great Diaghilev days. He also created a new ballet version of Rimsky-Korsakov's *Coq d'or*, a piece with which Diaghilev had already experimented. In Diaghilev's production the singers were put in niches on stage, where they sang motionless, while the story was mimed and danced. Fokine's new version dispensed with the human voice altogether. That made a curious impression upon those who were used to hearing the singers, but apparently I was the sole representative of that group who saw in that production an opera for the deaf-mute.

Bronislava Nijinska (Vaslav Nijinsky's sister) was a brilliant choreographer, and a feared disciplinarian. She was an intimidating apparition in her trouser-suits, with her long cigarette-holder and her whisper, above which her voice never rose. She re-established *Les Biches* and other former creations of hers, again from the Diaghilev era, and eventually produced a few new ballets, which, however, did not remain long in the repertoire.

Massine himself was a tireless worker and had a fertile fantasy. Curiously, and certainly unnecessarily, he needed to lean on another creative force, or rather another "authority", to feel at ease. This was, partly, the reason why he chose works by great composers of the past – by Beethoven, Brahms, and other such nineteenth-century Olympians – even if what he had chosen was not suitable for dancing. On their side the delighted management welcomed their use, because they were out of copyright.

As far as I was concerned, I had resolved, once destiny had placed me in this strange land, that I would try to understand what it was all about, and to be a useful member of the company as long as I stayed with it. So I did all I could to block the "symphonic" trend, and used all my persuasive powers to that purpose.

Massine, to my surprise, was quite receptive to my point of view; it turned out that he had no deep-seated reasons for preferring masterful symphonies to masterful ballet music. It appeared that he turned to Tchaikovsky's Fifth Symphony as music material for *Les Présages* simply because he had nothing else of quality to hand and because Tchaikovsky himself had given some sort of programme indications – the music's principal motif, which returns unrelentingly throughout the four movements, represents "fate" (a meagre enough excuse to try making a story or dramatic actions out of it) – and was then encouraged by the great success of that work to continue.

At that time the second symphony-ballet, *Choreartium*, had its delirious success in London, so it would have been quite futile to try to persuade Massine and his adoring entourage to stop creating further specimens of that ill-begotten species. Therefore I concentrated my efforts on helping to bring about a new symphonic ballet that *would* make dramatic and musical sense.

There was one great symphony just waiting to be dramatised, and, I thought, ideally suited to Massine's choreographic style. It was no less a work than Berlioz's Symphonie Fantastique.

Massine jumped at the suggestion. He took his time over his preparation and his work was detailed and arduous. He familiarised himself with the score as thoroughly as he could. So far into detail did he go that he asked me to provide him with a kind of "balletic" short score of all the polyphonic passages, to enable him to set movements for the various voices with the utmost correctness. I had fears that such, so to speak, "artificial preparation" would produce a stale, over-scholarly choreography, but, on the contrary, the work that emerged was spontaneous, direct, powerful, the best of the species – for me personally the only good and valid symphonic ballet. The splendid sets by Christian Bérard were also much applauded, as was the superb dancing of all the performers, headed by Massine himself in the role of the "Artist".

Among the most promising developments of those years was the slow emergence of David Lichine as a choreographer. He was already one of the star dancers of the company, very young, very handsome, very gifted. He wanted a chance to test his powers in choreography and was given one. His own first ballet was a small piece, danced in white, in inspiration not unlike Fokine's *Les Sylphides*, but by no means an imitation. It was called *Le Pavillon* and was done to a suite of piano pieces by Borodin, joined together and orchestrated by me. It had good success and stayed in the

155

repertoire for some time. After this start it was understood that Lichine would be given more opportunities. His imagination was very sharp and abundant, but his musical knowledge was limited, and he came to rely on me for advice. This led to some very interesting and successful collaborations between the two of us.

Little by little I became more intrigued by the creative aspect of the art of ballet, while conducting for it became – frankly – less and less interesting. Pride in my profession forbade that this boredom should become noticeable. During my school years I heard a maxim by Felix Mottl, who said that a conductor who cannot conduct the opera *Mignon* one hundred and fifty times with full enthusiasm and dedication should change his profession. I subscribe completely to this view, all the more so as my musical upbringing in the Kodály-Weiner discipline has left me with an abhorrence of sloppiness.

In our profession enthusiasm and dedication must and can be controlled and produced at will. Thus I have never given anything but the best I had in me, whatever I have played, conducted or written. If my contribution has been small, no matter. It is not quantity, but totality, that is the measure of human value in accomplishment.

16

As an orchestra conductor I learned a great deal during my time with the Ballets Russes de Monte Carlo. It was first of all invaluable as experience. The daily grind of unmemorable rehearsals and performances gave me a background of practical routine which so few of my young colleagues shared. There is so little to *know* about this young and tender art, and so much to *live through*. Nothing that has not passed through one's own mind and body means anything. During that time I learned how to face the best and worst orchestras, how to give unmistakably clear visual signs, how to rehearse a great deal of music in a short time, how to speak little and convey what is necessary in an authoritative yet casual manner, to react fast and decisively to what one hears, to anticipate and possibly forestall difficulties. All these knacks are the tools of the conductor, and lucky is he who can acquire them *before* he himself is in the most exposed situation. There is no school where they can be learned, and no teacher can teach them, for there is no norm that can be applied; all depends upon the mental and physical make-up of the conductor, and the problems are as many and present themselves in as many ways as they – the conductors – have different souls and bodies.

As a musician I profited from my association with the ballet because it made me turn back to creative activity. The numerous arrangements of other composers' music I made for ballet during those years were no substitute for original composition. Still, they kept my pen moving.

Other, non-musical, stimulation was not lacking. There was the world, which I wanted to know so badly, suddenly and casually spread out before me with all its wonders. There were languages to be learned. At the start of this period (in 1933) I spoke no English at all. My French was rudimentary, my Spanish non-existent. I picked them up fast, together with a smattering of Russian, which unfortunately I soon forgot, as I forgot the little Danish I spoke as a child.

The landscapes and cities etched themselves in my mind; the

157

people, often briefly and casually met, were an unending source of adventure and amusement.

Within the Ballets Russes there were several extraordinary subdivisions. One would think that the first of these would be the prima donnas with their tempers, intrigues, escapades. Not at all. Three of them, remember, were mere children. But what they failed to supply by being too young, their mothers more than made up for. These ladies themselves were far from old, probably in their late thirties or thereabouts. They were full of temperament, full of ambition for their daughters, and besides they had all the time in the world for keeping life back stage in a state of turmoil.

They were the great watchers of all posters, programmes and other printed material, and if they noticed the names of THEIR daughters being printed smaller than stipulated, or on the wrong line, pandemonium would break loose. "Slights" were almost a daily event, "scandals" occurred two or three times a week. Revenges on suitable scales were planned, and sometimes even carried out.

Once, a day before the company had to cross from the USA to Canada, one of the mamas was heard to whisper: "Did you notice my poor daughter's name left off yesterday's programme? Manager says printer forgot. It was done on purpose – oh yes, it was! But I know what to do. Tomorrow" – and in a toneless hiss – "tomorrow Tamarichka will lose passport!"

The slimness of daughters was a matter of honour to their mamas. At a time when, for some reason, the rivalry was especially acute – between the mothers, of course – each of the good ladies was to be seen before curtain time, on the evenings of their respective daughter's performance, sitting smack in the centre of the stage, with needle and thread, taking in the costume their child would be wearing a few minutes later and commenting in a loud and plaintive voice that the dress was *again* too large.

After some time this sport began to arouse general interest. More and more members of the company gathered round to watch and bets were laid, at higher and higher odds, on whose seam would split first.

One of the costumes did burst, one evening, in mid-action. The proudly pirouetting prima donna became, suddenly, a frightened little girl, yelling "Mamicshka!" and running at full speed off the stage.

New members of the company appeared, some to stay on, some to disappear again. One of the most interesting of these was a new star, Vera Zorina. She was one of the first non-Russians amongst the principal dancers. Zorina was a stage name, she was called Brigitta Hartwig, and had, I was told, a German father and a Norwegian mother. She was light blonde, fair skinned, very beautiful, very gifted and very intelligent. She won my friendship with one sentence. We were on an American tour, and found ourselves one Sunday in Buffalo, NY, with a free morning on our hands. I went to see the Niagara Falls, an overwhelming sight indeed, in spite of much human tampering with the wild beauty of nature. Looking at the cascades from the bridge confronting the falls, I saw a slender figure approaching. It was Brigitta – the only other person, apparently, who had bothered to make the short trip. She joined me and we looked in awe for a long time at the wonder before us. Then we walked back, together. We did not speak.

Suddenly she said: "We have a very good life, haven't we?"

One day I was entrusted to escort another new member of the ballet company from Paris to Monte Carlo, a trip we normally made overnight in a first-class carriage, which was almost as comfortable as a wagon-lit and much cheaper.

My charge's name was Sono Osato – no *nom de guerre* this time. She was a strikingly beautiful, sixteen- or seventeen-year-old Japanese girl. That is, her father was Japanese (a photographer in Chicago) and her mother was Irish-American. With her oriental features, white skin and enormous eyes she was a pleasure to look at. Moreover, she was excellent, amusing, company. I took her to the dining car, where we had a big meal *á la* French railways, after which we returned to our compartment and for some time continued in animated conversation. Then, without a moment's transition or preparation, she looked up towards the empty luggage net, climbed into it, curled up like a little monkey, and went fast asleep. She slept happily, until I collected her next morning at Villefranche, in time to get off at Monte Carlo.

Another excursion was a six-week stay in Berlin. For me this meant an unwilling return to the place I had so abruptly left not quite four years before. It was an unbelievable experience, to see

159

that country turned upside-down and now puffed up with a rude, cocky self-assurance.

Like all totalitarian systems, Hitler's dictatorship did not benefit the arts. Works were burned or banned, many of the finest artists left the country, either voluntarily or under compulsion. It was an epoch of sad decline. The appearance of the Ballets Russes de Monte Carlo was like a breath of fresh air and the applause which greeted it was what I can only describe as desperately ecstatic. Yet when we left, we felt relieved. We were treated with the utmost courtesy, but all of us felt like visitors in a prison, talking to guarded people through a screen.

Our last evening ended hilariously. As I have said, our success was pathetically great, and when the last curtain fell there was veritable pandemonium, an outbreak of over-enthusiasm that was as frightening as it was flattering. Everyone was on stage and the curtain calls had no end. Even de Basil joined the bowing line – he often did so, though audiences could never make out who that tall man in full evening dress was who suddenly mixed with the performers. The orchestra, which had remained in the pit, applauded. A rare event, for members of theatre orchestras are always envied as being the first who can go home. All of a sudden, they took up their instruments and, in an improvised gesture, played us a farewell tune. It was a popular German song, with appropriate words, played by bands in German ports to the passengers of departing ships. For the musical reader I quote its beginning:

Muss i' denn, muss i' denn zum städt – le hi – naus
(When I leave, when I leave my dear lit – tle town)

The audience started singing, and everyone was deeply moved. Then the mood abruptly changed as 2,500 Berliners began yelling, howling with laughter, guffawing and rolling about.

I looked around me and saw de Basil standing erect, solemn-faced; he believed he was listening to the German national anthem, and with outstretched arm was giving the Nazi salute.

Our bags were packed. We left early the next morning.

17

By that time I was eager to leave the ballet but had had bad luck. In Chicago I had concluded a contract with the local opera company, but it then got into financial straits and obligations were abrogated. I had an offer to go to Dallas, Texas, to take over the city's budding symphony orchestra. The letter of invitation landed in the pocket of de Basil, who kept it there until it was too late. Mishaps of this kind happened one after the other. In compensation, I conducted concerts for the various radio stations in New York, which then had their own excellent symphony orchestras. And I conducted concerts in Spain, and in my native town, Budapest. In London, I began recording in 1936 – the start of an activity I have continued and enjoyed ever since.

Then a new adventure loomed – a tour of Australia. The time: 1938.

I was sent ahead to prepare the orchestra, and so Klári and I left Marseilles on the P & O liner *Comorin*. The voyage lasted a month, with stops at Suez, Aden, Bombay, Colombo, Perth, Adelaide. Oldest of the Peninsular and Orient fleet, the *Comorin* was a creaky, obsolete vessel, but it had a charm of its own.

For me that thirty days at sea was a unique experience. I was cut off from the world, left to myself, unbothered by the normal daily duties of my profession. I took out the music manuscript paper which I always carried in the bottom of my suitcase, and started to compose, in a frenzied release, day and night. What I wrote made no sense for the moment. That did not matter. What was important was to bring to the surface ideas which had been accumulating and fermenting within me for years. Twenty years later that material became my first symphony.

On the pier in Melbourne, where we finally disembarked, we were met by a solemn gentleman in a dark suit, complete with umbrella and bowler hat. He introduced himself as Mr. Robertson, director of the Tait Company (later Williamson and Tait), which was bringing ballet to Australia. This was then the country's one and only theatrical organisation and very active and powerful it was. The Australian Broadcasting Commission (ABC), under the leadership of its superbly gifted director, Charles Moses (of whom I shall say more later) had just begun to take over the promotion of music, but the Tait brothers – there were four of them, one in London, three in Australia – owned and operated all the theatres in every Australian city and so controlled the destiny of a very large part of the performing arts in the Antipodes.

Mr. Robertson was courtesy itself.

"Mr. Doráti," he said, "the orchestra is yours. Please do with it what you want, rehearse as much as you wish. You have a completely free hand over all musical matters."

I was enchanted. This was the real New World, I said to myself.

How really new it was, I found out at the first orchestra rehearsal. I met a group of very nice people who knew nothing about orchestral playing at all.

As I gradually came to understand, there was no surplus of superior instrumentalists in Australia at that time. The best were employed by the ABC, which had its own orchestra in each of the larger cities, and there were very few left to choose from after that.

My decision was quickly made. I picked out the four or five players who *had* any quality and drew up a schedule according to which every member of the orchestra would work nine solid hours every day, Sundays included. First in small groups, led by my selected few and with myself going from one group to the other – thus my own working hours were some sixteen per day – then the entire orchestra together, starting from scratch – in every sense of the word – and progressing step by step.

Within two weeks the Tait brothers were near bankruptcy, and the orchestra was capable of giving adequate performances of the first two programmes to be presented.

The success was overwhelming. The Ballets Russes conquered Australia in a day. And the standard of the music was especially noted: it was the first time, apparently, that orchestral playing of an adequate quality had been heard in Australia in connection with opera or ballet. (Concert performances were different.)

It is possible that my reputation as an "orchestra-maker" – a term which makes me feel more angry than flattered – dates from that time.

162

In London Lichine had come up with a new idea: a light-hearted ballet about a ball given by a girls' school for a group of cadets. I liked it and proposed to adapt music by Johann Strauss (Jnr.), thus placing the story in the Austria of the later Hapsburgs, around the end of the nineteenth century.

The project was interrupted then. Now, in Melbourne, it came to fruition. The score and choreography were finished, and the ballet had its world première. Its title became *Graduation Ball*, under which it became well known all over the world. It was one of the most successful ballets of the post-Diaghilev period. And with good reason, for Lichine's choreography was nothing less than a masterpiece of tender, light comedy. He himself and Riabouchinska danced the two main roles adorably. They looked, moved, behaved exactly like the children they portrayed in exquisite stylisation, and the entire company matched them beautifully. Even today the piece is frequently performed.

My arrangement and orchestration of the music were also praised, and I could have earned a sackful of money on royalties from the many thousand performances the work has had. Alas, I lacked financial talent.

I was stupid enough to make a very bad contract with de Basil under which he was obliged to pay me no more than a pittance after each performance. What is more, I was shamelessly cheated by him and his Russian entourage. For a very long period de Basil managed to pay me nothing at all, using all kinds of excuses which I finally ceased to believe. Much later, during another tour of the United States, my patience ran out, and I staged what was probably the first one-man-sit-down strike in theatrical history.

I simply sat on my suitcase on the platform of a railway station, and in spite of de Basil's pitiful tirades, refused to board our train.

It so happened that Hurok was travelling with us that day. He watched the scene for some time, then began to speak to de Basil slowly and softly, in Russian. I understood snatches of what he said. He was "*ustali*" (tired) of this nonsense, Doráti was within his rights and would he, de Basil, pay him then and there. Otherwise . . .

De Basil, very sour and unwilling, bowed to the super-power, took out his bank book and wrote out a sizeable – indeed for him enormous – cheque. I put my suitcase on the train and we left.

An hour or so later Hurok strolled by where I was sitting,

stopped, bent down and whispered into my ear, "Now, my boy, when we arrive in XXXX, don't walk, *run* to the nearest bank and cash that cheque!"

It was his good deed for the day.

Another new production was planned and prepared in Australia with the choreography of Michel Fokine, who arrived in great style from America to start rehearsals. The ballet was to be called *Paganini*. The violinist was its hero, the music was Rachmaninoff's Rhapsody on a Theme by Paganini for pianoforte and orchestra.

I thoroughly disliked the project but I was voted down and, I have to admit, it proved a great success.

On his arrival in Sydney, Fokine received me like a potentate, in the ship's vast first-class salon. Passengers and crew had gone ashore; we were alone. There he explained to me the story of the new piece.

". . . that you should know interpret music better."

"Yes, go on, Mr. Fokine."

He went on, in Russian-English, concluding his account, "And now I will tell you my first idea of ending Balyet that you understand me better. My idea was" – he said "Idyea" and "Paganyinyi" – "that when Paganini dies, clutching beloved violin to chest, and curtain slowly falls, violin suddenly grows and becomes transparent, so Paganini in last second of Balyet lies inside violin like in glass coffin."

I swallowed hard, feeling queasy. But Fokine was flying high.

Enraptured, he continued, "When I have this idea – I cry. I go right away to Sudeikin." (Sudeikin, the painter, was designing scenery and costumes for the production.)

"When I tell him idea, Sudeikin, he cry. He deeply moved. After drying tears on face, Sudeikin rush for paper and pencil to draw first sketch of my idea. When he show me design, I surprise. I say to Sudeikin: but my dear friend, this no violin – this double bass!"

And this is why, thank God, Paganini could not be buried inside his "big violin".

Massine composed several new ballets during that period, amongst them one on an American subject, *Union Pacific*, which had quite a lasting success and handled, amusingly, the building of the trans-American railway from west to east and from east to west and the meeting of the two tracks. The music was composed by Nicholas Nabokov, who cleverly used one or two American tunes, and ingeniously conjured up an American atmosphere in his well-made score. Massine himself danced the incidental part of a bartender, and had, with a solo number called "Shuffle", such a success that it stopped the show every time. The applause that followed it was so insistent that, as the only exception to a very strict rule which categorically forbade encores, his "shuffling" always had to be repeated.

With the Australia tour of 1938 the peak period of the Ballets Russes de Monte Carlo came to an end and from then on decay set in.

Another Russian, a banker called Serge Denham, appeared from nowhere and formed another company. Massine and about half of de Basil's original group left and joined him, and took with them the name Ballets Russes de Monte Carlo.

The rest remained with de Basil and continued under a new name: The "Original" Ballets Russes.

The music department split, too. Efrem Kurtz went to Denham's company, I remained with the Colonel, my position – and salary – greatly strengthened. Denham did his best to make me move over to him, but I had no great desire to continue working with Kurtz, with whom I had a lukewarm relationship at best. It was not the fault of either of us. Kurtz was a gifted conductor, but I was clearly in his way. Both of us knew that the situation was not of our making and were perfectly willing to be friends. But we had very different temperaments, tastes and orientation. It was better for us to separate.

As for myself, I was more than ready to end that chapter of my life. But as conditions in the world went from bad to worse and as I had no other way of existing than through my work, I hesitated to leave the ballet before having found a new post in the musical world that was truly mine.

I was well prepared for the change. The endless hours on trains and ships, while never dull in themselves, had left me ample time to study.

165

And just as I packed my reading for a lifetime into four brief school years between the ages of fourteen and seventeen, so now, during my time with the Ballets Russes, I acquired a solid, thorough knowledge of the basic concert repertoire, committing to memory not only the symphonies of Beethoven and Brahms, and much of Haydn and Mozart, but a great many works from the orchestral literature of the eighteenth to the twentieth centuries. I also took care to keep my opera repertoire always in good shape.

I also did a number of arrangements and orchestrations, in addition to those I undertook for the ballet. I orchestrated, for instance, a sequence of chorale preludes by Bach, made an orchestral version of Debussy's Sonata for Violin and Piano, as well as, more rarely, composing music of my own, mostly small pieces of chamber music but also a divertimento for small orchestra in the Hungarian idiom.

To ensure that my departure from the ballet was not a jump into the blue, I conceived the plan of organising an opera company to tour Australia. The Tait organisation received the idea enthusiastically and I came to Europe in the summer of 1939 with their mandate to see to the assembling of the troupe, to arrange contracts, dates, details of the productions, scenery, costumes, everything. The principal singers we signed up were of exceptional calibre, as were the two producers and the scenic artist. A few singers for the smaller roles remained to be auditioned. For this purpose we rented the stage of the Zürich Opera House for a few mornings in early September.

The principals of the company were to meet in Zürich on August 31st. Before that, all of us went on a short vacation. Klári and I chose Italy. She came from a visit to her parents in Hungary, I from London, and we met in La Spezia, from where we went on to Forte dei Marmi, on the coast near Livorno and Pisa.

There, lying in the sand and looking at the stars, we discussed with friends the worsening world situation and decided that war was out of the question, once and for ever. We swam, we played tennis, we had an altogether splendid time, then went to meet our colleagues in Zürich.

Two days later, Hitler invaded Poland.

So there we were, Klári and I, on September 2nd, 1939, in

Zürich, hale and hearty, bewildered, like everyone else, with nothing to do, nowhere to go.

Our coping with the unbelievable and unbelieved situation was rapid and energetic.

18

FROM WHAT I HAVE SAID ABOUT IT SO FAR, IT WILL NOT HAVE emerged that, from the day I first set foot on American soil, I felt a great affection for that extravagant country. There was, indeed, no parallel to it anywhere. The moment in its history when I arrived, the Rooseveltian New Deal era, the magnificent effort of rehabilitation after the recession years was, especially, one of overpowering impact.

I never got completely acclimatised to America – true. But most probably I was not, am not, able to acclimatise anywhere. I left my own country by my own volition, and I never had a really permanent residence thereafter, until my most recent years in Switzerland, where, for the first time in my life since my early childhood, I have the feeling of being at home.

I had only one real sense of belonging; that was to my art, to music, which by its universality not only compensated me for the long lack of a home, but was probably the chief cause of my inner refusal to acclimatise geographically.

I first decided that I should like to apply for American citizenship as early as 1937. My so-called "first papers" were given to me in that year by the American Consul in Montreal, M. C. Cameron, who persuaded me to apply for them. He pointed out that I was already making a good deal of my living in the USA, in a field where fresh energies and talents were very welcome and had an important part to play. Did I not feel that I should make my adherence more permanent? I felt so and eventually did so. (That it took another ten years was due to my peripatetic life.) Ever since, I have tried to be useful, remembering always Kodály's teaching that everyone should "bring his brick to the building". And I hope that I have succeeded to some degree.

So there was nothing abrupt or illogical about my decision to go to America in September 1939. I was certain that I would soon find work and be able to start again. I was getting used to it.

The problem was, how to get there. Not only did I not have

enough money to buy our passages, but passenger shipping was partly suspended, especially in the North Atlantic, and the Italian ships which, for the time being at least, were making most of the crossings were overcrowded.

An American friend, Henry Clifford, came to our rescue. He was then curator of paintings at the Philadelphia Museum of Art, a wealthy lover of the arts, an ardent balletomane. He invited us to stay at his beautiful house above Vevey after the outbreak of the war, while we decided what to do next. Through his Italian connections he obtained passages for us all: Esther, his wife, himself and both of us. He also lent me the money for the passage, leaving it to me to pay him back when I could. (I was able to do so before the end of the year.)

So, after travelling by train to Milan and Genoa, we embarked on the *Conte di Savoia*. Conditions were very crowded. There were more than twice as many passengers on board as the ship was supposed to hold. The staterooms were split up by screens. Cubicles were erected on the covered decks. The luckier passengers had mattresses to sleep on, the rest had to make do with sacks of straw. But no one complained, no one minded. From Gibraltar to New York the ship sailed without lights at night; the evenings were long and the mood of the passengers subdued.

In New York luck was with me right away. One of the radio stations, the ABC, immediately engaged me to conduct a series of studio concerts. This was a good start. I could plan ahead without panic.

Next I took Klári, who had been feeling unwell for several weeks, to a physician. He examined her and said, "Congratulations, you are pregnant!"

This was great news indeed, and also a forceful reminder that one cannot "manipulate" God.

We had been married ten years. First, we had avoided having children because in our situation it was not "practical", as our elders held and as we unthinkingly agreed. Later we were willing, but no child arrived. Then – suddenly – at the most "impractical" moment possible, without a home, with the future hidden in the fire and smoke of the new war, here we were, blessed suddenly with offspring. I can, as I could then, imagine God with a mischievous smile saying, "I'll show them!"

Within a matter of weeks I had three offers of permanent posts. A newly formed dance company, the Ballet Theatre (later American Ballet Theatre), asked me to join them as conductor; the de Basil Company unexpectedly turned up with the prospect of a second Australian tour, on which they claimed my continuing services as music director; and simultaneously the Australian Broadcasting Commission, known as the ABC, offered me a concert tour to coincide with the same period.

This double offer was obviously the better one; yet I chose it not without misgivings, because I was unwilling to expose Klári in her condition to a long sea voyage. She, however, urged me to accept. For once, de Basil behaved as a true gentleman: on his orders we were provided with the best possible accommodation on both the trans-continental train, the famous "Super-Chief", and the Matson liner *Mariposa*. The Pacific Ocean was also true to its name. The crossing was like a beautiful dream.

Half of the company sailed with us, under my benevolent supervision. (I was scolded later for being too generous with advance payments, but it was too late, and a good time was had by all.) The other half arrived soon after us, and there we all were again, almost as if nothing had happened.

The double season that I was faced with went well. I had an excellent co-conductor, Max Goberman, who took good care of the Ballet while I was playing concerts with the ABC orchestras (though unfortunately he left before the end of the season after a dispute with the management). From Sydney we moved for a long stay in Melbourne, where – finally – Klári was taken in hand by the doctor who was to deliver our child. We rented a pleasant house just on the outskirts of the city, not so much for our own comfort as for that of the baby to come.

The child was in no great hurry to see the world. The pains announcing its arrival began on May 10th, and lasted through two days. As I had rehearsals for a concert during that time, the ABC and the telephone company installed a direct line from the conductor's platform to the hospital room, so that we could talk at any time and, by leaving the receiver off the hook, Klári could listen to any part of the rehearsal.

Finally, on May 12th, Sunday, "Mother's Day", a little dark-haired girl arrived. She already had a necklace, with a cross,

170

given by friends, and engraved; "TONIN'", to fit equally a Tonino or a Tonina, Anthony or Antonia, after my own name. This did not leave us any choice, but neither did it give us full satisfaction. The innocent child was named – after various grandmothers, godmothers and would-be godmothers – Antonia Klara Alexandra Magdalena Patrician Emilia, a burden she has carried with surprising calm ever since.

It was September, 1940, when we left for the United States, again splendidly taken care of aboard a Matson liner, this time the *Monterey*. On board the ship we met Yehudi Menuhin, who travelled with his first wife, Nola, and their firstborn, a daughter, Zamira, about six months older than Tonina. We approached each other hesitantly at first; the two babies, not music, was the common factor which first brought us together. It was the beginning of a very warm and lasting friendship. For the seven or eight years that followed we lived in close contact.

Those were years of exciting music-making. Partly through my mediation, Menuhin came to know and love Bartók's music; that in itself made for a strong link between the two of us. We performed the famous violin concerto, later known as Number Two, many times together – more often than I performed any concerto for any instrument with any other artist. We gave at least thirty performances of it, and recorded it three times. I think that around the first half of the 1950s we had approached that closeness of understanding and feeling of the work and of each other in it that should exist ideally between each soloist and each conductor all the time.

We also played chamber music together.

One evening a particularly illustrious company assembled at our house in Forest Hills, Long Island: Yehudi Menuhin, William Primrose and Grisha Piatigorsky. After some food and talk we sat down and played a piano quartet by Brahms; it went so well that we decided to play it again there and then. The second performance was even better. Excited and overjoyed, we embarked upon a third. When we were about halfway through, a police car drove up to the house, and an enormous policeman appeared in the doorway, shouting at us in a furious voice: "Shut that radio!!!"

We were several times guests in the Menuhins' lovely house in

Alma, California. Soon they had their second child, a little boy, Krov – and the three children – he, Zamira and our Tonina, were very close companions in their first years.

In New York, we lived not far from each other and often visited. At one birthday (whose, I forget) we came to them accompanied by a genuine gipsy band, which I had hired in an uptown Hungarian café. In the course of that merry evening Yehudi played an improvised solo with the band. This was too much for the double bass player. He leapt with his instrument into the centre of the room and played a virtuoso solo with the band himself, to be rewarded by Menuhin with a bearhug, and by the rest of us with shouts of praise.

During our visits to Alma I wrote some music of my own – mostly trying out various approaches to string writing – exercises, no more.

Looking back on a life now well on the way to its completion, I can see my friendship with Menuhin as one of those parts of it that enhanced the depth of its perspective, and that time of close association as a lovely cruise together, a voyage very similar to the one on which our friendship started.

The *Monterey* docked at San Pedro, the harbour of Los Angeles, at the end of another smooth crossing, and after a short season there we went east for another engagement in New York.

George Balanchine joined the company to put on a new ballet called *La Balustrade* to the music of Stravinsky's Violin Concerto. Balanchine – perhaps the most musical of all choreographers – was capable of arranging movements that were not only beautiful to look at and artistically valid in themselves, but were also coherent aesthetically as well as dramatically.

In my own view *Balustrade* was probably the best new ballet of that period, but that was evidently a minority opinion, for the piece earned no more than a *succès d'estime*.

Samuel Dushkin, to whom the concerto is dedicated, played the violin solo in the first three performances, after which Tossy Spivakowsky took his place with equal brilliance and authority.

Stravinsky, who diligently attended a number of dance rehearsals, conducted the first performance. From the second onwards I took over.

172

That was neither the first nor the last time that I met Stravinsky.

After his visit to Budapest during the period of my adolescence, I saw him again in Paris in the mid-1930s, when the Monte Carlo Ballet refurbished his *Firebird*.

I visited him then, humbly asking what were his wishes and instructions for the forthcoming performance, of which I was in charge musically.

He had many.

Very patiently he went through every bar of his score, pointing out and describing to me each detail and how he wished it to be executed.

To my surprise, in the process of this he changed about three-fourths of his own agogic and dynamic markings as they were printed in the score. Most of the long notes he wanted short, many of the legato passages he now wanted detached, and vice versa.

In my amazement I forgot my manners and asked him, point blank, perhaps somewhat impertinently, "But, Mr. Stravinsky, if you want it this way, why didn't you write it down like this?"

He was neither offended nor perturbed. He said, very pleasantly yet also somewhat haughtily, "You see, at that time I didn't know how to write it better."

Whatever one may say about Stravinsky's personality, he was certainly not overly shy.

To an interviewer, who, talking about a new composition, asked, "What were you searching for, Mr. Stravinsky, with this piece?" he replied, "I do not search – I find."

This was a proud statement. And it was at least partly true.

Stravinsky throve on the *trouvaille*. His sense of the "new" was uncanny. And not merely of the "new" only, but of the "new" which would be *en vogue* tomorrow.

I am speaking now of the younger man. With this gift of finding, of being the first, he became for a time dangerously close to dictating musical fashion. But by the time the fashion which he initiated took hold he had long since abandoned it and gone off in another new direction.

When I say that his boast of finding without searching only presented part of the truth, I mean that his *bon-mot* was applicable to his inventive gifts only. These were entirely original and spontaneous. For the fitting, correct *expression* of his ideas he did indeed search, earnestly, and often painstakingly.

173

This was the explanation of that set of instructions he gave me for conducting *Firebird*. (I count myself very fortunate to have received them. I kept them with me and always carried them out. I do not know how many conductors he advised in this way. But I am proud to be one of the few who are giving "authentic" renderings of that masterwork, according to the composer's wishes – although those who followed them by reading the score without further information might well wonderingly raise their eyebrows.)

This search for perfection was also the true reason for his later revision of the scores of *Petrushka* and *Le Sacre du Printemps*. He wished to improve them in two ways. First, to make them easier to conduct and play. In this connection he sometimes used his own conducting prowess as a yardstick. This was counter-productive, for he was not a very skilful conductor; he was physically not well suited to the work. In consequence some of the "simplifications" he arranged were either not necessary or not simple. But the major reason for his revisions was to arrive at the clearest notation possible of the essence of his thought.

Musical notation is by its nature imperfect, having a much less close approximation to musical sounds than letters do to words. Thus the quest for a perfect notation is a never-ending one. A complete solution is impossible. But Stravinsky, especially in his early years, was one of those, like Mahler, who went on trying to achieve one.

It is often said that he re-edited his *Petrushka* and *Le Sacre du Printemps* only in order to earn more money with a new copyright. That is not so.

It so happened that, owing to circumstances which I fail to fathom, his three masterpieces, the ballets *Firebird*, *Petrushka* and *Rite of Spring* were and remained unprotected by copyright laws. These works are performed constantly all over the world and should have brought in a fortune for their composer. Alas, Stravinsky's income from them was minimal, apart from the certainly modest initial commission; fees were virtually non-existent. No wonder that, from then on, he was intent on keeping things in order. He knew his worth and the worth of money.

That he had purely musical reasons for wanting to make changes in his early scores, I can vouch for personally. One of the changes for the second edition of *Petrushka*, he made in my hotel room in my presence. He came there because his own room, he said, was too noisy. He spent a good hour and a half on re-writing those few bars, talking to me in the process, or rather carrying on a monologue.

The passage in question occurs near the end of the ballet, at the moment when the puppet Petrushka's rag body is picked up and carried off by the magician while an astonished policeman looks on.

The music to this scene reads in the first edition like this:

"This," so Stravinsky mused, "is never heard clearly. The bass-clarinet cannot enunciate the syncopating rhythm against the bassoons.

"It would be better this way . . .

"No – this way . . ."

As he went on muttering, he wrote, slowly, carefully, a number of new versions. None pleased him until, after a long time of great concentration and much scribbling, he exclaimed, "That's it!"

He told me to take the new version down, and unfailingly perform it every time I conducted *Petrushka*. This was well before the appearance of the new edition in 1947.

I promised to do so and kept my word.

At the time when *Balustrade* was set to his violin concerto he was fifty-nine years old, very vigorous, energetic, witty – and as sharp as a razor. He had made his home in Hollywood, but travelled a great deal. He was always accompanied by his wife, Vera, and sometimes also by members of his entourage, Nicholas Nabokov, Boris Kochno, Eugene Berman the painter, and others.

He was very conscious of the war and the entering of the United States into the conflict affected him deeply. It was easy to suspect that he carried within himself a trauma from the First World War, in which, though he spent it in physical safety, mostly in Switzerland, he lost his homeland – and he was deeply, fatally, Russian. The cosmopolitan way of life that he adopted was his way of coping with a problem he never really solved.

The good-looking, smallish, white house on Wetherly Drive in Los Angeles was his refuge. Not that he could have lived a hermit's life. In his own way he was very gregarious, loved company, food and drink. But all of it had to be very much *his*.

An unconfirmed anecdote delighted me during those days. I call it "Two Russians in Hollywood".

There are two kinds of Russian exiles. The ones whom one meets and the others whom one does not. As a rule, the former are the fakes, the latter the real ones.

Two giants of the real kind made their homes in Los Angeles during the Second World War. They could hardly have been more different, except that both were master musicians. One was tall, stooping, sad of countenance, silent, a sublime virtuoso of the pianoforte and a composer of romantic, gushingly sentimental, pleasantly old-fashioned works. The other was small, straight, wiry, bright-eyed, sharp-witted and sharp-tongued, a fine pianist also when it came to his own music, and a composer daringly new.

The first was Sergei Rachmaninoff.

The second was Igor Stravinsky.

Both found refuge and as much privacy as they desired in the milling, motley pell-mell of Hollywood. They steered clear of the world of movies, which was, to a great extent, why they were able to live so peacefully in that warring world in a warring time.

As I have said, they were real Russians.

They had never met.

More or less immobilised because of wartime travel restrictions, they stayed at home, scarcely five miles from each other, no doubt knowing of each other but never thinking of getting personally acquainted.

Their friends found this an impossible state of affairs. They tried to bring them together. But both of them resisted.

"What could I talk about with that old fuddy-duddy?" Stravinsky was quoted as saying.

"What could I say to that upstart revolutionist?" said Rachmaninoff allegedly.

Thus, one or two years went by and the two great Russians still did not know each other, except by reputation.

Their friends, finally, decided to take action.

A lengthy period of intrigue ensued. Stravinsky was slowly, gradually, carefully persuaded by his friends that Rachmaninoff had no other wish in this world than to meet him before he died. And Rachmaninoff's friends ended up by convincing him that Stravinsky was thirsting to know him as a man in the Sahara thirsts for water.

Accordingly, both of them slowly relented, and agreed, for the other's sake, to a meeting.

This was arranged in the form of an intimate supper, with only a few others present, at the house of a mutual friend of both, a physician.

The evening was a colossal let-down. A disaster. The two shook hands morosely, murmured the most platitudinous of polite phrases, assured each other how glad they were to meet, and had nothing to say to each other thereafter. Conversation during supper was painfully slow and dull. First the weather was discussed, no great subject for surprises in California. Then the meal was praised, the hostess complimented. Pause.

Someone said another word about food. That theme was picked up again, very sluggishly, by the two guests of honour, one enquiring what the other liked to eat. It turned out that Rachmaninoff's favourite was black bread with butter and nothing else on it; Stravinsky liked honey. That was all. From there the other guests had to carry the conversation, punctuated by a few "yes's" and "aha's" from the two stars, until – at the first permissible moment after supper – the party broke up in the lowest spirits possible.

Three days later, in the late morning, a big limousine stopped before Stravinsky's house. As the driver held the door of the car open, the dark–clad, tall, stooped figure of Rachmaninoff emerged, holding a big, heavy jar in his hand.

He rang the bell. It was Stravinsky who opened the door.

"You said you liked honey. Here is some honey for you."

With this Rachmaninoff thrust the jar into the arms of Stravinsky and whilst he was hugging it – for once, speechless – turned on his heels and drove away.

This happened, so I was told, in February 1943.

Rachmaninoff died one month later.

Los Angeles was the haven of many other very prominent artists during those troubled years. It would suffice to mention Arnold Schönberg and Thomas Mann, but there were others: Heifetz, Rubinstein, Toch, Adorno, Korngold – the more I name, the more come to mind.

Some left as soon as the way cleared after the war – I thought, rather ungratefully.

Stravinsky was not one of those. He never gave up his California home.

He began to travel, extensively, as soon as he could. It was my pleasure to be his host during the late Forties and Fifties in Dallas and Minneapolis where he conducted his works. I also met him later in London and in Venice when his opera *The Rake's Progress* had its world première.

"No scandal this time," he said almost nostalgically, after the tumultuous acclamation he was given at the performance – referring to the unprecedentedly tempestuous reception of *Sacre du Printemps* in Paris some forty years before.

The last time I saw Stravinsky was at the Albert Hall in London, at a performance of that same *Sacre du Printemps*, conducted by Pierre Monteux on the occasion of a birthday. It could have been the eightieth or eighty-fifth of Monteux, or the eightieth of Stravinsky, or could it have been the fiftieth anniversary of the first performance of *Sacre*, when Stravinsky was eighty-one and Monteux eighty-eight? Whichever it was, it was a great occasion.

I had messages from Stravinsky later on, through Nabokov, who conveyed to me his congratulations on my "courage" in giving the first London performance of his *Flood*, and, in due course, his disappointment at my not having been able to lead that work to victory. It had a luke-warm reception and a poor press.

If I did not earn his esteem then, I certainly commanded his respect – though not on musical grounds – on another occasion, a few years earlier though still during the war, in Los Angeles.

He had, as his part in the war effort, started a chicken farm in his garden, of which he was inordinately proud. He talked much about it and his visitors were often invited to see the wire-fenced enclosure. Not the prime attraction of his home, as one silently noted. Several times I made the short pilgrimage to the chickens' dwelling, usually in the company of the master himself, Madame Vera and their Russian cook. Thus I witnessed various stages of chicken farming. Amongst others, the time of the young little yellow chickens, milling merrily about the place.

Following a nonsensical notion, I said, very nonchalantly, that I was able to tell, at that early stage, which of them would be a hen or rooster, respectively.

The master was astonished.

"Unbelievable. How do you do it?"

"Oh, just by looking at them. It's a gift."

"Extraordinary – will you show me?"

Without any hesitation I separated the little creatures into two groups, left and right.

"Hen – hen – rooster – hen – rooster – rooster – hen –"

The cook looked on with utter contempt, recognising me as the impostor I was, but Madame Vera, and above all, Stravinsky himself, looked at me with large eyes, full of admiration.

It was not my intention to deceive or to mislead these dear, wonderful people I so much admired. I had merely made a joke. But, overwhelmed with my unexpected success, I was weak and vain enough not to enlighten them.

No doubt my imposture could have been unmasked a few weeks later as the chickens grew up, but the incident was forgotten by then.

But not by the cook, who never spoke to me again.

19

THE END OF THE BALLETS RUSSES DE MONTE CARLO OR THE Original Ballets Russes arrived in Havana, during what was planned as a short visit, in 1941. The musical and theatrical life of that charming city had at that time a short-lived, euphoric up-swing. Its sleepy, third-rate symphony orchestra improved beyond all reason and hope under the leadership of Erich Kleiber. The emergence of Alicia Alonso, a Cuban prima ballerina of international standard, brought with it an unexpected blossoming of ballet culture.

A two-week visit by a world famous ballet company was thus both a logical and a sensible undertaking.

Alas, unexpected troubles arose within the company and the dancers, in a surprise move, went on strike. What caused them to take this then unheard of step, and how the problems were eventually solved, I do not know. My ties with the company were rather loose by that time, and when the trouble started I had left for New York where I had rented a small, furnished house for my family in Forest Hills, Long Island.

After a fortnight or so I was requested to fly back to Havana to conduct some benefit performances for the members of the company, who were penniless after their strike.

The performances took place and had their desired effect. The purses of the dancers were still very empty, but at least some temporary tinkling could be heard inside them.

While there, I witnessed a fine example of ingenuity.

David Lichine, who like the others was badly affected by the dancers' strike, made good use of the time on his hands. He went to an open-air night club in the outskirts of Havana and offered to stage a Cuban revue which would change the style of its nightly entertainment. The spectacle he put on was an enchanting *mélange* of popular dance and song, with dancers from the stranded company and natives of Cuba. It was an exquisite show, a masterpiece of its kind. With the grounds of the night club as a natural setting, the dancers moved gracefully on the grass, on the sand, dropped from the trees, the band played Latin tunes from a distance. Sometimes there were only whistles from the trees, then one small human voice – all done with the simplest means and altogether wonderful.

I thought our efforts in artificial theatrical settings very poor in comparison, and dreamt of the birth of a new art combining sound and movement and living nature. But nothing came of it.

Back in New York I worked on plans for the future. The concerts which came my way – the radio stations continued to re-engage me with increasing frequency – made my situation tolerable for the moment. But I wanted more security for my wife and child.

I had two tempting offers.

The Ballet Theatre (now the American Ballet Theatre) whose invitation I had rejected the year before, came back with a better proposition. They now wanted me as their music director. This was a good job which I felt I could not refuse, although my heart pulled me towards the other, which for the moment, however, was very nebulous and problematic.

A group of wealthy New Yorkers had the idea of organising a small opera company, in contrast to the monolithic Met, with young, unknown, and therefore less expensive singers, under first-rate musical direction. As their musical leader they wanted Fritz Busch, and, on Busch's recommendation, they also wanted me, though in what capacity they were not quite sure. They were very vague altogether; they knew little yet beyond their general intention.

This, for me, would have meant the way back to opera and "home ground", so to speak.

So, there was the daily bread and butter on one side, and a fine prospect on the other. Rather skilfully, I think, I managed to have both. I negotiated a contract with the Ballet Theatre which allowed for leaves of absence in case the opera project materialised.

Having obtained this advantageous position, I went to work at the Ballet Theatre with double energy, keen to do well. By that time I knew my way around the orchestral world (and underworld) in New York. When I first went there, in 1933, I was an easy prey to every kind of manoeuvre by the "contractors" – a very special kind of people – who found jobs in the orchestras which they were responsible for staffing for their entire families and a large circle of friends, regardless of whether or not their professional standards were satisfactory. By 1941 I was wise to all that and, moreover, knew a great number of fine musicians throughout the country (this knowledge and experience was to benefit me even more a few years later) and so I could offer the Ballet Theatre a first-rate orchestra from the start.

That organisation was very different from de Basil's. It was headed, as it still is, by Lucia Chase, who provided a good deal of the finances for her venture herself, and who gathered around her a very fine group. Some of them, such as the brilliant Oliver Smith, are still with her.

New choreographers appeared on the horizon, the most notable among whom were Agnes de Mille, whose work was perhaps the most important factor in the Americanisation (in the best sense of the word) of the art of the dance, and Anthony Tudor, a choreographer-poet *par excellence*.

Soon after the very successful New York season, which Hurok took over and presented at the Metropolitan Opera House, a lengthy stay of almost six months in Mexico City followed – a period wisely used for producing many new works as well as for extensive performances of the existing repertoire.

During that period I made three more major musical arrangements, two of them adaptations of music by Offenbach. The first of these was called *Bluebeard*, a long dance comedy, in four scenes, with Michel Fokine's superb choreography, Anton Dolin's equally outstanding comic dancing, and Irina Baronova's brilliant rendering of the leading female role. The piece scored a universal triumph and was performed throughout the world nearly as frequently as its predecessor by a few years, *Graduation Ball*.

On the strength of this success, Fokine was commissioned to create, in collaboration with myself, another comedy piece. I had several suggestions for a subject, of which I favoured *1001 Nights*, a free fantasy upon Johann Strauss's operetta of the same title (or *Indigo* as it was first called. This was Johann Strauss's first real stage success). The libretto was completed and I still think it a pity that it was finally rejected in favour of my second proposal, an adaptation of *La Belle Hélène*. That brilliant, frothy satire by Offenbach (not forgetting the work of Meilhac and Halevy, his librettists) in our

182

hands became a heavy, over-elaborate, over-long, cumbersome ballet monster. It had many delightful details (as, for instance, when the apple, the trophy awarded by Paris to Venus, was tossed about from hand to hand, thus initiating the first rugby game in the world). All the same, it was not stageworthy, and its première in Mexico City was a failure. We did not waste time on a post-mortem, but set out to correct, re-write and re-choreograph the piece. This work, undertaken jointly by Fokine and myself, was interrupted by the former's illness, from which, to our great shock and grief, he was not to recover. With him went a great epoch, that of the old "new school" of ballet. His work is still to be seen on the stage, admired, unavoidable, and indispensable.

The salvaging of *Hélène* was thereafter assigned to Lichine. From the ashes emerged a light, small, fast-winged Phoenix. Our new Lady of Troy danced through a funny, flimsy ballet, lasting scarcely more than half an hour. Lichine's choreographic ideas were very amusing, and the small, elegant piece was welcomed warmly and held its own for a long time.

Scenery and costumes for both *Bluebeard* and *Hélène* were designed by Vertès, the superbly gifted Hungarian painter and caricaturist, who had made Paris his home and was in America also for the duration of the war. His contribution to the two productions was above all praise. His appearance in the ballet world, in which many stars of the fine arts, from Bakst to Picasso, had already shone, gave great pleasure and satisfaction to me, for it was upon my recommendation that the commissions were obtained for him.

The third major work which I helped to create for the Ballet Theatre was a dance version of Moussorgsky's *Fair of Sorotchinsk*, also to Lichine's choreography. This was a most poetic and beautiful piece, of much higher artistic merit than most of the newer productions. Unfortunately – and I think that it was a great permanent loss to the ballet repertoire – it did not catch on, probably because of one structural fault in the libretto which would have been easy to correct, but which somehow was not spotted until Lichine, Dolin – who danced the main part: the Devil – and myself had all gone off in different directions.

The one ballet to which I would have loved to provide the music but didn't was Agnes de Mille's *Tally Ho*. She had sent the piece to another composer before we met. So I contented myself with

183

conducting it, as I did her sparkling and in many ways pioneering ballet *The Three Virgins and the Devil*, accompanied by the old Italian dances beautifully orchestrated by Respighi, her classic *Rodeo*, and others, many others.

Remarkable work was also being done by Anthony Tudor, whose *Pillar of Fire*, to Schönberg's Transfigured Night, *Lilac Garden* to Chausson's Poème for Violin and Orchestra, and above all, the unforgettable *Romeo and Juliet* to music by Delius are permanent monuments to ballet at its best at that time.

New and significant music by American composers also appeared in the repertoire. De Mille's *Rodeo* was danced to Aaron Copland's score, as was *Billy the Kid*, which had Loring's choreography. These pieces had not only American music, but also librettos deeply rooted in American life and folklore. By contrast *Undertow*, choreographed by Anthony Tudor, was based on a story of no national colouring of any kind, so that the music of William Schuman, which was deeply American without being nationalistic, seemed to me of even greater importance. It was a pleasure to contribute to making these works a success, but I received more than that. The lasting friendship that developed between Copland, Schuman and myself added an important new dimension to my life.

20

SOON AFTER OUR RETURN TO MEXICO, WHERE OUR LITTLE TONINA had her second birthday, came the shock of Pearl Harbor. War was upon us, and was, moreover, going badly. I felt part of the great high wave of patriotism, and wished to enlist. But the draft boards did not want me. I was found, to my great shock, too old, had a small child, and so on. I was told I could do better service to the country if I helped to keep life going by continuing with my profession. If the manpower shortage worsened, I could count on being called up later.

So I stayed with my music, rather forlornly and unwillingly. However, I was not the only one left out of the war. It was surprising how few changes occurred in America's everyday life. That showed the real inherent strength, the immense reserves of the country.

There was even time and room to launch a New Opera Company. It was under this name that the company sponsored by the wealthy group of New Yorkers whom I have already mentioned, came into being. The group was headed by Mrs. Lytle Hall and its moving spirit was Mrs. Yolanda Yrion, a one-time pianist, and wife of a director of Steinway and Sons. They offered me the post of director, combined with the conductorship of one of their first four productions.

Months of intense activity followed. Our conductor in chief was Fritz Busch, who conducted Verdi's *Macbeth* and Mozart's *Cosi fan tutte*, both in the production of Karl Ebert, mounted by Busch's son, Hans. The chorus director was Hans Peter Adler, who also conducted one opera, Tchaikovsky's *Pique Dame*. Under my direction Offenbach's *La Vie Parisienne* was given. As Busch was absent and could not be in New York until quite late, the casting of his two operas was done by Hans, who knew the productions as well as he knew his father's taste and wishes, and myself.

The choir was recruited by Adler, the orchestra was in my care, as was the general organisation. That was not an easy task because of the meddling of several board-members, especially Madame Yrion. Nevertheless, we progressed very promisingly.

We had rented the 44th Street Theatre, just off Broadway, which was inadequate but passable.

Casting took a long time, but we came up with a fine array of very interesting young talent. An arduous period of rehearsals followed, in accordance with our goal to present spotlessly prepared ensemble operas. The Mozart and Verdi works were sung in Italian, the Tchaikovsky and Offenbach in English. For this last a revised libretto was prepared, preserving the original idea of the plot but adapting it for American audiences. To do this for us we obtained no lesser person than Louis Verneuil. The producer was Felix Brentano, who used to be one of Max Reinhard's assistants. I rearranged the music according to the demands of the altered book and even provided a new overture on the main melodies of the piece, which Offenbach had neglected to do.

The success of the season was very rewarding. It is, perhaps, not surprising that with the Broadway audiences Offenbach's light, sparkling comedy – well presented, as the average performance level attained was very high – made the greatest hit. There was no comparison between the musical merit of the two masterworks by Mozart and Verdi, under the masterly direction of Fritz Busch, and the Offenbach comedy, yet so delightedly did the public take to it that we received an offer from a commercial theatre company to buy the production for a Broadway run.

My advice to accept this offer was ignored by the snobbish Board. Instead we extended our own season as long as possible but after about three more weeks we could not retain our hold on the rented theatre any longer.

As according to my contract I had to go back to the Ballet Theatre eventually, and as the future of the New Opera Company in spite of its initial élan and success seemed rather doubtful – it was indeed heartbreaking to realise that it was nothing more than a plaything of a wealthy but nonchalant coterie – I resigned as director after the first season.

The venture lived for only one more year, with much of the same repertoire; new was an English version of Johann Strauss's *Fledermaus*, under the name of *Rosalinda*. I again had obtained leave of absence to conduct *La Vie Parisienne* for two weeks, again its run was prolonged, and as I had other work to do after the agreed time, I was looking for someone to take my place. There was no dearth of candidates. My choice fell on a splendid conductor of approximately my age – perhaps a year or two older – who had arrived as an expatriate from Germany not long before; I did not know him personally, but very well by reputation. We met, and he was engaged upon my request. This was the first conducting appearance in America of Max Rudolf, my trusted friend ever since. His subsequent rise in the music world of the USA needs no describing.

Friends have since chided me – and, from a certain point of view quite rightly – for having completely failed to grasp the opportunity that the New Opera Company offered for the furtherance of my career. This opportunity, they said, lay not in directing an opera company which was nothing more than the whim of a group of rich people, but in making use of the connections which my contact with those people provided.

They were indeed an illustrious group, and perhaps my friends were right. But I simply would not have known how to go about such machinations, and indeed it never occurred to me to do so, for I have never believed in the "importance" of people so long as the word importance had to be put between quotation marks. I have always believed that the "thing" is important, not the man.

21

IN 1944 I LEFT THE BALLET THEATRE, AND WITH IT THE WORLD OF ballet altogether. By that time I had acquired an international reputation in that field, similar to that of Pierre Monteux, and Ernest Ansermet before me. Curiously that "fame" did me more harm than good. I found out, to my surprise, that the label of "ballet conductor" had a somewhat derogative connotation. In talks with my two distinguished colleagues we established that they went through the same experience. It took some time for all of us to live down that odd kind of celebrity.

Why?

Is not all music of the same worth? And is not every way of music-making of the same rank and value?

By and large, yes.

But everything has a reason, and it is never superfluous to dig a little for it.

In the first place, perhaps, one could consider that the average conductor is less familiar with the terms, techniques and indeed the "soul" of ballet than with those of the other stage music form – opera. We know what the singers do, we instruct them, learn their parts with them, breathe with them. Of the dance and dancing we know precious little.

In opera the stage, while providing the visual element, contributes essentially to the auditive sensation; in ballet the stage is entirely designed for the eyes, and does not contribute anything to the ear; thus, strictly speaking, it is outside the musicians' realm.

Dance is, in its deepest essence, harmony of movement itself, an art form which, while connected with others, is dependent on none. Dance at its most elemental can exist by itself. It needs no accompaniment of sound. In that pure form, it is one of the oldest manifestations of art, much older than music – which is the youngest of the arts – and older even, one would think, than painting and sculpture, the other visual arts. It is, in that form, also the art most closely bound up with nature and the earth. Through uncounted centuries, as the human intellect grew and the contact

188

of the human body with nature became more and more distant, the art of movement, the art of the body, underwent a gradual, basic transformation. It withdrew itself from nature, and, in the chain of interdependence, substituted sound-environment for its direct connection with it.

Then, in subsequent phases, the essence of dance – the art of movement – became interpretation of sound, transplantation of music into movement.

In this process the art of the dance inevitably lost much of its independence, and with it its primary role as an art form. Music, as music, does not mind if one dances to it or not. A picture or a sculpture does not change if a dance is being performed in front of it or around it. But in dance itself, that most frail of all the arts, as it has now become, the creative and transmitting (or performing) elements are so closely interwoven as to be hard to distinguish. Dance for instance, even today, has no notation (what exists in this realm has never gone beyond the state of experiment, or the very personal, private notes comprehensible only to those who put them down); the creative impulse can be conveyed to others in only one satisfactory way – by actual performance. The effect of the art of movement upon the receiver is as strong as it is fleeting. It is, moreover, greatly affected by "environment", be it visual (nature or painting), or auditive (nature or music). Thus, in the inter-relationship of music and the dance, it is not pre-established whether the movement shall be an interpretation, transvalidation of music, or the music an accompaniment to movement. Both can be the case, and the confusion or misunderstanding of that inter-relationship is often the reason for both components being seriously undervalued and thus mistreated.

The so-called "Russian ballet", of Italian origin, as it came with Marius Petipa and others to the Czar's court in the late nineteenth century, was definitely movement-accented. Music served for nothing more than accompaniment. It was ordered *"al metraggio"*, that is, furnished to measure according to the wishes of the choreographer, and provided little more than a rhythmic skeleton.

Thus Maître Petipa might have issued the following instructions to a composer: "Two introductory bars in four beats, then twice eight bars in the same tempo, a two-bar interlude, then repeat the previous sixteen bars; continue with sixteen more bars in the same speed but with twice as many accents, then two bars to resume the

189

main rhythm and close with repeating the first sixteen bars."

Who would guess that this description fits, exactly, the charming dance called "Les Mirlitons" from Tchaikovsky's ballet, *The Nutcracker*.

It is a mark of Tchaikovsky's great talent and fantasy that he could compose, on such commands, long, full-length ballets of great musical beauty.

He was, of course, a sublime exception in that period. Léo Délibes was another, and perhaps there were a few more. Adam's *Giselle* and all other scores I know from that time are inferior by far, and most were, at best, of routine quality and, at worst, trash.

Dancers, on the whole, are not a specially musical lot. There are notable exceptions, of course. George Balanchine in one sphere, for instance, and Fred Astaire in another. But most dancers are principally concerned with the movement, expression and culture of their bodies. Music for most of them (as I was disconcerted to find) is no more than a rhythmic background, a metronomic help. Worse, a good number of choreographers also have little understanding and regard for the music they work with. Neither have they any compunction about altering the speed of a musical phrase to fit a movement or a series of movements, regardless of the damage done to it. Perhaps this is not a cardinal sin when the music itself is of little or no importance. Also it may be conceded that when the choreography of a certain ballet was first conceived it did not ride rough-shod over the music, but that through the years, by a gradual process of erosion, it became so distorted as hardly to make sense – for example, the famous adagio in Tchaikovsky's *Swan Lake*. I can well imagine that at the première of that work, and for some time thereafter, this piece was danced elegantly and lightly, permitting the violin solo to soar in its fine, virtuosic passages; today it is slowed down to a sad circus caricature, pitiful to behold and to hear.

Diaghilev's aim was to combine the three arts of dance, music and painting on an equal footing, and his victorious realisation of this ideal made him the important figure in contemporary art history that he is.

His method was simple: he commissioned the best composers he could find to write new, original scores; the best painters to paint the scenery and costumes; the best choreographers to devise the staging and the best dancers to dance.

190

The commissions were a great challenge to the composers, the young Stravinsky, de Falla, Ravel and others. The results were a row of new masterpieces. These new compositions, in turn, were a great challenge to the musical performers. The true role of music in ballet as well as its true importance was re-established. One might have thought that from then onwards all would be well.

Not quite so. Two new dangers to the integrity of music in ballet developed. Not always were new scores commissioned for new ballets; of old ballet music only a very few works were usable; the demand for new ballets was great and growing, in consequence of which choreographers began to use music for their new creations that was not intended by the composer for that purpose.

As can readily be imagined, not every musical composition lends itself as suitable background for a danced performance. A composition that by its content, or through the description given it by its creator, suggests extra-musical associations would often lend itself better to visual interpretation than music that obviously exists for its own world only.

In Diaghilev's time very few such adaptations were made. I shall quote two of them to illustrate my point. Both had great success, both are still performed today, both are acclaimed as master-ballets.

The first is *Shéhérazade*, danced to Rimsky-Korsakov's symphonic suite of the same name. The choreographer here does not illustrate any of Shéhérazade's tales, nor does he follow the composer's sparse other suggestions. But, basing himself only on the work's title, he invents a full-blooded story of Arabian intrigue as relished at that time. Michel Fokine fitted his dramatic scenario to the music, depicting, not the story-teller Shéhérazade, but the passionate woman whose life is consumed in the flames of love and jealousy.

At no point does one feel that this dramatic plot jars with the composition or falsifies the composer's intention.

The other piece I wish to cite is *Les Sylphides*. This ballet, danced in white, is hailed the world over as one of the most graceful, perfect creations of its kind. As far as the choreography is concerned, this is certainly so. For me, however, its overall effect and value is marred, first, by the fact that Chopin's music, exquisite when played on the piano, is sadly distorted when performed by an orchestra (many fine composers have tried their hands at

191

orchestrating it, but in vain); and, second, by the sense of futility that hangs like a mist over the production. This is in the nature of things: Chopin's waltzes and mazurkas are *sublimations* of popular dance forms into the world of abstraction; Johann Strauss' melodies, no less inspired, cry out for movement and have their fulfilment in the dance as desire does in the embrace. Chopin's dance pieces originate from that embrace, but are lifted out of the sphere of the touchable, are disembodied in their own floating, fleeting world, without the need of physical contact or comment.

These two cases sufficiently illustrate, I think, the problem of music and – or music versus – the dance. My point of view is not only that of the musician, but also of one who desires to maintain every art's integrity in every combination.

The last major threat to music in ballet is of economic origin and concerns performance level.

With the commercial exploitation of ballet – that is, since the ballet's arrival in America – the neglect and disregard of its music was nothing less than shocking. It was a "sneak attack" of management upon naive and unsuspecting artists and unknowing public who were defenceless against such a practice. Things are better now, but not so very long ago I not merely heard but myself conducted such works as Stravinsky's *Petrushka* with about one-fifth of the required number of players in the orchestra. And, what is more, Stravinsky sat in the stalls, listening to the violence done to his music, and was as powerless against it as I was – for the moment. We had gloomy after-theatre suppers at excellent, small, mostly Russian restaurants and consoled ourselves as best we could with the famous exclamation of a former small-town theatre director: "Shakespeare must be performed well or not at all, but performed he must be!"

During that static period with the New Opera Company Klári and I took an apartment in Manhattan, with furniture made for us by a carpenter in Mexico and transported to New York, disguised as "props", with the ballet luggage. That apartment was near Central Park and the Metropolitan Museum of Art. That remained our address for several years, but we lived there for shorter and shorter periods as time went on.

After the New Opera venture I travelled so much and spent so little time in our new home, that we decided to move temporarily to California, where Tonina could grow up breathing cleaner air and living nearer to nature than she could in the stone desert of New York.

So we rented a furnished house with a small but nice garden on Sunset Strip in the Hollywood hills, sub-letting our New York place. It was good for Tonina, or so we hoped. She was a thoroughly delightful child, always well behaved, lively but never disagreeable or disturbing, with extraordinary self-discipline – certainly not a fatherly (or grandfatherly) heritage.

22

WHEN THE WAR ENDED IN 1945, OUR OWN SMALL FAMILY WAS SAFE and sound, free from physical need. But what of our friends and relatives in Europe? I worried about my sister in Germany. Then an acquaintance returned from Hungary with the sad news of my father's death. I had no reason to doubt the veracity of the information and was deeply grieved. The greater was my joy when, on one of my several journeys to Havana, where I was invited to go as guest conductor of the local symphony orchestra, I was handed a fat envelope, with my father's unmistakable handwriting. Breaking it open, I first looked at the date. My informant was wrong – my father was alive! Then I proceeded to read the twenty-page letter. It made me laugh and cry at the same time; its only subject matter was the string quartets of Beethoven. He was – I knew then – not only alive, but very much so. Just as, during the upheavals of 1918–20, he had found refuge in the museum amongst the paintings of the old masters, so now he had retired in the early 1940s into the realm of the most sublime sounds that any man could conceive.

During those years I was increasingly in demand to conduct concerts – the New York Philharmonic at the Lewinsohn Stadium, the Los Angeles Philharmonic at the Hollywood Bowl (once we drove with Menuhin for a whole day and night in order to arrive in time, having been ousted from our seats on the plane from New York in favour of other passengers with high priorities), in San Francisco, and elsewhere.

Then, in Los Angeles, out of the blue, I received a 'phone-call from Dallas, Texas. On the line was John Rosenfield, the music critic of the *Dallas Morning News*, asking me if I would be interested in taking over their Dallas Symphony Orchestra. It so happened that in the near future I would be flying again to Havana, and we agreed that I would break my trip in Dallas to have a conference with the orchestra's board of directors at the airport.

Because of the flying schedules of those days – the largest and

194

fastest passenger planes were the DC-3s, of which only a few were available for civilian traffic, and these few were mainly filled with so-called "first priority" passengers, travelling on real or faked assignments to help the war effort – the only plane I could take landed at two a.m. in the morning and was due to continue on at four. That was bad enough, but to make it worse, the plane did not even land in Dallas, but at the airport of its neighbour Fort Worth. To anyone who knew about the exaggerated, deadly rivalry of those two cities, this arrangement would have augured funereally for my future plans, but I was blissfully unaware of it.

During the flight I made a rough estimate of the yearly budget a symphony orchestra in a city like Dallas should and could have – I had been there several times, conducting performances of the ballet – and alighted from the plane with the figures in my pocket.

I was met in the hot, starry night by a group of about eight. I learned from them, for the first time, that Dallas had no symphony orchestra. I would be expected to create one. Rosenfield was the only member of the group on the tarmac who knew what a symphony orchestra was and the only one committed to the idea of having one – and a good one – in his city. The others present were businessmen and the like whom he was in the process of persuading to finance the venture. They were well equipped to do so, but ignorant of the "how", and "why", and "when" of the matter – in fact full of good will but still needing to be convinced.

And I was the one who was expected to convince them. At two a.m. on the still-hot tarmac of Fort Worth airport.

Sensibly, we retired to the airport bar, where beer and cold mint juleps – that delicious drink which I now tasted for the first time – made the rounds.

The conversation, conducted in a broad Texan drawl counter-pointed by my Hungarian-flavoured semi-English, went approximately like this:

"Well, Mr. Doráti, what would you think a good symphony orchestra would cost us yearly?"

I produced the small piece of paper from the breast pocket of my shirt and handed it over. "That much."

Impressed, they circulated the paper.

"Hm. And can you guarantee us that it will be a gooood orchestra?"

"Yes, I think I can."

"Aand, Mr. Doráti, what will you do if it is not a gooood orchestra?"

What would I do indeed? I gave the question serious thought. Then I spoke up.

"I hang myself."

Silence.

Then one of them said: "Weell, Mr. Doráti, could you go outside for a few minutes, while we talk this over amongst ourselves?"

I went out and walked around in the blue night, on the high, wet grass, to the accompaniment of the incredible noise of what seemed to be millions of cicadas and frogs.

After a short while John Rosenfield appeared and called me in. The spokesman of the group said: "You're hired."

Rosenfield often described this scene later, quoting me as having said in my earlier reply: "I'll cut my throat."

But he was wrong. I always hanged myself. It is my favourite method of suicide.

In the time that remained before take-off, I learned all that I needed to know.

After that letter, some years before, which had been confiscated by de Basil, another young conductor had been engaged. Under his leadership the semi-professional group which formed the orchestra had begun excitingly, then passed through stagnation to failure. The orchestra had then folded; it did not exist any more. The new board's intention was not to revive it in its old form, but to create a new one, on a fully professional basis. The length of the yearly season they had in mind would be about twenty weeks. They had a large concert hall in their fairground area and a smaller one on their university campus.

It was their intention to transfer the concerts to the larger hall, to mark the newness of their venture.

They had the necessary money. Nothing else. But by the time I took off for Havana they also had confidence that I could accomplish what they needed.

My stay in Havana was for a month. It was the month of Bartók's death, August 1945. A great sorrow, a deep shadow.

During those weeks the Dallas plans came together. It was decided to start the first season early in December – an audacious undertaking, considering that in August there was no orchestra at all.

The first task was to establish how many instrumentalists of high enough standards to be members of a professional symphony orchestra I would find in Dallas. So I went there and patiently auditioned everybody who came forward. It was amazing to find a good number – about fifteen – willing and able to be enrolled. Amongst them was one very fine violinist, Zelman Brounoff, who was good enough to be considered as assistant concert master.

The rest of the orchestra, about eighty-five, had to be recruited from elsewhere.

At that point the experience gained during my itinerant ballet years paid rich dividends. I knew many – far more than eighty-five – excellent young musicians all over the country, some just out of the army or navy, some just about to be demobilised, some about to lose their temporary positions in orchestras where they had replaced colleagues in the forces, some with touring companies looking for permanent positions, some just graduating from their studies.

I wrote, telephoned, travelled all over the country, waited at the dockside for landing troopships, recruiting my orchestra at a feverish pace. The task proved easy. Word passed from mouth to mouth with lightning speed. Soon I did not have to do the contacting any more; I was besieged with requests from would-be members for jobs in the new Dallas Symphony.

After a short, intense auditioning period the orchestra was assembled.

The next problem was how to get it to Dallas. Again my touring experience came to the rescue. We arranged to have a number of sleeping cars and a dining car attached to regular, scheduled trains, and these transported the whole orchestra, in one group, from New York, where it first got together, to Dallas. I say "we", because I had assistance by then. Above all I had official secretarial help. It was provided by Lester Solomon, one of my newly-engaged horn players, who had also been with me in that capacity during some of my years with the ballet. He was a very clever, alert, intelligent boy from Brooklyn, and as long as he stayed with me, that is, for the next four years, he was a tower of strength, roguish, inventive, kind and deeply loyal, my veritable Man Friday.

197

The arrival of the orchestra was a major event in Dallas. To find lodgings was not a great problem and we moved in right away to Fairpark Auditorium for a two-week rehearsal period before the inaugural concert.

That was a special evening before the regular subscription season began. The programme was:

> William Schuman: Prayer in Time of War
> Tchaikovsky: *Romeo and Juliet*
> Beethoven: The Third Symphony ("Eroica")

In its way this choice was a declaration of my intentions; it denoted an attention to contemporary music, inclusion of the romantic, and the overall accent on classical music, as a general policy for gathering, keeping, and nourishing a musical public.

We started by rehearsing the Beethoven work. The artists assembled were talented, young and keen. We rehearsed with shining eyes and glowing cheeks. The first sounds were even more pleasant than expected, and with each well-played bar our enthusiasm mounted. It was to the great credit of the young players that we went through the first movement without stopping. Then we began to attend to the detail, to polish, to beautify.

When it was time for a rest, I wandered around in the huge hall. It was anything but promising, a dilapidated barn, with a capacity of over 4,000 people. Its accoustics were passable. Surveying that unsightly shrine of our art, I saw a dark figure huddled in one of the aisle seats in the back row. It was John Rosenfield. He was in tears.

Tears of happiness, of course. To hear, for the first time, a real orchestra-sound emanating from a group that belonged to his beloved city was for John Rosenfield a moment of fulfilment. He had been dreaming of it, working for it, relentlessly, for many years. He was that very rare species, a "builder-journalist", a term coined by myself, for journalists are seldom builders and some are downright destroyers. Under the hat labelled "freedom of the press" they are apt to lose, or forget to acquire, the oxygen of freedom, self-discipline, without which its life-giving, life-preserving properties cannot live.

John Rosenfield was the opposite. A fiery Texan, and even more fierce Dallasite, he was for decades the sole mover of the town's cultural life. One can say that he had his finger in every pie but not that he was either a busybody or a self-publicist. On the contrary, he was seldom to be seen, he even moved unwillingly and with difficulty, for he was very corpulent, indeed obese. People came to him, rather than the other way round, and that in itself was not a too easy undertaking, for he was well hidden in the fortress of his small house amongst his large collection of books, gramophone records and small tropical fish, and protected by Claire, his wife, who was as frail as he was stout, but just as active and energetic. Or else he was sitting behind his desk at the *Dallas Morning News*, in a huge room with well over a hundred desks and continuously clicking typewriters.

Rosenfield, the paper's arts editor for many years, created its national prestige and used it for the best purposes. It was in large measure due to his efforts, tenacity and influence, that the institutions of art and education flourished and cultural activities multiplied during his time. The effects of his influence were evident everywhere. A museum of the fine arts existed thanks to his propaganda. There was the theatre; Dallas had one of the few really good repertory theatres in the country. And the other arts flourished alongside. Some of the best films had their premières in Dallas. The Metropolitan Opera came every season for a week. All the best ballet companies paid annual visits. A number of notable artists came to Dallas to teach and no great artist would not have come to Dallas to perform. But above all, there was his great passion: symphonic music and symphony orchestras. In his view, every city worthy of the name should have one. He measured the worth of a city by the quality of its orchestra.

Regretfully it must also be said that John Rosenfield remained the only really dedicated champion of cultural and cultured life in Dallas in his time. He succeeded in mobilising financial forces powerful enough to set things up. What he could not transmit to his followers was his own genuine, deep interest in and love of the arts, or the strength and the will to continue what had been started. Rich patrons of art, unlike John Rosenfield, often have mixed motives: personal vanity, local patriotism, self-advancement, to name but three. But in the course of the activities thus undertaken, many develop a real feeling for the cause they have embraced.

An elderly Dallas banker, J. R. Thornton, a rough and ready

self-made man, once said to me: "Ah'll give you money aaw–right, but you won't catch me at one of these concerts."

I angrily replied: "That is really all I want from you, Mr. Thornton – some money. At our concerts I don't want you – in fact I forbid you to come!"

At our next concert he was observed hiding behind a column in the back of the hall. He had come, of course, only to show us that he did not take orders from me, and he was careful to be seen by someone who would tell me of his presence.

But then, something unexpected happened. He liked what he heard. He came back the next week. And the week after. Thereafter he never missed any of our concerts. Not so long afterwards he was heard whistling, instead of "Pop Goes the Weasel", the first bars of Beethoven's "Eroica", as he walked to his tall office building on Main Street, under the tent of his ten-gallon hat.

The DSO, as we affectionately called it, rapidly became the city's foremost cultural asset, of considerable public relations value. Several industries decided to establish factories and other outlets in Dallas because of the orchestra's fast rise and expansion. This may sound improbable but I can assure the reader that it is true. The facts were public knowledge in the city as well as beyond its borders at that time.

For all that, the DSO was not supported as it deserved. The first president of its board, Gordon Rupe, Jnr., an investment banker of great ability, lost his hold because of his monolithic ways. His successor, Stanley Marcus, head of the well-known Neiman-Marcus store and a near genius in his field, appeared only moderately interested, though the personal glory attached to this honorary post must have been gratifying. Even the great tenor, Laurits Melchior, sang "Happy Birthday" for him, at a Dallas night club, after having just sung Tristan with the orchestra. It was, incidentally, one of the most remarkable interpretations of that ditty I have ever heard. Melchior's memory was notoriously not one of the best. So when he went up to the bandstand to do his "stunt" – carefully rehearsed previously – he suddenly forgot the words "Happy birthday tooo youuu", and sang "Tra la la la laaa laaa" to everybody's delight and hilarity.

Neither Rupe nor Marcus was successful in mobilising the big oil interests in the city, and other wealthy sources also held back.

200

This did not matter so much during the four years of my stay, during which the initial impetus of the venture carried it over all obstacles. But later the southern climate and the inertia that goes with it won out. Bad luck also played a part, but it was primarily the lack of real interest that prevented the DSO from developing as it should have done after its brilliant and zestful start. Instead, it limped along sadly, until it finally ceased to exist. Yet it had at the helm, for short periods at least, conductors as distinguished as Solti and Kletzky. All, apparently, to no avail. It is good news, however, that under the leadership of an energetic manager of vision and courage, it is making a new start as these lines are written.

In those days before air-conditioning, indoor activities were severely curtailed by the climate of the long, hot, Texan summers. All the same, we managed to enlarge our winter season from sixteen to twenty-two weeks. And each year from our second year onwards we added a special cycle of works to our regular season. The first was dedicated to Beethoven; the second was a Brahms cycle, and in my last year we introduced a festival of choral works.

The artistic level of our concerts was always high, with pro-grammes designed to please cultivated tastes. This was a calculated risk I took – and won. I have never played down to a public, and neither it nor I have ever regretted the fact. I have learned through long experience that the more simple an audience is in its tastes, and the more lacking in what is called tradition, the easier it is to lead it to the high strata of listening taste.

My programme policy was and remained to mix the challenging with the soothing, the new with the old.

In my view the aim of a performing musician should be to make the new familiar, and the known surprising, by releasing all that which is inherent in the music itself, with no devices or tricks.

The soloists we invited to come to Dallas were the greatest artists of the time. At our first subscription concert, in December 1945, Claudio Arrau played Brahms's Second B flat Piano Concerto. Yehudi Menuhin came every year. Rudolf Serkin, Zino Francescatti, Robert Casadeus, Grisha Piatigorsky, Yasha Heifetz and Nathan Milstein were all frequent guests.

The seasons being short, I conducted nearly all the concerts. A few great men were invited to visit us: Stravinsky conducted a concert of his own works, and Zoltán Kodály conducted his *Háry János* suite.

Both visits produced non-musical incidents. The Stravinskys had lost all their luggage on the train to Dallas, and the country-wide search that was instituted caused as much excitement in the city as the concert. Elaborate efforts were made to provide the Maestro with clothes suitable for the season, and quite a few shops and department stores were inconsolable when at the last minute the missing valises turned up.

Kodály wanted to meet an American folklorist. There was one in Texas, a jovial elderly man called Carl Lomax who collected folk ballads. With some misgivings, I arranged a meeting. Alas, Kodály was very tired after his long train trip, and Lomax had taken a good deal of refreshment while waiting. In consequence, after a few perfunctory words of greeting, the two folklorists fell fast asleep and snored happily at each other for a quarter of an hour, after which I plucked up my courage and broke up the meeting.

In our second season we began touring; first in Texas itself, "the Lone Star State" and, until the addition of Alaska, the largest of them all; then, gradually, throughout the American South-West.

Amusing – and at that time beneficial – was the rivalry between the Dallas and Houston Symphony Orchestras, a by-product of the general rivalry of all the Texan towns. Dallas first of all "conquered" Fort Worth – a subscription-concert series given by the Dallas Symphony Orchestra in the rival stronghold itself was the *coup de grâce* – then turned its guns on Houston. This was a hopeless adventure from the start, as Houston was larger and wealthier than Dallas, better located, and altogether more strongly equipped to become the leading city of Texas. But that did not deter the ebullient Dallasites, led, of course, by John Rosenfield, from entering the fray.

Houston riposted vigorously. The Houston Symphony had been in continuous existence for a longer period than that of Dallas, and had an unspectacular but steady history until then. Efrem Kurtz was now engaged as its conductor, and under his guidance it made great strides. Kurtz and I seldom met during that time – our work kept us apart – but, as I have already related, he had been for some years the senior conductor of the Ballets Russes and left ballet

202

conducting about the same time as I did. Neither of us had any intention of taking part in the Montague-Capulet comedy our respective fellow citizens were staging.

The young DSO began recording for RCA Victor barely six weeks after its first concert. This achievement was a near miracle. And even more miraculous was the fact that the first record it made, Bartók's Violin Concerto (now Number Two, then the only one), with Yehudi Menuhin as soloist, won the highly coveted "Grammy" award. Menuhin's declared readiness to perform with the budding orchestra was, perhaps, the decisive factor in getting those recordings launched, and his magnificent performance of the Bartók work was certainly as decisive in securing the prize, but the newly-started orchestra gave him more than adequate support: it was his worthy partner.

During the four years – which Rosenfield dubbed the "Eroica Period" – we recorded eight major works for RCA Victor. Among them was Kodály's *Psalmus Hungaricus* (sung in Hungarian by the choir of the University of Denton, Texas, with a real Hungarian, Gábor Carelli as soloist); piano concerti by Liszt and Prokofiev, with Arthur Rubinstein and the late, much-missed Willy Kappell; Aaron Copland's *Rodeo* (a very appropriate contribution from the American South-West), and more.

It was, musically, a period of great excitement, rapid advancement, a brief epoch of true *"Sturm und Drang"*.

During two of those four years, I was lucky in having as manager of the orchestra a young, gifted man who had an instinctive grasp of what I was trying to do. Lanham Deal was still wearing the uniform of a junior naval officer when he was introduced to me. He was in his early twenties and it was quite a risk to employ such a youngster without any previous experience whatsoever. But I have always held that experience is quickly gained. What matters is talent. On that basis I have supplied instant experience to quite a number of my chosen collaborators during the many years of my professional life.

Lanham was a truly devoted co-worker. I greatly regretted when he decided after two years to leave the orchestra and join his father-in-law's firm. Not much later, he, too, regretted that step and came back to music managing, which he still does, with much success.

Another stalwart helper and friend was my secretary, Wilma

Cozart, then fresh from Denton University, where she sang in the choir which I often used. After Lanham had left, she was the only help I had. Though only just twenty, she had great executive ability. I wanted her to take over the managership when it became vacant, but could not make the board agree to the appointment of a girl just out of her teens. So she remained my secretary, but ran, with my blessing and overall advice, the entire operation. At times it was awkward, to say the least, to watch her towering in intelligence, industry and wit over her nominal superiors.

Of the orchestra, as remarkable for its youth as for its performing standards, I asked a great deal, as I have from everyone with whom I have worked – almost as much as I have asked of myself. My conducting experience was by that time considerable. I had conducted concerts since my sixteenth year, if I count my schoolboy attempts, and had digested much of the standard and not-so-standard symphonic repertoire. Yet I felt very exposed when conducting so much of the symphonic repertoire for the first time in my life. And there is no amount of talent which would render that physical adeptness, that "carnal knowledge", unnecessary. This is a process very similar to the developing of mastery on various musical instruments, not only through learning them, but by performing them untold times, or the accumulation of flying hours for aeroplane pilots, and is connected in a similar manner to the mental work involved. The great problems of the conductor's work are, first, that it has no "en route" control, for it makes no sound, and further, that it cannot be practised alone, but only in contact with other musicians, for it is the contact itself that has to be practised. This renders the process extremely slow. The *bodily* mastering of orchestra conducting may take decades, although no "technique" worth mentioning is involved. Therefore it should be started at a young age, immaturity notwithstanding, and should be practised for a number of years as "hidden" as is possible. Few who begin late can hope to go through this process of physical adaptation in their lifetime. The young ones court the risk of physically outrunning the speed of their mental development. Therefore it is best for them to avoid limelight in the first decade or two of their conductorship (as was customary and natural in the "good old times"), to emerge at the right moment in full possession of all their powers.

What helped me in great measure during my first years on the

204

concert platform were those other years spent in the pit. The "1001 Nights in the Theatre" paid rich dividends now.

After my second season I had to engage a new concert master, or leader, as he is called in England. Rafael Druian, then perhaps twenty-one or twenty-two years old, was a rare find. Of Russian parentage, he spent his early childhood in Cuba, and grew up in Philadelphia, where he studied at the Curtis Institute with Efrem Zimbalist. In his upbringing an American to the bone, in his inner make-up a complex human being, very sensitive and very tender. A fine, searching artist and a splendid person, a collaborator, helper and friend as one seldom finds in a lifetime. He remained with me for thirteen years.

A remarkable import to Dallas – in fact, to America – was János Starker, the master-'cellist, who has since then made an international name for himself. For some time I was aware of that splendid young artist, and knew that he had left Hungary and had a hard time in Paris. I also knew of his great desire to come to the United States. My mouth watered at the thought of having him in my orchestra, and after much planning – getting him his immigration papers was no simple matter – I succeeded. He came to Dallas as solo 'cellist in my fourth and last year. We became close friends, and still often make music together. For twenty-five years he used to cable me from wherever he was on the anniversary of the day he first set foot on American soil. Now we both take it for granted that he *is* there. Not long ago, he gave the first performance of my 'cello concerto, and also recorded it.

A new series of children's concerts was started, in order to build up audiences for the future, in close contact with the school system of the city. The experiment was a great success. Children were directly encouraged to play musical instruments, especially strings. Each year a group of string players, selected from all the schools in the city, was allowed to play with the Symphony Orchestra at one of the young people's concerts.

This missionary activity yielded a variety of results.

On one occasion, the young "leader" of the group (there were as many as forty to fifty performers, all playing the melody of a simple, short piece in unison), who displayed a great deal of vigour and temperament during the rehearsals, played at the concert with such desperate passion, with such an indescribable expression of

205

involvement, suffering and annihilation on his little blond face, that I turned towards him in sincere astonishment and looked him up and down.

But no. He was too small: I could not look up at him – I had to look down – and downer.

And at the downest I saw the reason of his panic: under his little feet a small puddle was forming and slowly extending in eccentric shapes.

He played, the little fellow, played and played. What else could he do? He was a true hero.

Artist's life.

After the piece was over we shook hands, I hugged him and guided him forward to take his bow, manoeuvring him carefully round the puddle. My attempt at discretion was in vain: news must have travelled fast, for as soon as the applause had stopped, a cleaning woman of extravagant proportions appeared out of nowhere, with broom and bucket, and energetically mopped up the battlefield.

This was the only occasion in my life when I saw such an activity being greeted with thunderous applause. I am sure it was also a "first" for the charwoman. Too bad she could not give an "encore".

During our first season it was decided to commission one composition to be premièred by the DSO every year. The composers who were commissioned during my stay were Paul Hindemith, William Schuman, and Walter Piston.

Piston wrote an orchestral suite, patterned on baroque forms, a well-conceived, craftsmanlike but unremarkable work. Schuman gave us his Sixth Symphony, a complex, fine piece, its rich texture laid out in and woven across one huge movement. It was experimental enough to tax our young orchestra to its limits, but with assiduous rehearsals we mastered it – as I like to recall – rather brilliantly. Hindemith's contribution was his Symphonia Serena, a lovely work, and exactly what its title says: a serene symphony, without the "from despair through struggle to victory" background, that is, without the late-romantic pattern that in Hindemith's view has become the fatal disease of the symphony as musical form. It is a charming, intriguing game of sounds. The first and last of its four movements are for full orchestra, the second for strings, and the third, a march, for wind instruments only. It has become one of Hindemith's better-known works and I have conducted it in several continents.

The composers attended the first performances, with the exception of Hindemith. He was formally invited, as were the others, and he formally accepted – so we were puzzled and somewhat chagrined when he did not alight from the train on which he had told us he would arrive. The reception committee went home disappointed. Hindemith did not arrive with any later train either. He simply did not turn up and – what was even more curious – there was no word from him later. No apology, no explanation.

I wrote to him after the first performance, describing the event and enclosing the rave reviews, which he good-humouredly acknowledged. But still no reference to his non-materialisation at the première.

What happened I learned years later from Gerhard Samuel, my assistant and subsequently my associate in Minneapolis, whom I engaged fresh from Yale University where he was Hindemith's pupil. The story was this.

The composition of the Symphonia Serena went on, so to speak, in the class room. Hindemith talked about the work as it progressed, showed it to his pupils at various stages, and also mentioned to them that he would be absent for about five days, because he was going to travel to Dallas for the première. By train, of course; that is why five days were needed for the one-day visit. He added that he was looking forward to the journey, because his compartment would give him the quiet and seclusion he needed for composing a 'cello sonata, which he had been commissioned and had neglected to write. Now he was late with it and had to finish it as fast as he could.

He bade goodbye to his class and left. The pupils were astonished to see him back in the classroom on the third morning.

"Mr. Hindemith, what happened?"

"Why? What should have happened?"

"Well, weren't you going to Dallas?"

"Oh my God! I forgot! You see, I boarded the train – some of you came with me to the station – and began writing the 'cello sonata I told you about. When we arrived at Memphis, Tennessee, the sonata was ready, so I got out and came back on the next train. Now what shall I do?"

It was too late, so he chose not to do anything.

The Dallas concert seasons were short, and I had ample time and opportunity to accept other engagements. Offers and invitations became more frequent, and from May to October each year I conducted in many places, in the Old World and the New. In 1946 I made a brief guest appearance in London, at the behest of Yehudi Menuhin. It was not successful. I cannot complain; the defeat was doubtless caused by my own fault or faults, whatever they were. I was not aware of any particular shortcoming in my performance. The English simply did not like it. They were not willing to accept my transition from ballet conductor to the concert platform and that was all there was to it. Apart from the momentary displeasure that is caused by any failure, even the most trivial, I did not feel either hurt or offended. I decided not to return to England for a while and was confident enough, or young enough, or both, to believe that the time would come when I would be welcome in England on my own terms.

With guest appearances in Italy (Rome, Florence, Venice) I fared well, as I did in my native Budapest. I returned there as soon as I could – in fact my first visit, made in a private capacity, was only a few weeks after the end of the war. I found both of my parents alive and in fairly good health. I thanked God on my knees not only for having preserved them, but also for allowing me to take care of them thereafter. I also found my sister safe and sound in Berlin, her home for many years afterwards. The experience of that trip remained in my memory like the apparition of a ghost. Like millions of Americans, I was spared direct contact with the war; to see the destruction that was wrought upon Europe was a horrible shock, as was the revelation of the German concentration camps and extermination centres, the breakthrough of the Russians into the West, the collapse of an entire continent, and the bloody dawn of a new world.

What my parents and sister must have been through was too much for me to imagine. I cannot, may not, describe any of it in these notes. I would have no words for it, since I did not live through all that, nor witnessed anything even remotely similar;

and these notes are devoted to the narrow compass of my own experience.

That it was possible to continue our lives with a feeling of real togetherness, as warm as we had felt towards each other before the war, or even more so, is one of the rare graces that can be bestowed upon man. It is a miracle of nature when bonds of blood and spirit bridge the abysses of separation and of the different experiences imposed on each one by fate.

If my first return to Europe could be likened to a voyage to a scorched and unknown planet, the second, which took place soon after, was made with confidence, an open heart and outstretched hands. I went to make music, to bring a tonic to my friends – for all those people were my friends, or so I felt – and to help in every other small way I could. I brought along cane for mouthpieces of wind instruments, strings for violins or double basses, children's underwear, sugar, writing paper, razor blades, whatever could be crammed into the allowed number of suitcases.

I could now no longer travel on military planes, and as few, if any, civilian aircraft flew to Hungary I took the train from Vienna to Budapest. To travel those 120 miles took longer than today's air trip from London to Chicago (and that is without mentioning Concorde!). At the Austro-Hungarian border the train stopped for a few hours. The station there used to be decorated in a fancy way, according to the whim of a wealthy Hungarian magnate. A wrought-iron gate bore the inscription: ISTEN HOZOTT! ("God brought you!" – the colloquial Hungarian welcome greeting). And in that gateway a permanent gipsy band played Hungarian tunes whenever a train pulled on to the platform. There was no gipsy band now; there was no station building; it had been razed to the ground. The fancy ironwork was twisted, broken by blasts, hanging in shreds. Only those welcoming words were intact, bent in eerie curves, hanging incongruously on mutilated wire:

After what had happened, that grotesquely disfigured welcome was tragically out of place. It was rather for us who came from the outside to welcome that tortured land back into the world, our world, battered and ailing also but, in comparison with Hitler's world of the past six years, certainly near to Paradise. Yes, it was good to say "welcome back" to Hungary. It would have been better if Hungary could have stayed with us.

Quite a few old friends had survived. My teachers, Kodály and Weiner, were there – it was an emotional reunion. The former's recent work, Peacock Variations, I conducted. Its deeply Hungarian music at that moment made an unbelievable impact upon its listeners, so much so that we had to repeat it right away.

Kodály's comment upon that tearful, hysterical event was, "The second time it went even better."

When I first went there, in 1945, Hungary was like a butchered animal, gory and horrible. The country was fallow, unkempt, abandoned, the cities starving. There were carcasses of horses and dogs in the streets (human corpses were buried first), while the houses were gutted from bombs and fires. It was said that the Russians who "liberated" Budapest – and for the moment it *was* liberation – came into the city through the sewers. There were hardly any windows unbroken. Doors scorched, trees burnt – an incredible sight.

Yet the Opera House and the Academy of Music were intact (save for some very minor damage) and musical life was in full swing, as were the theatres, once the electricity supplies started again. Water was quickly restored, trams began to circulate; soon also there were buses (of incredible appearance, without seats and with rotten tyres, but still somehow contriving to move). Food was very scarce but life started up again, like a man emerging slowly from a coma.

In those surroundings we made our music.

The Allied four-power administration had started and worked reasonably well, but it was a foregone conclusion that the Russians would soon take over on their own. They knew it, and already regarded the place as theirs.

At an official function, with all the Allied chiefs present, the Russian – I forget his military rank – asked me in a booming bass voice: "How you like Russian occupation?"

It was hard to make him understand but I insisted on explaining to him that I hated every kind of occupation, and a Russian one more than most.

My remarks did not please the commissar. In reply he offered some criticism of the Americans: "Americans! – Americans only moniey, moniey – only love moniey. Russians – big heart, *sjertse* – love moosic – good man."

That "goodness" is vividly illustrated in the following anecdote: the siege of Budapest was raging. The Germans were deeply entrenched in the city and the Russian troops surrounding it could not enter for many weeks. Finally they found a way in to the main sewer and used it to take the defenders by surprise.

The population was huddled for safety in the cellars, where it remained for months, in indescribable circumstances, without food, heat, light. (My own parents were also cave-dwellers during the siege: they shared a small cellar with about fifty other people, so that only about ten could lie down to sleep at one time. They did not have a spare piece of clothing among them and their only food for the first three weeks of the siege was three cubes of sugar each per day.)

It was those cellar-dwellers who saw the Russian soldiers first, as they came up out of the sewers.

The rejoicing was ecstatic. The inhabitants weepingly embraced their Russian "saviours", kissed their hands, knelt before them.

It was a brief exultation. Within a few minutes the Russians had started to collect whatever small and valuable objects they found on the people they were "liberating". Mostly watches. The Russians were soon established as the most enthusiastic watch-collectors in the world. On their way from the Volga to the Elbe they must have appropriated many millions of wrist watches, pocket watches, alarm clocks, and other time pieces. The poor, freshly liberated cave-dwellers of Budapest soon got used to the Russian order: "*Davai tchas!*" "Give the watch!"

In one of the cellars, packed tight with tired, worn-out people, including many children, one enormous, giant Russian had just made his first rounds, yelling, in a tremendous Chaliapinesque basso his "*Davai tchas!*" refrain.

A baby, on the arm of its mother, frightened by that tremendous vocal explosion, started to cry bitterly.

As soon as the big Russian heard it, he ran towards the baby, took it from its mother, held it in his arms against his immense chest, and began caressing it and calling it endearing names:

"Oh my little dove, my darling, my little mouse, my sweet chicken, my butterfly," he chanted, tears of emotion streaming down his plump cheeks. The baby stopped crying and, nestling against the enormous Cossack's shoulder, fell exhaustedly asleep.

The big Russian looked lovingly at the baby infant sleeping in his arms, put his over-sized index finger across his lips to command silence, and continued to tip-toe round the cellar, whispering, in hardly audible yet unmistakable tones: "*Davai tchas . . . Davai tchas . . .*"

At the end of my first stay, the Hungarian musicians insisted on giving a banquet in my honour. I was horrified by the idea and besought them to abandon it. They needed the food, whatever there was of it, for their young, their sick and their old. My protestations were of no avail — a mule is a pushover compared to a Hungarian.

So the banquet took place at the site of one of the famous old-time open-air restaurants called "Gundel", a royal name in local gastronomy. At that time, however, it was a sorry sight. The yard was in ruins with shrapnel-holes in the ground, trees lying across smashed tables. The restaurant building was bombed, gutted, roofless, windowless, and instead of doors there were charred black holes. But never mind; there was enough room for a festive board seating about fifty, with snow-white tablecloth, impeccable china, every piece of a different pattern, but every piece *there*.

Suddenly, out of the holes that had been doors, half a dozen waiters appeared, with clean, white aprons and white shirts, carrying high over their heads large silver plates filled with all kinds of lavishly prepared, sumptuously displayed food. Nobody knew where it came from, and nobody asked. The plates were proudly carried around the table before being deposited on it, earning a loud round of spontaneous applause.

Old "Papa" Gundel appeared himself. He wore a big grey beard. I was told that one of his sons was a prisoner-of-war in Russia, and he vowed not to shave until the boy came back. He was seen, later, clean shaven.

In 1947 my entire family, that is Klári and Tonina, went to

Hungary with me. Tonina was then seven years old and it was the first time her four grandparents set eyes on her. The get-together, as expected, was an unqualified success. The only problem to be faced was that of communicating with my father, who did not speak English, while Tonina, who was bilingual during her first seven years, in her eighth year had suddenly decided "never to speak Hungarian again". Why, she would never tell us, but she had taken her stand with the utmost firmness and was not to be shaken. Later, at the age of fifteen, she was to change her mind, but for the present there was nothing we could do. She obviously loved her grandfather and sought his company, but speak to him in Hungarian – no. The old man, adoringly, did what he could in pantomime, but the budding relationship faltered sadly in default of words.

During one of those pauses, which got more and more frequent and more and more discouraging, Tonina had a sudden inspiration.

"I will speak Chinese to him!"

And started immediately: "Ching-chang-chung!"

Whereupon grandfather – deliriously happy – chimed in: "Ming-Mung-Mang-Mong-Meng!!"

From that moment, their Chinese conversations were interminable. Any intrusion by ourselves was contemptuously ignored. They understood each other perfectly.

In 1948 I made a further short visit – three days actually – but much resented in Dallas, where our season was due to start shortly. (John Rosenfield would not speak with me for weeks after that "desertion".) The purpose was to participate in the first Bartók Festival in Budapest and give what was, I think, the first performance in that city of the already renowned Concerto for Orchestra. By then everything seemed ready for the Communist take-over. I was not allowed to speak freely and when I disregarded a script handed to me to read during a radio interview and proceeded to give my own replies to the questions put to me, I was seriously rebuked by the authorities. I was no more willing to accept that sort of treatment from Russians than from Germans, so when I left I decided that if the Russian take-over really happened, I would not return.

It took place shortly after, as is well known, and I stayed away for eighteen years.

My parents came with me to the airport, and I saw them from the small window of the plane. To attract their attention I made circular movements on the window pane with the palm of my hand. They noticed it and began to make similar, parallel movements to mine. To intensify the contact, I changed the circles abruptly, from leftward to right, and back again, in complicated rhythmic patterns. They were "with me" all the time, imitating my changes instantly.

This way we "conversed" until the plane taxied round and we were lost to one another's sight.

That was the last time I "spoke" with my father.

In the spring of 1949 I had a sudden cable from my mother telling me that my father had had a heart attack and was in hospital. That day I had to leave with my orchestra for Oklahoma City, where we arrived late, having been held up by a terrible snowstorm, a very rare occurrence in that part of the country. We had lost instruments and music, but the local orchestra lent us both and we played an improvised programme.

The main piece in it was Brahms' Second Symphony. Silently I dedicated the performance to my father. He was very near me. I saw his face, with its put-on severity, when he had once loudly, almost harshly, declared that in music he knew no personal feelings: father-son relationship, love, and so on – all that was for the birds. He would listen to music as one should, with absolute objectivity and a cruelly critical mind – only to add later that he had seldom if ever heard a better performance of the work, whatever it was! Bless his objective soul!

When I returned to my hotel that night, there was a second cable from my mother.

My father had died that day. In his seventy-eighth year.

In his last letter to me he had complained that I didn't write to him. I hadn't for a long time. I was "too busy". Just at that time I had decided to leave my post and go to Minneapolis – a big change in my life – and he had heard it only from others.

Whenever my daughter does not write to me for a long time, I am especially careful to stay alive, because I don't want her ever to feel the way I felt then and still do when I think of that silly, small-minded, inconsiderate behaviour of mine.

As I do while I write this.

Tonina was five years of age when we came to Dallas and nine when we left. The fact that we, her parents, did not succeed in making a home in that city – and hardly ever later – was, probably, more of a traumatic factor in her young life than we thought it could be. While we felt her completely sheltered in our love, and were basking in her well-balanced, happy disposition, she often felt insecure and even abandoned – as it emerged from adult conversation, much later.

I had thought that the nomadic life we had led until then would change when we came to Dallas, and I had visions of a house, a garden, that did not materialise. For two years we lived in unsatisfactory hotel apartments – the name "Melrose", as our hotel was called, sent shivers down my back for a long time – and the house that John Rosenfield energetically got for us on a rent-buy basis and simply dumped us in for the next two fell sadly short of my dreams. Klári disliked being in Dallas altogether, and my complete dedication to my work there made her lonelier than ever, but she kept her disappointment as much to herself as she could. Yet all was not as well as it could have been, and time grew ripe for a change.

Not that I would have thought of leaving or seeking other pastures. The growth of my orchestra completely absorbed my attention. I loved it and was, mentally, prepared to lead it – together with myself – to natural maturity. (It is stated elsewhere in these notes, that I was – am – a late developer. By the end of the 1940s I had developed far enough to be aware of this.)

The 1948-49 season, which was to be my last in Dallas, occupied me fully. There was much of great interest happening. One of the season's highlights was the first performance in the United States of Bartók's *Prince Bluebeard's Castle*, to be broadcast on the NBC's "Orchestras of the Nation" series. In the spring a festival of choral works included Verdi's *Messa da Requiem*, Beethoven's *Missa Solemnis*, Haydn's *Creation* and Bach's *St. Matthew Passion*. Recordings and tours continued. The orchestra and myself were actively participating in the Rachmaninoff Competitions instigated by Olin Downes, music critic of the *New York Times*, and presided over by Serge Koussevitsky.

215

At the New York meetings of the organisers, at which I was the Benjamin, I met all my senior colleagues. It was an interesting round-table with Koussevitsky in the chair, surrounded by Szell, Reiner and others. My role was that of *enfant terrible*. When Szell produced a huge list of requirements which would qualify entry to the competition, I ventured the opinion that no one, not even he himself, could meet the conditions he quoted. That remark put me right at the bottom of George Szell's guest-conductors' list — so far down, in fact, that he never got to it during his lifetime. My next and final utterance made me unpopular with everybody else. When finally agreement had been reached on all points connected with the conductors' competition, I asked:

"And what will we do for the winner? Will each of us give up one week of our own concerts to invite him?"

The sad fact is that none of us volunteered.

It was at that meeting that Mitropoulos, conductor of the Minneapolis Symphony Orchestra, discussed his possible appointment to the New York Philharmonic. I had not heard of it before. Rumours somehow never reached me — they still don't — and if they do they usually pass by me unnoticed.

So I had indulged in no speculation about Mitropoulus's departure from Minneapolis, and it certainly had not occurred to me that I could be involved.

But it had to the Minneapolitani. I had conducted there several times for the Ballets Russes — perhaps also for the Ballet Theatre — in former years, and was engaged in 1944 as a guest conductor for a week of subscription concerts.

I have two memories of that event. First, the programme: Beethoven: Leonore Overture No. 3; Mozart: "Jupiter" Symphony; Richard Strauss, Suite from *Rosenkavalier*; Ravel: Suite 2 from *Daphnis and Chloe*. Second, an elegant reception for which I bought a hat. I never wore hats, and I have no idea why I bought one then. It was a black homburg, and I must have looked like my own caricature in it.

In spite of the hat, the overall impression I made cannot have been all that disastrous because one afternoon, in Dallas, my telephone rang and the manager of the Minneapolis Symphony, Arthur Gaines, was on the line.

23

I KNEW GAINES WELL. I FIRST MET HIM IN ST. LOUIS, THEN AGAIN several times in Minneapolis, a place I remembered with pleasure: the huge auditorium at the university campus spreading like a giant red fan when one turned audience-ward from the podium, and very impressive when filled with people in the evening; the fine and affable orchestra – I had heard its sound first during a rehearsal conducted by Ormandy more than a decade earlier, in the late Thirties.

It was precisely towards those sounds that the 'phone call of Gaines was going to lead me back. He wanted to know how long my Dallas contract was and my salary, and asked a few more questions.

A few days later he 'phoned again: "The matter of your appointment has gone quite far here, so would you send me a letter stating your ideas, plans – what you would want to do as our conductor, if you're interested."

Interested?

I was surprised and excited.

The Dallas years were good and rewarding in every way. The fourth of them was just drawing to its close. It had been a good beginning, and promised more. But to lead the Minneapolis Symphony was for me at that moment a great opportunity, a tremendous challenge.

I wrote to Gaines as requested, setting out my aims and plans as precisely as I could.

The reply confirmed my appointment. I soon went to Minneapolis, met some people, rented a furnished house for my family and myself and found a school for my daughter. Then I went to Buffalo, where the orchestra was on tour, to hear it. One member of the viola section fell from his chair during the concert, or his chair collapsed under him – so I added to my "aims and plans" the acquisition of sturdier chairs and, perhaps, steadier performers. Otherwise I listened with great pleasure to much lovely music; the main piece of the programme was Schumann's Third, "Rhenish"

217

Symphony, a very demanding work, presented with great strength. Later we had supper with Mitropoulos, whom I then met for the second time. He had bought himself a new pair of patent leather shoes of which he was immensely proud. He carried them in a sack of purple cloth, which hung over the back of his chair during dinner. He was most affable and witty, and gave me some inside information about the orchestra, his "legacy", as he said.

This was the beginning.

The Minneapolis years were, in retrospect, perhaps the most important in my development as an artist. Those were the last of my formative period.

Considering that I had my fiftieth birthday right in the centre of that span of time, this seems to be a dangerous admission, but I repeat, I am a late maturer. If I now show any signs of so-called maturity, it certainly did not emerge any sooner than my sixties. To arrive at maturity is, in any case, a private matter. It is also very difficult, indeed impossible, to determine the time of its arrival before the very end of life's journey, since it can hardly be estimated in absolute terms; the road towards maturity is certainly no less interesting, stimulating, worthwhile than maturity itself. Works of art created during formative periods of "storm and stress" have their own validity and permanence.

The development of a human being is a process like the fermentation of wine. The crucial, determinating factor is the quality of the grape. If the fruit is fine, the young wine made of it is very enjoyable. Some may even like it better young than the old and heady. And finally comes the time when . . . but by then, with luck, all of it will have been gratefully drunk – the best proof of the vintage's quality.

The challenge – yes, it was certainly great.

I became the successor – I had never been anybody's successor before – of one of the most exciting conductors of our time. At the beginning, at least, I was very conscious of this fact – perhaps too much so.

The comet-like, meteoric performers such as Mitropoulos reach their public, so to speak, directly from "outer space", with such a personal impact that the art they convey becomes almost secondary. That kind of artist is always a lonely figure. And a lonely figure heading a co-operative artistic effort, such as the performance of a symphony orchestra, is somewhat contradictory, at least as understood by someone of a different nature, for instance by me.

As I understand my profession, the conductor of an orchestra is a leveller, co-ordinator, balancer of musical sounds made not by him but by a hundred or so of his colleagues. He is also the one who gives the style to *their* – not his – performance, the individual and collective performance of many gifted people with as many different temperaments and musical inclinations as they are in numbers. It is his job to perceive and to develop the manifold qualities and conglomerate possibilities of the group and weld it into an inseparable entity, mixing his own initiative with stimuli received from the playing performers – of which he is *not* one. The living sound is produced by the orchestra, not by the mute gesturing of the conductor, whose movements are to be directed as reminders to the members of the orchestra exclusively, and must make sense only to them.

This was the kind of orchestra playing and the kind of conducting which suited my talent, my taste and my upbringing, and it was this manner of music-making which I strove to develop and bring as close to perfection as I possibly could, and even a little closer.

There was a lot for me to consider and to do when I took over the fine, experienced Minneapolis group. It had a great number of splendidly gifted artists amongst its members, many of them brought in by Dimitri Mitropoulos' predecessor, Eugene Ormandy, who is an orchestra-builder and maintainer *par excellence* – now the great "last Mohican" of the profession – and who unmistakably showed his "lion's claws" even at the very young age at which he took the helm of the Minneapolis Symphony for five years and placed it, once and for all, in the upper ranks of symphony orchestras.

There was no need for many changes, then, in the orchestra's personnel, apart from the routine turnover, which was not large. Minneapolis exercised a certain fascination upon musicians; it had a mystery, a lure, it was thought of as an oasis of the north. One came there willingly, in spite of the severe winters, the then rather short seasons, the none too generous salaries. Joining the Minneapolis Symphony was like getting a badge of honour. One went and one stayed.

Among the very few changes that I made at the start, the most notable were the additions of Rafael Druian, whom I brought with me as concert master, and Bernard Adelstein, who joined a year later as first trumpet. Their performance and general influence instantly brought new colours and new impetus to the orchestra. The performance style I was striving for appeared right away and developed with great rapidity, though not too smoothly at the start.

It was a great change for the orchestra – and unwelcome to some of its members – to have, suddenly, instead of the ascetic, Savonarola-like figure shrouded in cloudy mystery, a young man (for I was a young forty-five) who wished, as far as the public was concerned, to be just another member of the orchestra. For this exposed the orchestra to the limelight at each of its performances, and there is nothing more unmerciful than the limelight. Moreover, my way with the orchestra was very direct: I always tried to be unmistakably clear, and was sometimes blistering (I learned better manners later and offer apologies for early errors here). I was bent on thorough preparation and believed that music would make its own impact when it was presented understandably and convincingly on its own terms.

This new approach was well received by many – orchestra members and listeners alike – and opposed by some. But it won out, and a year or two later I could think that I had arrived.

My bodily arrival at Minneapolis was an event all of its own.

We came, my wife, my daughter and I – our two dogs and canary joined us later – by train, on the famous "400". We were greeted at the station by Loring and Mary Staples, he then president and she first lady of the Minneapolis Symphony. We drove through the night to our rented home on Lake of the Isles Boulevard. We tried to enter. The keys which the Staples brought did not seem to fit. There was a great bunch of them, many more than were needed, provided by the ever-absent landlord who probably didn't know himself which were usable and which were not.

Finally we found one that opened the back door. As soon as it opened, however, to our shock and dismay a deafening bell began

220

to ring. It was a burglar alarm. Within minutes the police arrived and began interrogating us with grave suspicion.

Loring deployed his best nasal lawyer's language and put them at ease; we entered the kitchen and soon all of us sat at the kitchen table, the Staples, the Dorátis and the policemen, drinking beer together and eating the goodies which had been placed in the refrigerator before our arrival by another couple who were to become close friends, Rosalynd and Leo Pflaum.

Thus passed the first evening of those eleven important, constructive years.

Next morning I went out to get the paper. The news was both flattering and bewildering.

Our arrival had made the front page – without the story of the alarm-bell – but the same page carried another headline which stated in large capital letters:
"MINNESOTA GOPHERS INVADE NEBRASKA BY AIR"

Good gracious, this was really bad! A plague or something, perhaps. I strictly forbade further unpacking in case we had to evacuate the house. Nebraska was not far away, and the belligerent Minnesota gophers could fly back any time.

It did not come to that. I soon knew who the Gophers were – the Minnesota football team – although I never learned who won the game in Nebraska.

The tasks that face the music director of an American orchestra are greater in scope and variety than his European equivalent has to deal with. One only has to consider the vast territory which is served by an orchestra in America, the great size of the music-loving public which depends upon that orchestra as the sole dispenser of symphonic music in an area perhaps as large as half of Europe or larger, to realise some aspects of what there is to do, some problems that must be faced.

One task I loved to face and to deal with, was extending the orchestra's repertoire; another was the working out of the programmes, which was equally fascinating and gratifying.

Every director has his own predilections, as is natural; and consequently after a long tenure any repertoire tends to become somewhat one-sided. It is, however, a wonderful thing to be at home in many lodgings in the beautiful mansions of music – to be a specialist in non–specialisation – and this is what I have tried to be during my entire musical life. The amusing result is that I have been, at various times, declared a specialist in different areas. Once I was an expert in Russian music, then a Bartók man. For a time it was Strauss, for another Stravinsky, for another even Respighi. Later it was Beethoven. And so on. At the time of writing this book I am supposed to be a Haydn specialist. I wish I were. I wish I were all that I have been said to be. The truth is that I am, or have become gradually, a musician of catholic taste, having cultivated my modest talents in such a way as to be at home in and at ease with several styles of music-making.

Even so, I do not think one can escape one-sidedness after serving the same public for a good many years. There is only one remedy, and it is widely applied today: the engagement of a number of guest conductors to supplement the repertoire of the resident music director with works of their own predilection.

At the start of my time in Minneapolis there were several avenues open to me, and I went off in quite a few directions at the same time. Looking back over the programme books of those years, I can affirm that the fare I offered was varied and of good quality. The pleasure of planning and the fever of execution of that repertoire are still with me. Indeed, what could be more exhilarating than to be allowed to present such firsts as Stravinsky's *Rite of Spring*, Bartók's Concerto for Orchestra or Mahler's Third Symphony?

At least one memorable world première took place during my first season: that of Bartók's posthumous Viola Concerto, with the splendid William Primrose, who commissioned the work, as soloist. I took great care over the selection of each of my "firsts" and every season had one or two. Yet in my eleven years, only one other work besides the Bartók became for a while part of the symphonic repertory, Gunther Schuller's Seven Studies after Paul Klee. In comparison with the wasteful ways of Mother Nature and the casualties involved in the survival of the fittest, two new works within a decade which became popular successes does not make such a poor showing.

The press was friendly, my acceptance by the audience seemed complete.

Outwardly, my start could hardly have been more propitious.

222

Yet I felt uneasy. And I was right. As it turned out, I was far from being accepted immediately. I learned much later that a minority of the public felt it an affront to have a young, and as yet unknown, man follow the great Mitropoulos and refused to come to my concerts at all. Another small group did come, but only to find fault. This I did not mind, because my task was (and is) to give pleasure, and we all know that to condemn is as great a pleasure as to praise.

In spite of this reluctance of a few diehards, our public grew considerably, because a great many young people were drawn into the orbit of the orchestra. That this was so was a direct result of what we produced, for publicity and PR activities on the scale we have them now were non-existent in those days.

The members of the orchestra, by and large, did not warm to me right away either. The rather strict discipline I demanded from everyone – myself very much included – was quite a shock after the much looser reins of the previous decade. To that came my regrettably short temper – a cross I have had to carry since child-hood, and have only mastered quite late in life. In Minneapolis, it was certainly counter-productive. So, during my first season, there were rumours of secret meetings at which proposals were made to have me fired. One day, Claudia Cassidy, the much-feared Chicago music critic, 'phoned to ask if reports of my resignation were true. "No," I told her. "They are not. How could I think of going when I have barely come!" And indeed I had no such thoughts: my spirit was high and I looked ahead with confidence to getting a real grasp of my job.

That moment arrived before long. It was after a performance of the *Rite of Spring* in my second season that the members of the orchestra came to me and said, "Now we are *your* orchestra." This was good to hear, and I was moved almost to tears.

It was always very important to me that the members of my orchestras should understand me, and know that my complete effort, my entire energy, talent and initiative, had only one goal, to make the best music, and that I was not trying to make music without them, aside from them or even against them, but *with* them, and more than that, *through* them. It is obvious that in order to be able to produce good music in that manner, I had to have orchestras of reasonable quality, good morale, great strength and even greater potential – and, perhaps above all, great pride. It was these co-efficients which I always tried to foster in the orchestras under my care, perhaps not very skilfully at first, but improving with the years.

Our path – for it did become *our* path soon – turned rapidly upward. The concerts at home gained in popularity, the programmes – sometimes called "bold", sometimes called "made with a ruler", sometimes called "fun" (how happy I was if I heard that!) – got hold of our music lovers. The tours, on which the orchestra went every year, were successful, and not only that: they were lucrative (those were the days!), and the two months on the road every year were a time we all looked forward to and enjoyed. We travelled on special trains, or in a suite of special cars attached to regular trains (three sleepers, one parlour and one dining car!), in which we quite often lived for several days in succession, returning to it after the concerts to sleep. We hardly noticed the train pulling out of the station, almost stealthily, during the night, and often woke up some few hours after arrival at our next stop.

The orchestra gave a good number of children's concerts each year in Minneapolis and St. Paul. It gave me a special delight to conduct these; I was also the commentator, and I was told that I did that rather well. At any rate, I never felt that I had any problem in communicating with the young people, either musically or verbally. I kept my talks to them on a personal level, never trying to teach, but to elucidate as clearly and as briefly as I could. My foreign accent was never a handicap.

For about seven years out of the eleven I conducted these young people's concerts myself, before handing them over, gradually, to Gerhard Samuel, my very able associate.

I was never burdened unduly with extra-musical duties in Minneapolis. The board did not require me to take an extensive part in fund-raising activities and the like. Yet I, on my side, was keen to extend the appeal of our music, to escape from the ivory tower of the materially privileged and make our concerts an integral part of the life of the people, one of whom I felt (and still feel) myself to be. So I not infrequently addressed various gatherings and clubs, and lectured at Northrop University, where I was made a professor for the time of my tenure and where later a fellowship in my name was established. I enjoyed taking part in campus activities, including, on one occasion, conducting the brass band at a football match.

Where I never compromised was in my guardianship of the level and the integrity of our music-making. We never had a sloppily prepared concert, there never was a single piece on any of our programmes to which my most conscientious judgment was not applied, and never did a soloist appear with us or a new member of the orchestra join us who was not, in my opinion, worthy of the invitation.

Those are unbending standards, and I have tried to apply them everywhere. What *was* special to Minneapolis was the absence of obstacles militating against their fulfilment. If ever there was a completely unprejudiced, understanding and broad-minded board of directors of a symphony orchestra, which knew what its job was and what it was not, it was the board of the Minneapolis Symphony during my times.

Power is always in the hands that have the money. The money behind an American symphony orchestra is provided and controlled by its board of directors. How easy it is for its members, collectively and individually, to exert their power to achieve personal aims, and how difficult it is for a musical director to oppose them if those aims do not serve the best interests of his orchestra.

Never, in Minneapolis, did I have to suffer that embarrassment. Not once in eleven years was any pressure exercised to influence or hinder me. Everything that belonged to the musical and artistic side of the life of our orchestra was freely talked about with the board, we did nothing it did not know about.

So the money raisers raised money, the managers managed, the directors directed, the music-makers made music.

Too good to be true?

Well, time, in passing, embellishes the past. But the nature of that embellishment is such that it makes the essence of the past shine through with greater clarity, while the non-essential fades away.

Thus, thinking back, I may forget unimportant details, but I do remember well all that is worth remembering.

A matter that we discussed with increasing intensity, and from my side with increasing frustration, was that of the poor acoustics

225

of Northrop Auditorium and the need for a new concert hall.

Far be it for me to think ungratefully of that venerable place. It had its role to play in the Minneapolis Symphony's history, and played it honourably. But it must have been clear from the very start that the immense, fan-shaped, disproportionately low-ceilinged hall was not meant for music. What it *was* meant for, I never could make out. It was built as a multi-purpose hall, and like many such buildings was not really good for anything.

What a feast it was to our ears, hearts and minds, to our collective morale, when we performed on tour in New York's Carnegie Hall, Boston's Orchestra Hall, Chicago's Symphony Hall, or the Herodus Atticus Theatre in Athens – when our sound, which we so carefully cultivated in the "vacuum" of Northrop Auditorium, suddenly blossomed out. Our ears could hardly believe it for the first few minutes, and when our own sound fully entered our consciousness, we felt as the boy on Columbus's *Santa Maria* must have felt at his look-out post at the moment when he cried, "Land! – Land!"

The board did see my point; it was sympathetic to my pleas. But it was scared by the enormous expense that a new building would involve. It spent generously on expensive "improvements", new acoustical shells and the like. They did not help at all, as I knew they wouldn't. A fundamentally bad hall can never be made into a good one. The so-called improvements are only changes. One poor sound is replaced by another, different, poor sound. This difference is heard, for a short period of time as an improvement, but all too soon it becomes evident that it is not. The only possible remedy for a bad concert hall is a drastic one – dynamite.

Thus I considered the money spent on improving Northrop Auditorium a well-meant but foolishly incurred expense. What I did not know then – and begin to know now – is that there is a time for everything, that ideas, like babies, have their gestation period. Well, my baby turned out to be a very large and superlative elephant and accordingly needed greater gestation time. I now bask happily, if belatedly, in the glory of the new Minneapolis Orchestra Hall where I conducted with great pleasure and satisfaction in the year of its opening, 1975.

As time went on, one of the MSO's most important activities became our recordings, which spread the name Minneapolis Symphony throughout the world. They were made for two years with

RCA Victor, then, permanently, with the newer and smaller Mercury Records.

The approximately one hundred long-playing records we made became an important contribution to the recording panorama of that time. The great variety of repertoire which was provided on excellently recorded discs, using the latest technical equipment then available with exceptional skill, and with the greatest care taken over every musical and technical detail, made our discs welcome to many melomanes. Their "living presence" (the commercial slogan that was created by appropriating a remark of one reviewer) of our records made them a household name. The number of people who were actually "brought up" on the Minneapolis records of the 1950s is astonishingly large.

The pillars of strength of all that activity, from the recording company's end, were two young people, now a married couple with wonderful children, Wilma Cozart and Robert Fine, both well-nigh unsurpassable in their respective fields. Wilma, who was my secretary in Dallas, continued in that capacity for one year in Minneapolis, then went to New York and entered the recording world. She later became vice-president of Mercury Records and is now retired from professional life. Robert Fine was and is one of the most gifted sound experts, well known and respected in the profession.

Nothing can better illustrate the success of that fine collaborative effort than the fact that even today a great number of those records, after many re-issues, are still on the international market, beautifully holding their own against many newer recordings.

Another major event around the middle of my tenure was the change of manager.

The profession of symphony orchestra manager is as complex as it is rare. No more than a small handful of people embrace it in one generation and I would think that it is much more difficult to find a good manager for a symphony orchestra than a good conductor.

The manager must be a good businessman, a good administrator, an executive – but not without musical sensibility. He has to guide the business life of his organisation within an agreed established budget; he is responsible to the board of directors, generally a group of businessmen highly capable in their own field

227

but incompetent in that of music; he is also responsible to the music director, generally a fine musician but incompetent in business. And finally, along with his colleagues, he is responsible to the public. Even this very rough, incomplete sketch of the manager's duties shows why there are very few men who can master them successfully.

Minneapolis was lucky to have Arthur Gaines for a long time, in fact for two lengthy periods, as its symphony manager. He was, by my time, the doyen of American orchestra managers, a big, bald-headed man with a walrus moustache, an earthy figure of great strength, and a good deal of old-fashioned wisdom. He was completely uneducated in music, but had a great love for it that was absolutely genuine, and through many years of faithful listening he gathered enough experience to become quite competent and well informed as far as orchestral music was concerned. By profession, he was an accountant. He had a clear head, and was an able executive with considerable natural authority. In the early postwar years of the 1950s he was the ideal manager. His problems began when times changed. Radio and TV were advancing relentlessly, the press was no longer what it used to be, the customary method of transport changed from rail to air, the labour unions gathered power. The world around Arthur Gaines was suddenly no longer his. All this did not make him suffer, for he took scant notice of what was going on. But he became, gradually, a lonely figure.

The atmosphere in his efficient, sparsely-staffed office was austere – the only light relief in it was Frank Meyer, the public relations officer who worked on a part-time basis, an equally large man with a kindly smile.

It was a typically mid-Western outfit, and I did not enjoy their full confidence. Although I had been an American citizen since 1947, they looked on me as a foreigner, and though I was forty-three when I came, they considered me somewhat too young. Being of a different temperamental make-up, I was, in short, something of a black sheep, a man to be watched.

During an ordinary work-meeting at Arthur Gaines's office one afternoon, his secretary interrupted us, rather breathlessly.

"Mr. Doráti, the FBI is on the 'phone for you."

The FBI meant little to me – little more, in fact, than a group of initials. But the effect of that "three letter word" on my companions was terrific. All conversation stopped, and as I picked up the 'phone a deathly silence fell.

"Hello."

"Mr. Doráti?"

"Yes."

"Mr. Antal Doráti?"

"Yes."

"This is Mr. XYZ of the FBI speaking."

"Good afternoon, Mr. XYZ."

"Mr. Doráti, could I have a few words with you at your convenience?"

"Of course."

"When would it be convenient?"

"Well, right now if you wish."

"May I come to see you?"

"Yes, come right here to Northrop Auditorium, the right side front office."

"I'll be there in one hour."

"Thank you, thank you," etc.

The next hour was perhaps the longest single hour in my life. Conversation came to a complete standstill. No work was done. The eyes around me pierced me with looks like tiny arrows. Lips became thin, pale, opening with difficulty for a word that had to be spoken at intervals to keep up the civilities. I was indeed, at that moment, a potential traitor or a possible spy. For this was the middle of the so-called McCarthy era, when almost everybody was under suspicion for something or other.

Finally Mr. XYZ arrived – dapper, dark-suited, with the obligatory black briefcase. He could have been played by David Niven, only Niven would have been better in the part.

"Mr. Doráti."

"Good evening, Mr. XYZ, will you please sit down?"

A short cough.

"Mr. Doráti, could I see you alone?"

That made me snap.

"No, Mr. XYZ, you cannot. I am fully at your disposal, but we must talk right here, in front of my friends."

"But, Mr. Doráti – it – it would be much better if we could talk eye to eye."

229

"No, Mr. XYZ, I am sorry, we have to talk with all the eyes here looking and all the ears here hearing."

"But – really – please . . ."

"No, Mr. XYZ, you must understand that I consent to talk to you only with my friends present."

"But . . ."

"No but, Mr. XYZ. The only other way I could suggest would be communicating by correspondence, and you may rest assured that I will distribute copies of your letters and my replies to all those here in this room."

"Those" were Arthur Gaines and two ladies, secretaries. They watched in silence. It was a very tense moment.

Mr. XYZ swallowed a few times, his adam's-apple moving up and down like a semaphore. He wilted, visibly. Then, he began fumbling in his briefcase and after some searching he pulled out a bunch of papers that looked like – and was – a music manuscript.

"Well – Mr. Doráti – could you please look at this. It is a symphony which I have just composed . . ."

Curtain.

There was no reason for me to go to jail, after all. As for Mr. XYZ, on the evidence of his symphony, I am not so sure. But I let him off, with clemency.

After that incident, my position in the MSO's offices was much strengthened. Perhaps I was even fully accepted.

I was in Stockholm in 1954 conducting a concert in celebration of the 800th anniversary of Sweden's capital when I received a cable telling me that Arthur Gaines had suffered a heart attack. He lingered on for two more years, but never worked again. The MSO had in him a loyal and strong friend, a faithful servant who guided it well for a long stretch of its way.

It was not easy to find a successor. Finally, after long deliberation, we chose Boris Sokoloff, who managed the orchestra for ten years or so. He had a fine musical background, being the son of the Cleveland Orchestra's first conductor. Although he himself did not become a musician, he always remained in the orbit of music.

With his narrow-set, dark eyes he is an austere-looking man, but his nature does not correspond to his looks. From the first he was pleasant company, knew the symphony business inside out, was of a resourceful turn of mind and, above all, anchored firmly in our times and moving along with them.

Perhaps his greatest managerial achievement during my time was the European and Middle-Eastern tour of the MSO. It was a great event. The emergence of a first-rate symphony orchestra from the American Middle-West must have surprised many people. The New York Philharmonic undertook a European tour under Toscanini in 1930, but I do not know if any other orchestra from the USA had crossed the Atlantic after that, before we did.

Never will any one of us who took part in the event forget our first concert, at the Herodus Atticus Theatre in Athens, where, under the moonlit Parthenon, six thousand people gave the orchestra a standing ovation lasting the best part of one hour and producing seven "encores", being brought to an end, finally, when the orchestra played the Greek National Anthem and marched off the platform, leaving the still cheering audience behind.

Other events of that tour also remain clearly etched in my memory:

The concert in Baghdad, where the dogs along the river barked as loud or louder than we played.

The evening in Teheran in front of the Golestan Palace with the peacock throne, in the large open square with traffic diverted miles away to ensure silence. The Shah was present, in resplendent uniform, stretched out comfortably with his entourage in red plush armchairs under the trees, asking for Berlioz's Hungarian March as an encore and signing his autograph after the concert.

The night out of the "1001 Nights" in Lahore, where we played under a giant improvised tent sporting all the colours of the orient; where our first trumpeter, Bernie Adelstein, was escorted by a military guard to the tower, which – reluctantly, on my orders – he had to climb by a step-ladder to play the signal in Beethoven's Third Leonore Overture (the only place and the only time in history, I believe, when that signal, which is meant to be sounded from a look-out post, was played in its proper place!), and where Bob Tweedy, our tympanist, used electric hair dryers to keep his kettle drums in tune in the humid, hot night.

Our visits, discussions and musical exchange evenings with several groups of raga players of India, which gave unexpected glimpses into the nature of India's music. What *they* liked best in our repertoire – they came to all our concerts – were the rhythmically complete contemporary works.

It was also in Lahore that one of our violists, Michael Danesuk, bought himself a souvenir: a strange piece of complicated winding tube of a lead-like material, allegedly an ancient Hindu musical instrument. Personally, I gravely doubted that attribution and rather suspected the long, twisted tube structure of being a strayed piece of modern American plumbing. But the proud owner dismissed my sceptical thoughts and carried his trophy around in his hand, as it was too bulky to fit into any piece of luggage.

He arrived with it, accordingly, at Bombay Airport, where we had a long wait while changing planes for the flight back to Europe.

Among the passengers also waiting in the same lounge as ourselves was Mrs. Pandit, Jawaharlal Nehru's sister. She had visited Minneapolis several times during her many travels, and was delighted to find herself in the company of the Minneapolis Symphony Orchestra during the long, dull wait.

Soon she noticed – how could she not have done? – the monstrous souvenir of our colleague. She went up to him and asked what it was.

"An ancient Hindu instrument, Madame, a great rarity," replied Danesuk proudly.

It cannot be established how well versed Mrs. Pandit was in ancient Hindu music and musical instruments, but her eyebrows rose a good inch higher than their normal position.

After a short moment of silent contemplation, she asked, "Would you mind playing a tune on it?"

To the astonishment – and subsequent hilarity – of all of us looking on, Michael obliged.

What followed was the most extraordinary performance of the entire tour. To begin with, Danesuk was a violist and not a wind–instrument player. Further, the tubing he tried to play on was – let's face it! – no musical instrument at all. The result of his efforts was shattering. The sound he produced was like the death-cry of a hippopotamus run over by a bulldozer. Perhaps not a great credit to ancient Hindu music but overwhelming in its own way.

That adventurous tour gave a great lift to the Minneapolis

232

Symphony Orchestra. For the first time its performances were exposed to the reactions of people of other cultural climates than its own, and the happy response which the orchestra received from Athens to Zagreb made its members prouder, better people and artists – and poised them for the greater heights of accomplishment soon to be reached at home.

As the horizon around the MSO widened, so its own scope enlarged with the years. It introduced concert performances of major operas never heard in the twin cities before, and full productions of small-scale operas were also tried. They included Menotti's *The Old Maid and the Thief* and *Amahl and the Night Visitors*, his touching one-act piece based upon the biblical story of the Three Kings, and – one of our most important experiments – Stravinsky's *Persephone*.

It was, incidentally, these smaller works that introduced our daughter Tonina to her future profession of stage and costume designing. Then aged about fifteen, she was allowed to work as assistant to the stage director of one production and, returning from a rehearsal one day, declared: "This is what I want to do."

One very important event in my personal life as a musician took place during my time with the MSO: my return to composing.

I must mention here that I was a very prolific and perhaps not unpromising composer in my early youth. At the age of twenty-two or twenty-three, however, I abandoned composing, for a number of reasons – mostly, as I will relate later, of a neurotic nature – and devoted all my talent and energy to conducting.

I did, though, feel, in my innermost heart and mind, always a composer in exile. And yet, with all my desire for it, I could not compose – I was held back by invisible chains.

And then, suddenly, in the middle 1950s – it was like a miracle – the chains fell away. From one day to another I knew that I could and would compose again. And without delay I launched into the heart of this profoundly exciting and absorbing life of creative activity open to me once more.

It did not happen by chance – nothing ever does, everything has its merciless logic – and I owe it to the truthfulness of these notes not to by-pass this private matter, because, although intimately personal, it is directly connected with my musical life.

(At this juncture I wish to say that when I refer to my creative musicianship, to my composing and compositions, I do so without "illusions of grandeur". Writing music is an integral part of my life. Without it I would not be me. Therefore I must include it in my story although, in the flow of the years, composing did not become my only, nor outwardly central, activity. Alas. But the music that I write contains my creative seed, and my compositions are brought into the world as children of my mind and soul. As I write the story of the parent, the child must be mentioned because he is his, not for his ultimate merit. If my son is not Alexander the Great, that makes me no less his father.)

My composing capacity in fact re-emerged as self-defence against an illness that befell me in the mid-1950s. By God's special grace not only did I gain back that lost part of my life, but even my illness, which could have crippled me, left me unscathed.

What I had was an attack of Menière's disease, a disorder of the balance nerve situated in the inner ear. This disease is not fatal and exhausts itself with time. But almost always it leaves the victim's hearing badly damaged or extinguished.

That I was one of the few to be spared that fate was a near miracle. I am convinced that what helped me to defeat the illness was not, in the last resort, medication – although I had much of that, faithfully and competently administered – but my fierce determination not to give in, to fight and fight and fight it. This I did, day by day, hour by hour, never stopping – and won.

And in this fight, my greatest weapon was composing. I began again – finally! – to write music. Thoughts poured out, freely, without obstacles. I wrote and wrote, fiercely, madly, day and night, whenever I could snatch an hour, a moment. It was my way back to health.

The physicians were amazed, shook their heads, and decided that I had not had *real* Menière's disease after all. Well, so much the better. For me it was real enough.

Since that time – my fiftieth year – I have produced rather more than one work a year, a total of twenty-five to date.

Two major works of mine were given their world premières in Minneapolis. One was *The Way*, a full-length cantata for orchestra, choir, two solo singing voices and narrator, on the text of Claudel's

234

beautiful poem "Le Chemin de la Croix". The other was my only symphony to date. Both were more than kindly received, and the latter was recorded.

During my decade in Minneapolis there was ample time from late spring to early autumn each year, when the orchestral seasons stopped, to accept other conducting engagements, and from 1955 onwards to continue with my composing.

I made my conductorial debuts in Boston and Detroit, re-visited Washington, the Philadelphia Dell summer concerts, the Hollywood Bowl and other places. New horizons opened up in other parts of the world.

Holland, for a ten-year period, became almost my second musical home, with many concerts in Amsterdam, The Hague and one or two in Utrecht. I also started recording for the then very young Philips Company, a relationship that has continued in an interesting manner to this day.

The most important new prospects, however, opened up in London, where I was received with open arms when I came back about eight years after my first short and unsuccessful visit on the concert platform.

This time a close and productive contact was quickly established with the London Symphony Orchestra. I conducted it in many concerts and recordings and, though I never had an "official" position with it, I was its more or less permanent conductor for some five or six years, touring with it in Europe, Israel, Japan and in England itself. It can be said that the period of our close collaboration coincided with that of the orchestra's rise to the top international rank.

I also conducted in turn every London orchestra, and most of the provincial ones. With two of them, the BBC Symphony and the Royal Philharmonic, close relations were to develop in future years.

Another visit had further consequences later: that to Stockholm in 1954, on the occasion of the city's 800th anniversary. It was an intriguing, interesting, and musically not unrewarding excursion to that handsome city and its Nordic world of unbearable darkness and intoxicating light. Little did I know that later, for seven years, I should be the principal conductor of the orchestra I then worked with for a few days.

In the Latin countries my circle of acquaintances widened with concerts in Madrid, which I still visit from time to time, but more importantly in Latin America.

Once more I returned – for the last time – to Havana and again visited Mexico City, which had grown enormously since I was first there, but its symphony orchestra had remained unchanged.

The quality of orchestral playing in the Latin-speaking world is, somehow, organically under-developed. This includes the Latin countries of Europe as well as Latin America. One can hear occasional fine performances from the orchestras of the Teatro alla Scala in Milan or the Teatro Colón in Buenos Aires, and sometimes (though rarely) at other places. But the general level is never higher than, for instance, one of the third-class orchestras in the USA and often inferior.

Thus the trips I undertook to South America in the 1950s were less rewarding musically than for their revelation of a new world so far unknown to me, for South America is like no other part of the globe, and South Americans are like no other kinds of people.

The first South American city I visited was Buenos Aires. I went there several times and conducted several orchestras. The most satisfactory was the orchestra of the Teatro Colón; the fine acoustics of the theatre itself were surprising considering its vastness. The city is splendid, its streets wide and spacious, its architecture like that of a conservatively modern city with French affinities. The people on the whole looked sad and depressed; the men, with their scarves worn outside their overcoats, had a ceremonial aspect.

Once I went to Cordoba in the interior of Argentina, at the feet of the Andes. The orchestra I had to conduct there was pathetically poor, but I did not regret my visit, for I saw landscapes of incomparable beauty. The real reason for my going was that I wanted to see the home of Manuel de Falla, who lived there in exile after the Spanish Civil War. Full of pity and compassion, I made the pilgrimage to the house where he lived and died. Looking around, I could not but admit that he had chosen his place of exile very astutely. My admiration did not change, but I could pity him no longer.

Santiago, the Chilean capital, interested me most with its extraordinary human make-up. The very thin top layer of the people are the finest and most delightful to meet. I met them superficially only, with the exception of the one person who became one of my most cherished friends and will remain so, in spite of the many years that sometimes pass between our seeing or hearing from each other.

Montevideo, Caracas and Bogota completed the range of my Latin American tours.

In 1959 I had received an invitation to teach the summer course in conducting at the Mozarteum in Salzburg. In spite of grave doubts about my ability as a teacher, I let myself be persuaded by the directors of the Mozarteum to accept. I should not have done so. As to teaching, I still maintain that it is not my line, yet some young conductors assure me that they have learned a great deal from me. But in Salzburg a very mixed group of pupils attended the first lesson. It turned out that the Mozarteum accepted everybody for the course who sent in the fee for it, without further examination. When I remonstrated with the directors, calling this procedure by unkind names and questioning its morality, I received no satisfactory explanation.

My conviction that conducting cannot, and therefore should not, be taught, grew stronger during that summer, though later I had a few experiences that made me partially relent.

Salzburg itself, in spite of the turmoil of the festival period, exuded all its charm. I met there and became friends with two great artists, Oskar Kokoschka and Giacomo Manzù.

Kokoschka was holding a course in painting in the castle of Hohensalzburg, in which I wanted to enrol as his pupil, but, unfortunately, I had no time. Tonina, who is very gifted in drawing and painting, and was on her way to become a professional designer, attended and found the course both enjoyable and fruitful.

It was pleasant to receive another invitation for the following summer; on that occasion to conduct the world première of a new opera by a young Austrian composer called Heimo Erbse. The name of the opera was *Julietta*. Its text was adapted by the composer himself from a short story by Kleist. It was an interesting attempt at a contemporary *opera semi-seria*. The performance was well cast, carefully prepared and competently presented. It was murdered, gruesomely, by a hostile press. This has often happened to good operas, which later re-emerge from their ashes. *Julietta*, regrettably, did not withstand the assault. Only the performers emerged unscathed. In fact, their success was as great as the opera's failure, an extra bit of cruelty for the poor composer.

After the first night I received a visit from Andre Mattoni, one of the aides of Herbert von Karajan, who was then musical director of the Vienna Opera House, asking me to join that institution as regular conductor. This offer, in combination with the steadily growing demand for concerts in Europe, seemed to present exactly the change I was looking for. Klári, who all her life had longed to live in Rome, suddenly saw her wish approach fulfilment and was all for our moving back to Europe. My tenure in Minneapolis was approaching its natural end, and Vienna, as long as one is well away from it, is a great lure. So I agreed in principle to make the move at a mutually convenient time – perhaps within two years, and we shook hands with Mattoni. There was no reason to doubt his word, and I began to plan accordingly.

The last months in Minneapolis were given over to a passionate leavetaking in which I was unabashedly sentimental. We made our last tours together, our last recordings – amongst them that of my First Symphony, which we had premièred shortly before, in the spring of 1960. There were endless farewell dinners with tearful speeches, honours of all kinds; and on one nice, early May day we boarded the plane that took us away.

I was in a sombre mood, brooding, not about the future, but about the past. A decade in a human life is a long time. I had had a job to do in the period that had just ended. How well had I done it? There is no complete success, no complete satisfaction (though there *is* complete failure). Achievements are always a mixture of things done well and badly, as wars are a series of battles won and lost. The sum total decides the final victory or defeat.

One has done much, yes. But how far was that from what one set out to do? The chain of little achievements, did they measure up at all against the supreme achievement of one's dreams? How far was I limping behind the self that I wanted to be, that I was going to be in some future already behind me?

After a few days in New York we went straight to Rome, to establish our home there. This was more difficult than we had expected.

24

THE FIRST NEWS THAT REACHED ME AFTER LEAVING MINNEAPOLIS was that the State Opera in Vienna had made other plans and my contract there would not materialise. Apart from a momentary disappointment I did not mind this very much. In fact, subsequent contracts showed that this set-back was a blessing in disguise, for as it turned out I am completely allergic to the special Viennese spirit which always ruins my visits when I go there to conduct.

True, Vienna is a unique music city. Haydn, Mozart, Schubert, Brahms, Bruckner and other great masters lived there, and it is quite in order that the Viennese musicians of today should be proud of this heritage. But pride without humility is conceit and – well – worthless. It is, possibly, my personal reaction to the Vienna music mentality of today that is unjust. I tried to change it, but could not.

My European network of engagements expanded rapidly – too rapidly, in fact. News of my year-round availability spread fast, and soon I was conducting concerts around the calendar-clock, somewhat indiscriminately, I must now admit, but with a sincere, unblasé pleasure in being wanted.

The freelance life was very agreeable, and the new places and new orchestras most stimulating. I began to give concerts in Paris, and this became a yearly event. In Germany I conducted regularly, taking in one or two cities every year. In the East-European block I went to Prague, Warsaw and Bucharest and later to Budapest again. My engagements in Italy increased and several at the Opera House in Rome were added. That house achieved a high level of performance for a brief period under the directorship of Massimo Bogianckino and it was a pleasure to conduct there during his time. Copenhagen and Brussels were two more cities I visited regularly. The concerts and recordings in Holland continued, with one, for me, memorable operatic performance in Amsterdam (of which more later). Criss-cross touring with several orchestras has opened new horizons and provided a wide range of new experiences,

239

musical and otherwise. They also brought to the fore some extra-musical effects that music can have upon human relations, and the existence and possibilities of what could be called music diplomacy.

International tours of symphony orchestras are often official good-will gestures, and in such cases it is an accepted custom that the visiting body performs the two anthems, first the one of the host country, then that of the visitor.

The effect of this procedure is not always the same.

The London Symphony's visit to Israel under my direction was the first time that an orchestra from Great Britain had appeared there, and the event was not without significance.

Naturally, we had the two anthems in our luggage, the Israeli Anthem, the "Hatikva", having been rehearsed with special care. We had done more: we had asked one of the foremost British music arrangers to make a new orchestration of it for us. He did a most accomplished job; in fact, his ambition made him overshoot his target. Not only did he fashion sounds of most orgiastic splendour; he also employed imitative counterpoint. Thus, in our performance, the theme of the anthem was repeated – in imitation – one bar later. We liked this very much, and proudly performed it – to the horror of our first-night audience in Tel Aviv which filled the large concert hall to the rafters. They thought that we were unable to play their anthem "together".

After this "shameful failure" of the "otherwise so wonderful orchestra" had been aired in next morning's papers, we quickly asked for the local version of the anthem – and succeeded in satisfying the audiences with it from the second night onwards.

For an example with a different outcome let us go back for a moment to the Middle-Eastern tour of the Minneapolis Symphony in the mid-1950s, also a first occasion, this time for an American orchestra, in that part of the world.

In preparing for the event, I naturally asked the embassy of the countries we were to visit – Lebanon, Syria, Iraq, Iran, and so on – for their national anthems. Looking through the scores, I found all of them poorly orchestrated – indeed, unfit for performance by a full symphony orchestra.

That situation had to be remedied.

And I had the right man to do the doctoring.

The librarian of our orchestra, an elderly man then, had formerly been one of its trumpet players, and since his retirement as a performer looked after our music library like a ferocious watch dog. He was born in Germany, and after more than half a century in America still spoke with a heavy German accent, using strange turns of speech like "the onliest thing to do" and other gems of the kind. He saw only out of one eye, but with that one he saw a lot. His bearing was gruff and outwardly rather unfriendly, but there was no favour he would not willingly do for his colleagues, and his loyalty to "his" orchestra was boundless. Above all, he was a splendid musician and also a competent orchestrator, with several excellent arrangements to his credit.

He was called Hermann Boesenroth, but his surname was practically forgotten. He was our indispensable "Hermann".

I called him and showed him the anthems.

"What do you think of them, Hermann?"

"No goot."

"Hermann, have you a view on how a national anthem ought to be orchestrated?"

"Yes, Maestro, I hafe."

"Tell me."

"Every instrument plays all the time like crazy."

That convinced me.

"Hermann, you're the man! Take these anthems and orchestrate them for our tour."

Soon the new scores and parts were set out in his scrupulous handwriting, and when we tried them the anthems sang out, with a convincing ring, the praises of their countries.

Thus equipped, we left Minneapolis on our historic tour.

It turned out to be a genuine success, much talked and written about. But the truth is that we hardly needed to play our programmes at all in order to win our public. That was done, every time, during the playing of the national anthems, at the start of our concerts.

The audiences stood enraptured, goggle-eyed, transported into the seventh heaven. Those countries were young, their national consciences newly awakened, and their anthems were not yet casually accepted parts of a routine ceremonial but the living songs of their land. And it was the first time a large, fine orchestra had ever played them.

241

That was the real sensation of the tour, the real gift we brought them. Not only the audiences but the various authorities were swept off their feet. The state-controlled radio stations, the military, the governments sent emissaries with requests to have our rendering of their anthems immortalised.

We obliged as well as we could. At the end of some concerts, we repeated the anthems so that they could be recorded. Or we had copies made of our score and parts for them.

For some years thereafter, and in some countries – who knows? – even today, the official versions of the Middle-Eastern national anthems were those played in 1956 by the Minneapolis Symphony Orchestra.

That tour, as the various US foreign services reported back, "did more good for our international relationships than a dozen conferences". And to think that it was all due to Hermann Boesenroth!

In 1960 I went for the first time to Israel – on that occasion with the London Symphony Orchestra.

It was an arduous, concentrated, short season of about eight different programmes in no more than two weeks, as exacting as it was successful. It gave me an exciting first glimpse of that unique country, the greatest, most daring and most precarious experiment of our century.

My Israel experience was and is – for our contact and friendship continue regularly – one of the most remarkable.

In 1960, when I first went there, the country had already passed its first, heroic, period of being launched. This is a better word than "founded", for Israel was founded in biblical times, and still existed in Jesus Christ's time as Judea. Its resuscitation, as initiated by Herzl and his group and as carried out step by step until 1946 when the new state of Israel came into being, was one of the most singular of historic feats. Its final outcome is, alas, still in the balance.

What the new Israel has done for its land can be seen at a glance when approaching it by air. As the plane begins to circle in descent over Lod airport, it circles, in fact, over the entire country, and the arriving guest can clearly see its borders: Israel is green; where the yellow of the sand starts, the neighbouring Arab countries begin.

242

The degree to which the Israelis have conquered their country is as little known and appreciated as it is extraordinary.

And vice versa; the soil has conquered its conquerors too, much more than in any of the new countries. But then, Israel – as I said – is not exactly a new country, it's a renewed one.

I was fascinated to observe the change in the new Israeli generation, the Sabras (those who were born there are called by the name of the cactus flower) and even in those who went there young enough to come under the spell of the earth of Canaan. Their sudden identification with their soil is beautiful to see. They are a different race, erect and primitive in spite of their exaggeratedly high IQs and cultural heritage. As their ancestors were driven away from the soil and so to speak banished into the intellectual spheres of life elsewhere, so a great many of the new Judeans came hurrying back to "Mother Earth" and walked it with "bare feet".

A young Israeli, who came to America a long time before I ever set foot in Israel and was extolling in my presence the virtues of his new country, lit up that very point with a sharp beam by an involuntary *bon-mot*, as he pounded the table in excitement and exclaimed:

". . . And you will see, Sir, you will see . . . that if we continue as we are going, we shall have, very soon indeed, our first – illiterates!!"

What is behind the history of the Jews? How could they have suffered as they did? How could their land have been destroyed and they themselves have been driven out, then to return and remake it after two thousand years?

Races, nations, have their lifespans, like dynasties, families or individuals. When a race or a nation dies, it ordinarily dies of "old age". It is ripe to die when it does, and its way of dying is to be absorbed by – or rather first conquered, then absorbed by and mixed into – a new, fresh, potent race.

Thus the Persians were ripe to fall to the Greeks, the Greeks were ripe to become part of the Roman Empire, Rome was ripe to be conquered by the Visigoths, and so on.

The Jews, I submit, were not ripe either as a race or as a nation, to be obliterated or absorbed when conquest overtook them. They spread over the globe in the act of self-preservation, and their vitality could not be extinguished.

243

They continued living in the "deep freeze" of their dispersion, but could not live out their normal lives, could not be used up, could not grow old, until they resumed their former life and began to breathe again. This new life that they achieved thirty years ago will carry them back, as a race and nation, to the natural, normal, ineluctable, destiny of all nations, all cultures, all people.

Or so we hope – because another untimely Diaspora could have no better result than a new span of frozen eternity, and probably worse.

What I have tried to describe here is known in folklore, which echoes it in many tales; in that of the *Flying Dutchman*, and others.

The Jews are a people of great musical affinity and talent, though because of their long separation from the soil their creative ability has developed less forcefully (and less fully) than their performing genius. Jewish musicians of high attainment abound everywhere and every city, large and small, which has any Jewish community at all, has a core of a music-loving and understanding public.

In Israel itself there is one special reason for the love of music. Almost everyone there has come from somewhere else, of his own will or driven. The old countries are not easily forgotten, the memory of them lingers for generations. But everything that kindles that memory is, for many Jews, either painful or offensive or both. With one exception – music.

Music can be recognised and remembered without opening up old wounds – it carries no memories of humiliation, affront or grief.

The Israelis turn to music as a natural fountain of solace, the only pure relief they have. One would have thought that as the older generation died off, this would change. But over the seventeen years which is the timespan of my own observation, it seems that the new generation has inherited to the full the love and attachment to music of the old.

No wonder, then, that at an early stage, the Israelis set up their own symphony orchestra. It existed, in fact, before the state of Israel itself. It was then called the Palestine Philharmonic, and was founded by Bronislav Hubermann, the famous Polish violinist.

He was a fine, impassioned artist, of an unruly mind, who involved himself deeply in such idealistic schemes as the Pan-

244

European Movement, in which he was very active, and then in his own beloved project, the Palestine Orchestra, to which he devoted all his colossal energy.

He succeeded brilliantly and the first concert of the new orchestra, under the direction of Arturo Toscanini, no less, was an event noted all over the world.

The orchestra has been most active ever since. It has toured practically everywhere (except possibly in Africa), and has made its mark throughout the world.

It is of almost top quality, and will, as far as can be foreseen, stay so permanently, by reason of its inherent human make-up.

If we are ready to accept the idea that the Jews are the salt-and-pepper of humanity, we also have to concede that any food that consists of salt and pepper only is hot stuff indeed.

When I joined the BBC Symphony Orchestra in 1964, I was called into a directorial meeting and asked to say what I thought would be needed to make that fine orchestra even finer.

My answer was: "A dozen Jewish string players."

If I were to be asked the same question by the Israel Philharmonic, my reply would be: "About two dozen Anglo-Saxons, please."

The Israel Philharmonic Orchestra is a remarkable organisation, for its strong and weak points, equally. It is well known that no symphony orchestra can exist without large subsidies, from whatever sources they come. The only one which can maintain itself almost without outside help is the Israel Philharmonic. It virtually lives by its sale of tickets, which is unheard of elsewhere. Also unheard of is the number of season-ticket subscribers: some 36,000, and this in a country of a mere 2,500,000 inhabitants. As a consequence of this, every programme has to be performed twelve times until each subscriber has heard it. But this routine is bad for the performers, who have difficulty in concentrating on the same music played so many times in a row. So now a compromise has been reached. The main works in each programme are given twelve times, the surrounding numbers are changed after six performances.

The two Richards, Wagner and Strauss, are not performed in Israel. No law decrees this; they are simply not played, and any

245

attempt to do so would certainly provoke open hositility in some circles. There was and is much controversy about the issue. It is pointed out that Wagner's anti-semitism was theoretical rather than practical and had no connection with the Hitler régime; that Strauss was not an anti-semite at all and that his co-operation with the Nazi government, though certainly contemptible, did not in itself hurt anybody (as neither did Strauss himself), and that, furthermore, if such taboos are to be set up, they should be extended to include more than those two composers. But the unwritten ban remains.

Those who suffer most from it are the members of the Philharmonic Orchestra, for whom it would be very good to be able to include the difficult works of those two masters in their repertoire.

One day that ban will stop by itself. But until it does, as I have often told zealous Israeli music lovers, it is better not to interfere.

When I went first to Israel with the London Symphony Orchestra, I had already been invited to conduct the Israel Philharmonic, which I did, for the first time, shortly afterwards, still in 1960. Thereafter I came back every season for ten consecutive years, and conducted it on several tours. After 1970 my visits became somewhat less frequent, but our contact is still very close and personal.

To make music with the IPO is not a smooth process. The orchestra is moody and its manners are poor (as are those of the Israeli public which, apart from brilliantly fulfilling the public's first and foremost duty of being present, contributes precious little to the lustre and atmosphere of a musical event).

I demand more of the IPO than of most orchestras, because I know their well-nigh unlimited potential and am for ever discontented with their biblical display of human shortcomings.

In the Bible, I am reminded, much the same sort of thing occurs, and the story ends, with monotonous though alarming regularity, by Jehovah's wrath being aroused, the lazy chosen people being punished; catastrophe; repentance; forgiveness; and so on, *da capo*, *ad infinitum*. And this is the remarkable part of the story: through all of that the chosen people remain, for ever, "chosen".

The severity I have in my heart towards the Israel Philharmonic is that of love and pride. I wish I could protect them from their own

246

momentary failings as I would if they were my next of kin; and I dream of the splendour of this small group of people to shine forth like a beacon of complete achievement in the newly-born Israel.

In 1960 the Amsterdam Opera Company asked me to conduct a new production. Since my early Münster days I longed to return some time to opera not only as conductor, but also as producer (stage director). My relations with the Dutch musical world were so cordial at that time that I dared to propose a family project, an opera production done entirely by Dorátis: my daughter, Tonina, would do the scenery and costumes and I would be in charge of both the music and the stage. The idea was accepted and Verdi's *Simone Boccanegra* was chosen.

What resulted was one of the most memorable events of my musical life. When, nowadays, interviewers ask me about my happiest moment on the podium, I tell them it wasn't on the podium but in the pit, and it occurred exactly at the moment when the curtain rose for the third act of *Simone* and Tonina's splendid décor was roundly applauded.

That production was, in fact, a *tour de force*, achieved in the face of every sort of handicap. To begin with, the building itself, the so-called Stadschouwburg, was as big a hindrance as can be imagined: the stage was narrow and deep, and very poorly equipped; the orchestra pit was a small cavern, placed far too low and under the stage rather than in front of it. The orchestra was incredibly weak; it seemed incomprehensible that such a body should have been tolerated when, less than a thousand paces away, the public could hear the magnificent and proud Concertgebouw Orchestra. The chorus had little to brag about; and the cast, though young, ambitious and not without qualities, was far from first rate. Scenery and costume workshops produced only mediocre work. These were the ingredients we had to work with, and from it came a splendid-looking and adequate-sounding production that was repeated many times in successive seasons and was included (twice, I believe) in the fastidiously-selected programme of the annual Holland Festival.

The reason for this success was the probably unprecedentedly close collaboration of the scenic designer, costume designer, director and conductor, and their stubborn insistence on proper execution of their ideas.

247

The collaboration was simplified by the fact that the four facets of production involved only two people, and further by those two being members of one family, father and daughter.

If I dwell on that collaboration for a moment, it is because the occasions must be extremely rare when the entire production staff spends no less than six months in the closest contact in order to establish, co-ordinate, harmonise each moment, each detail of the entire material.

That is what we did, and that is what showed.

Our dramatic scheme was to bring the five tableaux of the opera – prologue and four acts – into the span of a single day: dawn – morning – noon – evening – night, also symbolising the career of its hero.

This scheme, which gave the entire drama great visual unity, was emphasised by backdrops of one basic colour for each of the five scenes, summarising, as it were, the time of day in which it was played.

The costumes of fourteenth-century Genoa were stylised and divided into colour-groups which made the adversaries in the plot easily distinguishable.

The reality or immediacy of the action was emphasised by means borrowed from expressionism and surrealism. I quote only two examples of this procedure. When, in the prologue, Simone discovers that his beloved Maria, daughter of the patrician Fiesco, has died – the focal point of the entire tragedy to follow – the producer is hard put to it to enable the audience to live through this moment of shock and grief with the hero of the drama. Most of the time a funeral cortège is passing across the stage, a not very effective device, for it is not at all clear whose corpse is being carried on the bier. In our production Simone entered Fiesco's house in search of his beloved, with a burning torch in his hand, and wherever he went, up and down staircases, looking into rooms, the wall of the house became transparent so that his progress became visible, until he came to the room where Maria was lying on her deathbed, with two nuns praying at her feet. Simone beheld that terrible, unmistakable sight. The torch fell from his hand, the house went dark; and he stumbled out into the night, towards his destiny.

The other moment when these expressionist methods were used occurred in the third act finale, when Simone, by then Doge of

Genoa, tries to reconcile the warring political factions of his city and crush the outbreak of a revolt. He then sings the deeply moving, heart-rending arioso: ". . . *e voi gridando: pace!*" – "I cry out to you: peace!" This sentence, clad in a superb, heart-felt melody, which signifies the climactic moment of the development of the hero's character, and shows him as the great spirit, the great mind into which he has matured, needed the strongest focusing possible. To give it the most immediate impact and to emphasise at the same time the universality and timeliness of the message, we lifted it out of the dramatic continuity of the play. Suddenly the stage went dark; Genoa, its senators and its people, became black shadows, mere silhouettes who could belong in any age and place. The ducal robes of Simone were hidden for that moment – all that could be seen was the transfigured face of a man who confronts us, and, stepping outside the artificial bounds of the theatre, urges us, with as profound an emotion as the human voice is capable of uttering: "Friends, people, make peace" – "*e voi gridando: pace! – e voi gridando – amor!*"

The lights came up gradually when that phrase had ended, and the drama continued.

Later, I was asked, at a meeting of the directors, what my advice for the institution's future would be.

I replied, "Go bankrupt – and start again."

Thus ended my brief popularity with the Amsterdam Opera.

In the mid-Sixties the period of my yearly guest appearances in Holland temporarily stopped. This had to do with the sudden and rude elimination from office of the man who had first brought me to Holland and who became a close friend, Anthony Adama-Zylstra, now retired and living in Fontainebleau. At that time he was director of Scheveningen.

Scheveningen, a name very difficult to pronounce correctly by anyone who was not born Dutch – it was the shibboleth used to detect undercover Germans during and after the Second World War – is a seaside resort and a suburb of The Hague, then extremely popular and with an international reputation. It has a fine beach, a row of large hotels and a great variety of entertainments, from symphony concerts to an excellent circus.

It must be very rare that so much should be concentrated in the hands of a single director, but that was the case in Scheveningen.

Anthony Adama-Zylstra was at the head of all the commercial and cultural activities of the place and it flourished largely thanks to his ingenuity.

He fell victim to his own qualities and his own achievement, which became so conspicuous that a group of real-estate entrepreneurs thought they could do better and bought up Scheveningen from under his nose. But they could not do better and now the once so popular concert seasons of Scheveningen have stopped altogether. It is hardly surprising that a number of artists did not feel like returning for a while, once their friend was no longer there.

For other reasons besides my co-operation with Tonina, the Amsterdam *Simone Boccanegra* remained for me one of my finest experiences during those years. It showed how a high-class performance can be achieved without star performers through thorough rehearsing, and proved once more the validity of the ensemble principle.

In the same class – applying my own measures, and not seeking either to explain or to justify them – was the first performance at the Rome Opera House of Stravinsky's *Oedipus Rex*, with the uniquely impressive and stunning sets and costumes by Giacomo Manzù. This was the eminent sculptor's first foray into the field of the theatre, and an unqualified success. I had the pleasure of conducting the production during two consecutive seasons.

The first time it was paired with Dallapiccola's *Il Prigioniero*, one of the few contemporary masterworks of operatic literature, which I had conducted previously at one of the Holland Festivals and later presented on the concert platform in Washington, and also recorded.

Dallapiccola came to both the Amsterdam and Rome performances and did much to help us present an authentic performance.

The next season saw the unusual pairing of *Oedipus Rex* with Strauss's *Elektra*. This was decided upon after much deliberation with Massimo Bogianckino, then artistic director of the Rome Opera, under whose leadership it rose, after a long period of drifting, to an eminence which it has failed to sustain since he left.

In retrospect the choice does not seem to have been happy, for *Elektra* is enough by itself for a full evening. Nevertheless, it was an experiment of memorable dimensions and impact. Our Elektra was Inge Borgkh, whose characterisation of the part was unerring. The scenic aspect of that production was, again, of personal interest to me. This time I did not act as producer, nor did Tonina design the sets, but the whole production was executed after my *ideazione*, as the Italians so beautifully put it.

An emergency conference was called by Bogianckino, who announced that there was no money for sets or costumes for *Elektra*. What other opera could we do instead? Many were mentioned, but upon closer scrutiny it appeared that none could be produced without sets and costumes costing more or less the same. At last, out of sheer desperation, I came up with the proposal that we should do *Elektra* with a minimum of scenery, by showing not the royal palace of Mycenae but its courtyard, an open place surrounded by a low wall and only the entrance gate of the palace itself – an open-air set as it were, under a steadily moving cloud-scape, projected upon the cyclorama in such a manner that the colours and shapes of clouds should harmonise with, or illustrate, the action and the music.

This idea was accepted and subsequently long rolls of film were painted with clouds of fantastic shapes and colours, and the projecting of them carefully timed so as to match the prevailing moods of the opera.

The device worked very successfully. Not only was it an interesting novelty in itself, but it also served as a sharp contrast to the elaborate construction of Manzù's sets.

Conducting engagements in London at the Royal Opera House, Covent Garden, would have been routine occasions, save for the fact that I was allowed to make a new English translation of Rimsky-Korsakov's *Le Coq d' or*, which was, I hope, refreshing not only for me but also for the audience. At my side to help me was Jimmy Gibson, of the Covent Garden music staff, who put my translation indefatigably into correct English. So correct, in fact, that I had to undo some of his doings more than once to make the text "livable". It was an entertaining task that resulted in a lively performance. After the first night Sir David Webster, then director of Covent Garden, remarked, "One should ask all conductors to make their own translations, then we should always understand what is sung."

Well, that would be one way to a most desirable end.

Conducting opera in Hamburg and Vienna was disappointing, and a lesson to learn. I should not have needed it, had I not been so foolish as to agree to conduct without or with sadly insufficient rehearsals. I was persuaded against my better judgment by Rolf Liebermann, then opera director in Hamburg, who no doubt meant well, as many conductors are able to conduct in that way – in fact, it is what suits them best. But not me – and I should have known that my strength is in thorough preparation, through which I can produce performances that have their own special flavour. I should also have known that this method does not mix with the prevailing routine of the large opera houses. So after those few evenings I said goodbye to "routine" for ever – only regretting that I had once dirtied my hands with it.

A splendid example of non-routine work in the lyric theatre was an evening at the famous Maggio Musicale in Florence, which I led at the request of its then artistic director, Roman Vlad.

"How many rehearsals do you want to hold with the orchestra and how much time do you need to have with the singers and dancers for a programme containing *Erwartung* by Schönberg, *The Miraculous Mandarin* by Bartók, and *Volo di Notte* by Dalla-piccola?" he asked me over the telephone.

I made a quick count, weighing up the state of the orchestra and the difficulty of the works, and stipulated: "Twenty-six orchestra rehearsals and six weeks' rehearsal time altogether."

"Have you six free weeks next May and June?"

I had.

"It's done," he replied and put down the receiver.

The six weeks were exciting, the performances good and successful, the costs staggering, but borne with elegance. As Mario Labroca, another friend of my Italian period and another prominent personality of the musical life of Italy, said in another context about the Italian music establishment, *"Siamo poveri ma signori."* "We are poor but we are gentlemen" is not a good translation of that sentence, for *"signore"* cannot be adequately translated. There is no word with the same flavour in the English language. (The Hungarian has one, but that word would be of no help here.)

252

With all my delight in the beauties of Italy, of its three millennia of culture, its language, its landscape, its fine arts, its music, with all my devotion to a handful of Italian friends, I never could feel at home there.

Yet I lived in Rome for a decade, from 1960 to almost 1970. We moved there from Minneapolis at Klári's wish (to which I offered no resistance) and settled in one of the most spectacular corners of the city, one of those from which one can clearly see why it is called "eternal" – and also why on deeper examination our dream of "eternity" must be judged misdirected.

It was wonderful to be able to contemplate the Roman Forum and the skyline of the entire "*Roma eterna*" from one's windows and roof every day. This awesome and beautiful view was a most powerful reminder of a great past, a sublimated image of three thousand years of civilisation in white marble ruins. Turning to the left, one saw the Campidoglio – its backside, to be exact; a fine, majestic sight, even so, of the building from which Rome was governed for about thirty centuries. Turning about, one confronted the gardens of Lucullus and the ruins of the Palatine Hill. Looking down, one found oneself above the Basilica Giulia in the Forum, with a good view of the Phocas Column, the Arch of Constantine, the temples of Jupiter, of Castor and Pollux, of the Vestal Virgins, and more. To the west one saw the top of the Aventine Hill.

All this was magnificent, eye-filling, thought-provoking. At the end of the train of thought the inevitable questions came up: "And where did all this lead to?" and "What will come next?"

When the eye has taken in and absorbed all the melancholy beauties of man-made glory destroyed by time and even more so by the human lust for taking things apart, an unquenchable craving for nature's God-made beauties fills the mind – or no, it is not the mind, it is the heart that becomes so ready to watch the small movements of a blade of grass in the morning breeze.

Friends – one has very few friends, no matter where one lives, and they are always very special people, never typical of their surroundings, but of the radiation that emanates from each person and forms affinities, reaching out for hidden kinships like invisible tentacles.

My Roman friends I have named already. Mario Labroca, who

253

died in 1974, was one of the last of that group of Italian musicians around Alfredo Casella, who in turn was on the periphery of Stravinsky's circle. The influence of Casella and his friends upon the musical life of Italy was very positive and would have been great if the political, and subsequently the economic, decline of the country had not stifled it, together, probably, with every other line of progress.

Labroca was a composer himself, of minor importance, but sincere and *soigné* in his work. Not very fertile. He was also an interesting writer, with sharp insights and a brilliant pen. His few volumes of essays, short articles and stories are a valuable contribution to the picture of musical Italy in his time. Early in his life his activities were channelled into managerial, organisational realms. He held a number of important posts, such as his directorship of the Maggio Musicale (it was in that capacity that I first met him in the 1930s). Then came a long stretch as director of the Italian State Radio (RAI for short), directorships at the Teatro alla Scala in Milan and at the Teatro Fenice in Venice.

One other person with whom if not a close friendship, at least a close acquaintance, developed was Giacomo Manzù. Our relationship was particularly close during the brief production period of *Oedipus Rex* at the Rome Opera House. While not a spectacular one, it was, perhaps, the most meaningful of my various associations with other artists of my time.

He intrigued me no end.

When I came back from one of my orchestral tours I would 'phone him and he would come, with his wife Inge, for lunch or dinner, arriving punctually, one might almost say austerely. He would stand for a moment in the doorway, a rather short, solid, but wiry figure, his dark, sparse hair crinkly and growing long over the back of his neck. His face was strong, energetic, watchful. It was full of wisdom – peasant wisdom.

While his verbal repartee is not the quickest, his riposts through his art can be very cutting indeed. About these feats of swordsmanship-in-sculpture, however, he is more silent than his statues.

Once, in his studio on Monte Avetino, Manzù showed me an enchanting group of two figures in clay. They were a girl and a boy, lying in the grass in a beautifully chaste embrace. The two youthful figures were as fresh and innocent as dew. The group had been commissioned, he told me, by an American university called Wayne

State, in the city of Detroit. Some time later he mentioned, amongst other things and not like anything that is important, with a shrug, that Wayne State had refused the sculpture as being immoral. That was all he said. He never brought up the subject again, and I completely forgot about it.

Until one day, when my destiny had me live in Detroit for a while. I was walking on the campus of Wayne State University, and stopped short at a bronze statue of a girl lying on the grass. It took me a few seconds to recognize my young friend out of Manzù's studio. She was alone. Her young boyfriend had vanished.

But had he?

As I looked around further, I saw behind the girl, about ten yards away, another bronze figure: a crouching, leering, faun-like male, on the jump, ready for rape and violence.

It seems that this version of the group *was* acceptable to the University authorities. I could almost see Manzù's quizzical smile as he made the new, "acceptable" version of the two figures.

One of his most celebrated works is the bronze door on the left front entrance of St. Peter's, with its twelve panels depicting scenes from the Old and New Testaments. The old masters often involved their own, images in their large paintings or sculpted compositions. Manzù did not do this. Nonetheless I think I have spotted him – to my great delight – peeping out from the skin of one of the little animals to be seen below the panels. He is a porcupine; and he winks at me, secretly, every time I pass that great door. That mischievous wink is my more or less steady companion. I think of it in situations when it is difficult to decide what to do – to be amused or angry, to laugh or to cry. It helps me to do the former.

25

WHILE WE RESIDED IN ROME THROUGHOUT THE SIXTIES, I WAS working mostly elsewhere.

I was not in tune with the way of music making in Italy, especially in symphonic music, and conducted there as little as possible.

Step by step, my centre of work became London.

The affection I conceived for that great city when I first went there during the 1930s increased during my long absences. When I began to go back regularly for an ever-increasing number of guest appearances I felt that I was going home, and was deeply happy, as I am now, every time I am in London.

Orchestras are curious beings, and the London orchestras are more curious than most. They would never thrive elsewhere. They can live, like the koala-bear, only in their native habitat. And for them that habitat is not Britain as a whole, but strictly London itself.

Between them, they provide one of the most exciting activities in that friendly monster of a city. Besides offering extremely high-class orchestral music, they are also a constant topic of conversation and argument. Much of what would normally belong to their private lives is discussed in public, as for instance fees and salaries, and what should be made public about them – for example the hardship of their rehearsal conditions, the fact that almost every concert they give is dangerously under-rehearsed and its achievement is a day-to-day miracle – is kept under the seal of strict privacy. They are respected, loved and speculated about.

It is said periodically that there are too many of them and that one – or more – should be eliminated. (The number of the proposed victims varies, as does their identity.) Actually, none of them can be "eliminated", that is, forced not to exist, except through an act of murder. These orchestras, like all other living entities, were born naturally; they live by their own strengths. They have the right to live out their lives until they die as naturally as they came into being.

At one time I told an official enquiry that to cut off one symphony orchestra from London because there seemed to be "too many" would be as stupid as finding an animal whose natural endowment was five legs and cutting off one of them because most animals have only four. London, with all its orchestras, is such an animal. We should accept the fact, and glory in it.

There are seven full symphony orchestras in London. Two are at the opera houses, Covent Garden and the Coliseum. The other five are the BBC Symphony, the London Philharmonic, the London Symphony, the Philharmonia and the Royal Philharmonic.

How splendid it would be if someone were to write a book giving these their full history. The resulting volume would be as entertaining as it was informative. But that someone will not be me. I will just say as much about them here as I think will suffice to make the reader understand why they are so special.

My first point is that, throughout the world, symphony orchestras are fully subsidised (by governmental or private means or both) and their artists salaried.

Three of the London orchestras are maintained on this pattern: those of the two opera houses and that of the BBC. The other four – and it is those who work the miracles – are co-operatives, owned and directed by their members. They do indeed receive subsidies, but not enough to guarantee their members a regular – that is to say, a salaried – existence. They are paid when they play and have no basic assurance how often they will play during any given season.

The economic and artistic administration of these four orchestras is thus very complex: long–term planning is hard to carry out, because the orchestras have to be ready to grab work opportunities as they come along; orderly programme planning of any sort is extremely difficult, because every programme has to be "sale-able", and because each of the orchestras contributes only a part of a general programme presented in one and the same concert hall, the Royal Festival Hall, and prepared in various rehearsal halls, not in the concert hall itself, which is shared by all and which cannot accommodate any participant for more than one rehearsal per performance.

That under these circumstances the Royal Festival Hall can boast such extravagantly rich and varied concert seasons is a feat that merits more admiration and respect than is actually given.

All the orchestras naturally want to present the best guest soloists, instrumental and vocal, but – at least in the 1950s and 1960s – could hardly afford to pay the cost of those in the top class. Some artists did appear with them at vastly reduced fees, because they loved these orchestras and loved London. For the rest they had to make do with those they could afford, among them a number of very fine young artists as yet unknown, which of course had its own advantages.

Again, the co-operative organisational structure of the four orchestras so constituted makes it very difficult to handle them managerially and direct them artistically.

In rehearsal and performance the London orchestras are the quickest, most adaptable, most disciplined, most co–operative and most agreeable groups to be met with anywhere, and their achievement in performance often surpasses the keenest expectations.

The problem of direction is that the directors, or boards, of the orchestras, who are most acutely and actively interested in guiding the destinies of their organisation, are, almost all, performing members of their respective orchestras and, with a very few notable exceptions, not competent managers. Nor do they have the time to be. So they engage managers from outside whose life they make utterly miserable by interfering in matters that should be none of their business. Thus to be the manager of one of the London orchestras has become the most dreaded appointment in that rather thinly-manned profession, and it happens very rarely that it is held for any length of time by anyone.

Also – and this is perhaps the most negative aspect of the orchestras' self-government – it sometimes happens that those orchestra members who take on directorial positions are not of the highest class musically. Thus a hierarchy of mediocrity can develop within these orchestra boards, with a tendency to perpetuate themselves rather than the organisation.

When this happens, the orchestra goes through a low period, lasting, often, for several years. So far, a strong revival period has always followed, beautifully demonstrating the orchestras' great inner strength. After a time of relative stagnation, the better, progressive elements take over, and an era of *élan*, achievement and general progress occurs. These periods always carry the orchestras to a higher level than they had reached at their earlier best, and – a special joy to behold – such a leap ahead carries the other orchestras along as well, by inciting them to similar achievement. The usual problem is for one of the other three orchestras, after a while, to "overtake" the one in the lead and thus there is a leapfrog-like development between the four orchestras. The general result is an exciting, pulsating musical life of a very high order, the like of which it is hard, if not impossible, to find elsewhere.

During the time of which I have knowledge, the best example of this sort of development took place at just about the end of the 1950s, when the performing standards of the London orchestras improved most radically, with the London Symphony Orchestra leading the way.

The first concerts in which I conducted the LSO were successful rather than good. But they were good enough to continue, and my at first casual visits soon became regular.

Soon I began to conduct recordings with them for Mercury Records, the American company which made my Minneapolis recordings. Thus started a very close collaboration with the LSO that was to last until 1964. The concerts – in London, throughout Britain, on the continent of Europe, in Israel, in Japan – are now memories. More durable are the many records we made, most of them still in circulation.

It was during that time that the LSO entered the ranks of the world's first-rate orchestras. I do not claim that this is my doing. The way those orchestras work effectively limits the power and influence of any single conductor. But although bereft of any executive authority, a conductor could – and can – show the way forwards, kindling the desire and providing the energy and atmosphere which will lead the orchestra's members to bring about the necessary improvements both within and by themselves.

This transformation – one of the finest I have ever witnessed – took place during my years.

The appearance of Ernest Fleishman as the LSO's new manager when John Cruft left to become a member of the Arts Council also proved momentous, for his gifts as an orchestra manager are well-nigh unique. He fully sensed the upward trend of the LSO, understood what it was about, and fostered it by taking an extremely firm stand, alongside myself, for quality. With his great organisational ability, resourcefulness, and energy he was of immeasurable help to the orchestra.

He was not always easy to get along with. But neither was I. And regrettably neither of us restrained our clashing temperaments. The result was that the "storm and stress" period of the orchestra often became much more "stormy" and "stressful" than was necessary. No single incident proved fatal to our relationship, but the gradual erosion which it suffered was undeniable.

This was the situation when one day a cable from William Glock arrived, asking me to conduct the BBC Symphony for two weeks. The two-week visit was soon repeated, and more and more occasions were added. Soon I was the *de facto* permanent conductor of that orchestra, and it was quite natural that after one year I was asked to become its official conductor-in-chief. The invitation was limited to three years. I accepted the post with pleasure, including the limitation, for having been with the BBC for one year already, I considered that three more would probably be long enough.

It was like a marriage with the bride seven months pregnant, because the very intense rehabilitation period of the BBC Symphony Orchestra was already in full swing at the time I was officially appointed.

The central figure in that revival was William Glock himself, who held the post of controller of music at the BBC and whose dream was to restore the BBC Symphony to the glory of the days when it was, for a while, the first orchestra in England, and the only one that Toscanini, when invited to Britain, would consent to conduct.

The post was of great complexity and the imaginative Glock (now Sir William Glock) was just the right man to make a success of it. His problem was that while the task in hand needed an executive who also was something of a musician, he was a musician who was also something of an executive. He had, indeed, great executive talent, but his passion was music. Thus he became easily engrossed in musical matters, which a true executive would not have bothered with personally. He had an incredible load on his shoulders, some of it of his own making. But I think he has always liked it that way: and, if so, he is lucky, for it is impossible for him to change his ways; he is always overloaded and keen to carry more.

He is also a pianist of considerable ability, and still plays in public now and then – with trepidation. One of his great predilections, which I fully share, is the music of Joseph Haydn. But this does not hinder him from being a stalwart defender of the music of our own time.

While Glock's responsibilities at the BBC were wide-ranging, my personal collaboration with him, though very close, was of course restricted to matters concerning the BBC Symphony. We spent countless hours – mostly late in the day and sometimes well into the morning – discussing its plans, and once or twice a year he came to my flat in Rome, where, closeted in my room, we arranged the season's programmes, a task to which we were both deeply devoted. We understood each other well and worked in fine harmony.

The name of William Glock was first mentioned to me by a mutual friend, Roberto Gerhard, the eminent Spanish, or rather Catalan, composer who left his beloved Barcelona at the time of the Civil War and made his home in Cambridge. We first met in the early 1930s, before that war broke out, when I was in Barcelona with the Monte Carlo Ballet and commissioned him to write an original score for the company. The name of the piece would have been "Mont Juic" and I saw sketches for it during return visits. But the war put an end to the project, and it was never revived.

In about 1957 Roberto was at Ann Arbor, a very active university town, as guest professor at the music faculty of the University of Michigan – a very active institution – and we met when I gave a concert there with the Minneapolis Symphony. It was on that occasion that he spoke to me in glowing terms of William Glock, who was then just about to get his job at the BBC. Roberto prophesied a veritable renaissance of England's musical life in consequence of that appointment.

He was not far from the truth.

Before my time the BBC orchestra had relaxed somewhat but had not lost its former fine qualities. A few changes in personnel were necessary, but not many. Glock had already engaged a new leader – as the concert master is called in England – before he contracted me, and had made a brilliant choice in Hugh Maguire. He also engaged an excellent new orchestra manager in the person of Paul Huband, who energetically revitalised the organisational affairs of the orchestra.

Thus in all directions much progress was being made. All that was missing was – a live public.

The microphone will not do – a gadget does not react. As long as performers are human beings, they will need a human audience. (In the same way, to my mind, an "electronic" performance is completely wasted on a human receiver. It should have an electronic public.)

I had to learn that truth in practice, while making music for the microphone.

Once I became acutely aware of the problem, I discussed it very seriously and in depth with William. He saw my point and wanted to do all he could to bring the orchestra into more direct contact with a live audience; in fact, to transform it into a "public" orchestra. But this could not be done.

For all that, we did not give up, and chalked up several victories in a basically stalemate situation. Thanks to William's efforts, the BBC Symphony did begin to play for far more live audiences than before.

The public concerts at the Royal Festival Hall in London had to remain at their former number, twelve per season. But there were other avenues. We increased the number of our concerts in other cities in England, going on brief tours several times each year. We also toured the continent of Europe, and, as our crowning achievement, made a very successful trip to the USA – the first the BBC Symphony Orchestra had undertaken to the New World – where we presented programmes devoted to the music of the present century. It was in the course of this tour that we gave the world première of Roberto Gerhard's Concerto for Orchestra, in Boston, and presented Jaqueline du Pré in her first American appearance, in New York, to mention only two of several interesting and important musical events connected with that visit.

The BBC Symphony also entered into the circle of my recording work and several records – such as the complete *Miraculous Mandarin* by Béla Bartók, Roberto Gerhard's First Symphony, and the prize-winning Chronochromie by Olivier Messiaen – preserve the memory of that exciting collaboration.

262

When I accepted my three-year post with the BBC, I knew that the life of a freelance conductor, of which I dreamed, would remain a dream for some time. I knew that at least for the next ten years or so I would prefer to take care of one orchestra only (or two, as it turned out).

So I planned accordingly and, when the three years were up, was ready to take on my next post.

26

I HAD NOT BEEN BACK IN STOCKHOLM SINCE 1954, THAT PLEASANT week, with its sunlit nights – it never got dark; one could read without lamplight all the time – and the cool North Sea breeze sweeping around the corners of that somewhat aloof, handsome city.

Music was made, there, comfortably – one could almost say nostalgically – with a kind of apologetic talent.

I felt I had been a success, that I would be invited again soon, and I was looking forward to some return visits.

But no word came, and Stockholm faded into a pleasant, pale blue-and-yellow memory. So much so that when, ten years later, in 1964, out of that pale blue-and-yellow, an invitation for a week arrived, it was more disturbing than agreeable. Yet all circumstances and conditions being right, I accepted.

After the first rehearsal three members of the orchestra wished to see me. They asked me whether I would be their principal conductor. This abrupt offer amused me more than it flattered me, and I did not take it too seriously.

I said a few friendly words and proposed that we should allow time for getting better acquainted.

The next day the managing director of the orchestra, Johannes Norrby, came along with the same proposition. These talks continued throughout the week, reinforced by the good playing of the orchestra during the rehearsals and concerts and the prevailing aura of good will and success. When I left, I was willing to continue negotiations. These lasted for nearly a year and ended with my acceptance.

So, after my BBC term, I was ready to go straight to Stockholm. Saying goodbye to the BBC Symphony was, again, a tearful affair. During the last weeks of my last season, William Glock very kindly arranged a concert of my works – we performed the Madrigal Suite and the Symphony in Five Movements – and members of the orchestra played my String Octet at a programme of chamber music. These went well and were well received. It was an emotional moment. When the last concert arrived there was a little ceremony afterwards, at which Hugh Maguire made a moving farewell speech. In my reply – during which I had to stop several times to find my voice – I said, as I very sincerely felt, that happy and grateful as I was for all that had been achieved, I deeply regretted that I had not been able to do even better for the orchestra.

I still feel the same way, and am constantly watching from a distance to see if one of my successors succeeds in what I failed to accomplish – that is, in liberating the BBC Symphony from its "slavery to the microphone". So far it has not happened, but perhaps one day it will.

My new Nordic world I found fascinating, and my tenure began auspiciously. The Stockholm Philharmonic was scheduled to play the United Nations concert on October 26th, 1966, in Paris, a week or so after I was due to arrive. I thought this would be an opportunity to make a small tour in France and possibly in Western Germany at the same time.

The suggestion was taken up, and so the previously rather retiring, stay-at-home Stockholm Philharmonic left its visiting card not only in Paris, but in Strasbourg and other French cities, as well as in the German Rhineland.

When we returned to Stockholm I found a cable from Hurok, my American manager, offering us a tour in the United States. I went to the Konserthuset – the orchestra's concert hall and also its offices – waving the cable like a flag of victory.

The victory was to be won two years later.

It is no small matter to send a European symphony orchestra across the Atlantic from its comfortable nest into the aggressively competitive life of the New World. The directors of the Stockholm Philharmonic, excited as they were by the prospect of touring the USA, were also rather frightened of it. So was the Minister of Education and Communications, to whom the matter was in due course referred since the orchestra was, and is, in large measure subsidised by the state.

None of the authorities seemed to believe that the Stockholm

265

Philharmonic would be good enough to handle such a tour successfully. This irritated me no end, for I would not have joined it if I had not been convinced of its very high potential.

The problem was not that of subsidy.

"Do you think our orchestra is good enough to undertake such a tour?" the Minister asked.

"Your Excellency, on the day of our departure it will be."

"What guarantee can you give us of that?"

In 1945 the same question had been put to me on the airport of Fort Worth, Texas, on a hot summer night, and my reply to it had gone down well. So I repeated it, changing its wording to conform to the local climate.

"My presence."

"And if you fail?"

"I shall commit suicide, of course."

My threat was not put to the test, luckily, for the tour was a resounding success. So much so that it was repeated, with the same or greater success, two years later.

The Stockholm Philharmonic proved to be a very fine body, much superior, indeed, to what it believed itself to be. Once the players themselves realised what they could accomplish, their confidence grew and the general level of their performance grew also. Gradually their feeling of being isolated, abandoned in a faraway corner of the world, vanished, and they came to believe what I often repeated to them: that in our time and age one is as isolated as one wants to be, no more and no less.

The limits of their development were drawn not by their musical ability, but by the inner and outer climates.

The long, dark winters of the north are depressing and just as inimical to the "lively arts" as is the great heat of the south: both thin out the blood and make men lazy.

It is true that our culture comes originally from the hot countries but it has moved into the temperate regions and has developed and flourished there at its best.

The north has its own rich culture as it has its own unique magic, which mixes badly with that of the warmer regions and has responded "coolly" to the invasion of the southern cultural influences. The last words of northern culture in our time have not yet been said, and the future may have magnificent surprises in store for us from that part of the world.

In saying that, I am not thinking primarily of music, or the fine arts as we know them; my fantasy is kindled by the stirrings of new art trends in textiles, architecture, films. A reminder of the indigenous strength of the north is not out of place, especially in connection with the arts, for up to the present Scandinavian art has been more or less a pendant to that of the more southern parts of Europe. We can expect much new inspiration from that region – or rather, our grandchildren can.

For the time being the social climate of the north seems to me the chief obstacle to free development of the arts, at least in Sweden. That vast and thinly populated country is, in a way, its own victim. Its trouble is, mainly, that it didn't have any trouble for a very long time. It is the country that has enjoyed the longest stretch of peace, or perhaps it would be better to say the longest time without wars. For Sweden's long peace does not exactly correspond to that blissful image that the word evokes in the minds of those who so crave for it and have had so little of it.

Where Swedish democracy will lead is difficult to foresee, and certainly I am in no position to prophesy its future. One thing seems certain – that the present state of affairs is not a final destination.

Looking around the earth's five continents, the thought is inevitable that once again on the revolving turntable of history an epoch of systems and ideologies is coming to its end and an era of individual leaders is bound to come.

Why?

Because the *demos*, as a body, cannot govern, and therefore the working power of democracy as such is fatally weakened. Its splendid, true and powerful premise was poorly stated at the outset. "All men are created equal" is such an obvious untruth that it cannot serve as a basis for a social structure. Ironically, this is, I think, a semantic problem, no more. I am convinced that those who thus formulated that basic democratic principle meant the right thing, namely that "human dignity is unassailable" or "the worth of a human life is absolute" or another sentence that would explain that *"being* human" is of equal value in spite of the differences of "human *beings*". Under the prevailing formula democracy is a fragile system, in its essence only valid for one

267

generation at any given time – a generation that has experienced the opposite. No one I have spoken to, read or heard about, has understood democracy, unless he has come to it from the other end. No one who is born in a democracy is, or can be, a democrat, for he will not understand that being part of one means active contribution to it, and not a "free ride".

It is, of course, impossible to generalise about character and establish ethnic or national types of clearly defined profiles. Still, it can be said that the Swedish are a rather withdrawn and sensitive people who are easily hurt and not aggressive or spontaneous enough to defend themselves or to fight back if attacked – or if they feel attacked – in a like manner. They carry their hurts within themselves for long periods of time, brooding, suffering, sometimes scheming.

The match of that northern atmosphere and my own very different temperament was not an easy one; the difference between their organised *laissez-faire* and my vehement professionalism was tremendous.

That nevertheless seven good years of superior co-operation resulted – and more, a lasting and, I can safely say, mutual, affection continues to the present day – proves that a meeting upon a high level of communication did take place, notwithstanding the difference or, perhaps, because of it.

At the time of my arrival the managing director of the Stockholm Philharmonic, as well as of the Concert House itself, was, as I have said, Johannes Norrby. He held that post for over thirty years and was, besides, director of Stockholm's excellent Philharmonic Choir.

His father was a clergyman, and he himself had many callings besides music, among them botany. He told me that he became director of Sweden's most prestigious orchestra by answering an advertisement. There was, surely, more to it than that. His main interest was vocal music. He sang in many vocal ensembles – including quartets with Jussi Bjorling, who in his short life became one of the most celebrated Italian (!) operatic tenors of his time – and trained and conducted many choirs in Sweden.

His long régime at the Konserthuset was an unqualified success. It was not an easy position. Owing to the peculiarities of the

Swedish character no business there is ever cut and dried. The skill with which Johannes navigated the lagoons of administration was as phenomenal, in its own quiet way, as the seafaring feats of the Vikings.

Indeed, going in and out of his calmly ordered office, one had the impression that little if anything ever happened there. What one saw was the exact opposite of the great modern executive hustle, with six telephones ringing at the same time, scurrying secretaries and barked-out orders. But everything went on without a hitch, in even-tempered understatement, always somehow on schedule.

Yet Johannes, in his special, Nordic way, could also lose his temper.

Our very close friendship started on one of those rare occasions.

One evening I was in a foul mood. It is not important to explain why. My reactions to the lapses and imperfections of the players were unfriendly and counter-productive.

After the concert Norrby came into my room. He sat down heavily; he is a rather short, stocky man, with a great, bald head and round face, of enormous bodily strength and movements that reflect it.

In a voice that had descended to deep bass out of sheer anger he said: "It is a crime to conduct an entire evening without a smile."

I sat there, opposite him, wearing *my* darkest face, unrelenting, silent.

After a long time, he said, still in a tragic voice: "Let's go and have a drink."

We went. And in the course of that drink — and several more that followed it — a deep understanding and friendship was born. Each of us profited from the other's way of life, philosophy and outlook. Johannes, I think, learned something about my fanatical, unrelenting quest for perfection — never to be attained, ever to be pursued — and he helped me greatly on my road towards self-control and a readier understanding of other people.

This friendship was most welcome to me at that particular time. Its soothing wisdom was there, unbeknown to its dispenser, as a quiet background against the turmoil through which my private life was passing during those years. My long marriage, which had started in youthful bliss, was now ending in agonising pain; it would have been difficult to believe that this could ever happen. It would have been even more difficult to imagine that out of the almost unbearable suffering – caused and endured – a new, hitherto unknown world of harmony and serenity would emerge, as blinding at first as the pain was numbing.

Nothing in life happens without cause, and the roots of this personal upheaval could of course be traced. But I am not writing in this book about my innermost private life, and so mention of these events must be made only in passing. If this is to be a truthful chronicle I cannot omit them altogether, for they have, obviously, their bearing on my musical life, which is my main subject matter.

To say less would not be possible.

To say more would be too much.

Not only does nothing in life happen without a cause: also, nothing in life happens without effects. Thus during those years of stress, the emergence of a new dimension of my musical life, a re-orientation, a new start, has to be noted.

A conductor, as I see it, has also to be a champion, a warrior, a defender of a cause. Conducting alone would not be enough. This probably has something to do with the inherent insufficiency of conducting as a profession. Basically, it isn't a profession at all. It is merely a musical occupation, and of course all conductors *are* defenders of a cause. Most often the cause is the conductor's own career. But there are others as well, such as serving a composer, a great master whom one worships. Moreover, there are several choices. It is a splendid and worthy task to devote a lifetime to the performance of Beethoven's works, for instance. It is equally worthwhile to put oneself at the service of a revered master who is not recognised, or has been forgotten, by the public. It was my lot – of which I am proud – to be a disciple and propagator of Béla Bartók's music from my early youth. It was a great task to pave the way for him, to be his advocate before a multitude of people, who, I felt, *had* to know what Bartók wrote and to become his friends and followers.

This battle was won in the Fifties. A decade after his death, Bartók was universally recognised and admired, his music widely performed.

I do not know how my performer colleagues felt when such a

task was achieved. Satisfied? Triumphant? Perhaps. I felt somehow flat and let down. My feeling was similar to that which I experienced at the end of each school term, when I had successfully come through it. I was sorry it was over. My question was always, "What next?"

That was easy to answer during my school years. But now, "what next?" was a great problem.

I had to admit in all sincerity that after Bartók no other contemporary composer in need of a champion interested me sufficiently to make me go into the ring for him. The very young ones, by the nature of things, were not for me to serve: to discover, perhaps, but not to promote; if for no other reason than that their works were not yet written.

It is in the nature of things that the creator has to supply the material to the performer. The latter, if he aims at achieving definitive performances, must do more than study and learn one or two of his composer's works. He must be familiar with the latter's complete personality, which can seldom, if ever, be grasped through a single work. Not only does the composer need years to build up an *œuvre*; the performer also needs years to assimilate that *œuvre* so as to make himself ready to provide its re-creation.

From this it follows that the apostles, the disseminators, of a great composer's work must be of a somewhat younger generation than himself.

To turn to the great masters of the past is but natural. But my *condottiere* nature needed a new battlefield. This the old masters scarcely yielded. They were already fully known.

Or were they?

Of one of them, at least, this could not be truthfully said. And so I returned to the renewed study of one of the classics for whom I had a very special adoration during my childhood and who, as I came to realise more and more as time went on, was much misunderstood and neglected in our own day.

In my parents' home we had played, in the family and with my father's pupils, all the string quartets of Joseph Haydn. This left an indelible impression on me.

It was to Haydn's works that I now returned. And they opened up before me a new, hitherto unknown world, filled with the delights of harmony, form, sentiment, wit, passion, serenity.

The symphonies I looked at first. I knew some of them, perhaps more than most people often hear. But I had only an inkling of the treasure that lay hidden in that pile of scores, some of which were rather difficult to obtain. They came in several different editions, some rather badly manhandled, "re-edited", in nineteenth-century fashion.

Fate came to my aid in the shape of Universal Editions in Vienna, which had just issued a complete edition of the scores of all of Haydn's symphonies, carefully edited from their original texts by Robbins Landon. This was my cue – I did not have to wait any longer.

Seeking to bring this immense volume of 107 works before the public (there were more than that in the end), I realised that performing them in the concert hall would take many years, probably more years than I have left. So I conceived the plan of recording them. I had by then made well over 300 records, so I had enough experience to know the ways and means of organising such an undertaking. I worked out a complete schedule, to the last detail, including the timings of all the symphonies, the timings of the proposed recording sessions, the orchestra with which I wanted to make the records – everything. I then began looking for a recording company that would be interested. Having just concluded a period with an exclusive contract I was now a freelance recording conductor and could go anywhere.

This was the first time that I approached recording companies – before, they had approached me. But my time as a "travelling-salesman" did not last long. The third recording company I approached showed interest.

The new young director of Decca Records, Ray Minshull, took to the idea with enthusiasm. His elders and superiors were not easily convinced, but he succeeded in winning them over. So, after about a year of negotiations, the recordings of the complete edition of Haydn's symphonies began.

This was the start of an extremely harmonious collaboration, which continues in full swing as I write these lines. Not that I would have given up my freelance status, but the relationship is even closer the way it is.

Ray Minshull proved a fine and active partner, receptive to ideas and not without his own. He is also an excellent recording director, though we have not worked together in that way. My recording director at Decca is James Mallinson, still very young, although now eight years older than when we made our first record together.

Thinking back upon the recording directors I have worked with, I have to admit that I have been lucky. From Wilma Cozart, Harold Laurence, van Gineken at the start, to Erik Smith, the last so far, they are a splendid collection of people to whom I owe deep gratitude. James Mallinson has even within this very distinguished group a special place. A small present I once made to him I inscribed "to my young brother-in-arms". I cannot describe him better.

Our main work, and our first, was the complete edition of Haydn's Symphonies on records. Although it is not the first to have been done, it is now regarded as the one and only. As far as I know, it is the most complete version to date, and, one can say, the "definitive" one – until another, even more "definitive" one, comes forth. And so on.

Haydn's "complete" symphonies consisted, at the end, of the following material: the 104 symphonies already known; the two newly-discovered early, pre-Eszterházy symphonies called "A" and "B"; the "Symphonie Concertante"; alternate versions of Symphonies 22 (the "Philosopher") and 63 (la "Roxolane"); three additional (discarded) finales of Symphony 53 and the first – later altered – version of the finale of Symphony 102.

To record all these took three and a half years. As a member of the orchestra, an amateur statistician, reported, this meant 281 recording sessions, or 843 hours.

If I dwell on this event in my professional life, I do so with good reason. It was, in my evolution as a musician and a human being, of crucial importance. I believe that I understood this unique opportunity, and that I allowed the wholesome, nourishing influence of the experience to penetrate into me as far as my modest capacities were able to accept and digest the strong food.

Belatedly, I became what Leo Weiner, my chamber-music teacher, prophesied in one of his rare, generous moments that one day I would become – a good musician.

I can say that now, without blushing.

Also, I think, a better man.

To describe the influence Haydn's music had on me would mean to describe, first, that music itself. Alas, I cannot. The history of it has been desc,ibed, its musical, aesthetic, comparative analysis provided, in masterful fashion. The great five-volume work by Robbins Landon, now almost complete, is perhaps the definitive opus on the subject.

But the innermost content of this music defies any other approach but the musical, as does Mozart's.

It was my incredible privilege to have been permitted to experience that gigantic *œuvre* from the inside, to have been occupied with each note of each movement of each symphony in detail. There was no bowing which I did not think out in its practical and musical context to the best of my ability: no phrasing, no agogic instance of any participating instrument, that I did not devotedly consider, in the symphonies both taken as individual entities and as parts of the whole range. I worked out the interrelation of phrases, movements, complete symphonies to each other and to their composer. His life, the years he spent during the creation of this huge cycle, the incoming and outgoing influences – whatever could help me to penetrate into the core of these great works I took into account.

This description does not convey much: it is the normal way to study every score. My object in bringing it up here is twofold: first, to show that if the method of study was nothing out of the ordinary, the amount of it was unusually great, as was the energy needed to find one's way through such a vast, virtually uncharted field; and secondly to emphasise that during all that time of preparation – and later during the three and a half years which spanned the performances – no thoughts other than purely musical ones entered my mind in their regard: no literary or other analogies or comparisons; only the music.

This is also why that music defies verbal description. There are no words for it, there are no necessary associations with extra-musical thoughts or pictures that would fit. One cannot talk of sunrise, fate, and so on in connection with Haydn's symphonies; they are what they are: music, musically expressed.

Only two other composers, Johann Sebastian Bach and Mozart, had this same quality of the absolute.

Even when dramatic situations in operas or other music for the stage are being illustrated, they are stripped to their purest essence which tolerates, and even demands, that purely musical approach.

When Haydn writes music to a play called *Il Distratto (The Absent-Minded)*, he succeeds to perfection in letting us feel the subject matter, but he does not try to illustrate. He "musicates". At one point only does he make an obvious joke: the violins play a wrong chord, and then tune up; they "forgot" to tune their instruments before starting to play.

Also hard to convey in words is the great, once-in-a-lifetime experience of being closeted with that kind of absolute music for now over a decade. Of course, this is open to everyone, but it seems that a special incentive is necessary to gather the courage actually to undergo it.

Another aspect of the experience will be easier to describe: that of watching a great mind, as it developed over a long lifetime. Haydn wrote his symphonies over nearly forty years. We do not know for certain whether or not he wrote any before 1757 – if he did, they are lost. We know that he wrote his last symphony – the great "London" – in 1795.

Thus, he composed symphonies from his twenty-fifth until his sixty-third year. (Mozart's entire life was three years shorter than that period.) From the first note of his first symphony until the final one of his last an enormous development took place in the man and in his music.

From the start to the finish he trod a path, not straight but unbroken. To observe his progress at every turn, to follow, re-live his gathering of strength and experience, the unfolding of his mind, his sentiment (his soul I would say if I dared), to watch his talent flowering into genius, and to be allowed to employ one's own small capacity in attempting to show all this to others is an exhilarating, unbelievably, unimaginably beautiful experience.

To find the orchestra to fulfil this gigantic task was another problem. It had to be one which was at home in the style required or at least was not alien to it, and which had the potential to acquire it.

It also had to be one which had enough time to devote to such a project, if the work was to be accomplished within a realistic period.

A normal symphony orchestra schedule is too crowded to allow for nearly three hundred recording sessions within the time I wanted them to take place.

A special orchestra was needed – special in every way.

There was one.

In 1956, during the tragic Hungarian uprising, many thousands of people had left their country for ever. Among them were about eighty very fine young Hungarian musicians who then gathered together in Vienna and decided to form an orchestra.

This was not as easy as it at first seemed; their struggle for survival was pathetic.

To their great good fortune an enterprising man heard about them: Nicholas Nabokov, who was then presiding over an institution in Paris called "Congrès pour la liberté de la culture" – the Congress of Cultural Freedom.

Nicholas Nabokov, a cousin of the writer Vladimir Nabokov, was one of the most colourful people I have ever met. He came from a family of affluent Russian nobles, and left Russia during the 1917 revolution.

He composed several operas, ballets, and works for full orchestra and chamber orchestra, and had a moderate success. The best known of his work is probably the ballet *Union Pacific* which he composed in 1935 for the Ballets Russes de Monte Carlo, as I have described earlier.

During his adventurous life he taught at American universities, wrote at least two books – one a recently published and splendid volume of memoirs – and did an incredible variety of things. At the end of the Second World War, as a civilian member of the US occupation army in Europe, he controlled theatrical and musical activities in Germany.

His interest was catholic, in fact had no limits, neither had his gregariousness and his gift for verbal communication. He knew about everything, from the secrets of the Pyramids to the private life of Buddha and Solzhenitsyn, and was personally acquainted with everybody from Stravinsky to de Gaulle and Pius XII.

Nicholas pricked up his ears when he heard about the Viennese Hungarian Orchestra, which by then called itself the Philharmonia Hungarica. Here was a freedom-seeking group of artists who were

276

trying to establish themselves and make a livelihood in the dream-land of liberty in which they had just arrived.

He flew to Vienna, met the group, liked it, and swung into action, asking the Rockefeller and Ford Foundations for subsidies to help them on to their feet. The foundations were interested – the refugee Hungarian cause was much on the public mind – but wanted an orchestra specialist's opinion. Would it be a worthwhile effort to subsidise it?

Nicky turned to me. I was then in the Middle East, on tour with the Minneapolis Symphony, and very willing to stop over in Vienna on my way back.

Hearing the orchestra, I found it promising enough to recommend. What it lacked most was discipline – which I thought it would easily acquire once its existence was secure. (As it happened, it did acquire many fine qualities over the years, but discipline – never.) On the strength of my recommendation, Nabokov then put through his request for a subsidy to the two great foundations. It was granted on one condition – an absurd one. We – Nabokov and I – were to guarantee that within three years from that time the Philharmonia Hungarica would have a permanent residence somewhere.

What could we do?

Nothing.

What did we do?

The wisest thing possible. We went to Grinzing and got thoroughly drunk on "Heuriger", the young local wine, as dangerous as it is delicious – and gave our guarantee.

Our consolation was that even if after three years we did not succeed in finding a permanent home for the orchestra, we couldn't be shot – and anyway by then it would have survived long enough to prove its worth to the world.

We were lucky. The place *was* found. It was our own and the orchestra's good fortune that the young managing director whom we engaged for the young orchestra was nothing less than a special kind of genius.

His name is Heinrich Kraus, to which he now adds the titles of Doctor of Economics and Law, and the official Austrian distinction of Professor. Since that time he has gone far: for some years he was economic director of Vienna's famous Burg Theater, and today is one of the two co-directors of the more modern Theater in der Josefstadt. He it was who found the Philharmonia Hungarica a home in the small city of Marl in Westphalia. Even more important, he has got it officially accepted as one of the symphony orchestras supported by the West German Republic.

Unfortunately the city of Marl, while doing everything to make their new orchestra feel at home, failed to provide it with a concert hall. The existing Municipal Theatre was judged good enough for concerts, but wasn't. With the lack of a proper place for performing orchestral music, it was impossible to develop a musical atmosphere in the city, recently invaded by a number of large industries and correspondingly culture-hungry.

But the expected cultural "boom" did not materialise. The small community of Marl stagnated. No more than ten concerts could be given there during one year. The Philharmonia Hungarica had to make its living outside its city, and became what is known as a touring orchestra. Its inherent talent remained surprisingly strong and powerful, but the quality of its actual performances dwindled, due to insufficient leadership.

Yet it was *the* orchestra to play the Haydn symphonies for their complete recordings.

I thought of it at once.

First, it was a group not dissimilar in race and temperament to that which played these symphonies under Haydn's own direction – and I was certain that after the accumulated musical experience of two centuries, it would play them very much better.

Second, it was the one orchestra which had the time to do it. It went on tours every year for the best part of the season. One could also engage it for "tours" into recording-land as well, with the added advantage that it could remain at home at the same time.

Third, the outlay would be acceptable to the recording company, which might undergo a risk in the hope of a profit, but was no Maecenas.

My proposal was accepted by all, and regretted by none. The beginnings were full of problems, but they were overcome. A splendid recording hall was found by Decca's sound-wizard Kenneth Wilkinson in the St. Bonifatius Church in Marl. The orchestra gave exemplary performances, the recording company gained confidence. In spite of Ray Minshull's missionary work, the senior directors did not at first agree outright to record all the symphonies. But I cheerfully accepted part-contracts, being cocksure of final victory. In the end the entire series was finished in what could indeed be called record time.

On the day of our last recording session (December 2nd, 1972) Decca presented us with a "silver disc", commemorating the sale of 500,000 records of the series. The "gold disc" celebration of 1,000,000 sales took place not long afterwards, and the second gold disc is due any time now, as I write this.

In my thank-you toast to the orchestra I said, "From now on you have a new problem. You will always have to play as you did on these records."

Three more events concerning my private life fell into this period, the end of the 1960s and the ensuing four years, which must be mentioned here, briefly.

One is Tonina's marriage to Ralph Brown, Jnr. in London; the other the birth of her son, Nicholas, in Rome, two years later.

It is not my good fortune to see as much of them as I would like to. Our periodical visits allow me to glimpse the emergence of a very interesting, promising child, and give at least a taste of that ultimate dimension in life of being an "ancestor". A grandfather is the youngest representative of that species. I also hope that young Nicholas is conscious of having what he calls – in Italian – a *"nonno"*.

The final event is the advent of Ilse.

She hails from Innsbruck, the capital of the Austrian Tyrol. Her name is Ilse von Alpenheim, which she continues to use, as she always did, in her professional career as a pianist.

We first met in Salzburg in 1959, when she came on a brief visit. I was ill at that time and sat there saying little. She was beautiful and friendly, very quiet. If, at the end of that short, formal visit, anyone had told me that this young woman would be my wife, mate, friend and partner for the latter part of my life, I should have recommended that he be sent to a lunatic asylum instantly.

We met again, professionally, about two years later, to do a concert together in Zürich. It was a thoroughly agreeable musical experience. I liked her natural, quick-witted, always alert musicianship, and enjoyed her well-judged, spontaneous yet disciplined performance and the beautiful sound she elicited from her instru-

279

ment. During the next eight years we met sporadically, and had some intermittent professional correspondence which yielded nothing, for our paths in the concert hall did not cross again.

What happened in the summer of 1968 cannot be either explained or understood.

Witnesses, hostile or friendly, have proposed various theories, from the sudden last sexual flaring-up of an ageing man to witchcraft, exercised maliciously – and successfully – by a vampire (the kindlier theories are less interesting). Even we ourselves have tried in vain to discover the logic appropriate to the process that brought us together. Yet there must be a very high logic somewhere, to something that has made such good sense.

It can be seen in chemical experiments that two fluids, each of them turbid, when mixed together, yield a third, new, completely transparent liquid.

Transposed into the phenomena of human nature, this is what has resulted from our union.

27

When I left Minneapolis in 1960, I thought that my professional life would from then on take place in Europe. But soon, gradually, a return to America began to shape up.

After 1960, I first returned to the USA with the BBC Symphony, a memorable tour of which I have spoken already. Then came two visits with London's Royal Philharmonic, followed by two with the Stockholm Philharmonic. Also I again began conducting American orchestras, amongst others those of Chicago, Boston, Los Angeles and Washington, DC.

It was there, in 1968, that I was asked if I would take over the directorship of their National Symphony. The pattern repeated itself: I had not thought of a new permanent post in the USA; I did not want it, but was then persuaded to accept.

Little did I know what hornets' nest I was stepping into.

The outgoing régime had left behind a decidedly sulphurous odour. The 1969–70 season had been marked by a long, odious strike of the orchestra personnel and a near bankruptcy. The legacy of all this was a discredited, disoriented, discouraged bunch of performers, a less than competent board, a justly hostile press and a distrustful public.

At the time when I was approached, I was not aware of these circumstances, in spite of various messages of warning, some well meant, some doubtless less so. Had I been, I should surely have refused to go to Washington, and my life would have been perhaps simpler as a result.

Simpler, yes, but not fuller. Looking back, I can see that I did not merely occupy a post in Washington, but that my presence there had a special purpose. In retrospect I believe that destiny ordained that in my seven-year tenure of that appointment I should make my most important professional contribution so far, and I am profoundly grateful for the opportunity.

It was, also, in spite of all the inherent problems, a very happy period of my life.

The discouraging factors were amply compensated by the truly spectacular growth of the National Symphony Orchestra from practically nothing into a splendid body with more than a strong claim to international status. The magnificent individual and collective spirit of the orchestra and the fine human relationship that soon developed between us were invincible.

It is no secret in musical circles in the USA that the board of directors of the National Symphony and I did not get along. Basically the question never was, who is right? In fact, there was no question at all. There was, instead, a difference in attitude and purpose. They hired me to do a job. I tried to fulfil a mission.

Already, long before I went to Washington, I had the reputation of an orchestra maker or orchestra doctor. Since the success of the National Symphony during my years with them, I am probably branded with that irritating epithet for life.

In fact, I have no secret, no method, no special trick or technical faculty to make an orchestra play well. No conductor has that. Knowledge of one's material, rehearsal-planning, and so on will not suffice. The gift is to make an orchestra *wish* to play well, because, if it so wishes, it will do so. What a conductor must be able to do is to interest and involve an orchestra. That is not as easy or obvious as it may seem.

An orchestra is a complex body of many very gifted, highly skilled artists.

The duality of an orchestra player's life as half individual and half group member makes for the development of complicated personalities. While the performer's achievements are often lost in those of the group, his disappointments remain always intensely personal. This gives a sharp, defensive edge to his critical disposition, an added degree to his resistance and an overdose of sensitivity.

That is a thick wall to penetrate.

It is the conductor's task not only to penetrate it, but to tear it down, for this self-protecting mental mechanism must vanish during the hours of performance of a fine orchestra. No matter what happens during twenty-two hours of the day, from eight to ten in the evenings a perfect working commune has to exist on the platform.

Here, in a nutshell, is the inside job of the orchestra conductor.

There can be as many approaches to it as there are personalities attempting it. Mine, which I willingly state for possible use by others, is simple: thorough preparation, complete dedication and utter honesty.

The greatest compliment I ever received – I record it here, though it exposes me to the reproach of being vain – was spoken by a member of the Washington Orchestra to a colleague as they walked to the exit in Constitution Hall after one of our concerts. He was overheard to say: "I am ashamed of myself that I did not always play like this."

Constitution Hall, the home of the DAR – no, not the initials of a people's republic beyond the Iron Curtain, but those of the venerable association of the Daughters of the American Revolution – is a splendidly placed white building on Constitution Avenue, between the equally splendid buildings of the International Red Cross and the Pan-American Union. It was no more intended to be a home of music than its neighbours. Nevertheless, it was the arena of Washington's music life for four decades or more. I conducted in it the first concert I gave in Washington in 1937 and the entire first season of my music directorship there in 1970-71.

A rectangular auditorium, a parallelogram turned with its long side stageward, in an overall colour scheme of white, blue and dust, adorned with innumerable stars, spangles and banners, it has acoustics to take one's shirt off: its stage, or concert platform, is too small; its backstage non-existent.

It is elementary that music cannot flourish in a place where it cannot be heard. Would anyone think of trying to display a painting in a room that is completely dark? Yet, time and again, for years and decades in a row, music is listened to in rooms that are "pitch-black" for sound.

In all probability I would have failed in Washington, or would have fled prematurely, if I had had to continue in Constitution Hall. But luck, as so often, was with me, and soon I had a powerful ally: the Concert Hall at the new Kennedy Center.

Washington's single great and decisive contribution to its own cultural growth, the J. F. Kennedy Center for the Performing

283

Arts, was long in coming. Over the years, during my visits to the city, I saw its scaffolding and steel frame in various stages. When I was told that it would be opened in the autumn of 1971, I did not believe it.

On a rainy day in 1970 I and a number of other interested people were shown through the half-ready building by Roger Stevens, the moving spirit of the entire project and now the Center's chairman-director.

During my first year with the NSO we met Roger Stevens and his wife socially and talked at length of the Kennedy Center, as it was to be. He was rather taken aback – and others with him – when I said that the Center must be the home of the NSO. I, in turn, was taken aback by their being taken aback. Only then did I realise how low the local opinion of the local orchestra was, and how little confidence the community leaders had in its future.

It is impossible to overstate the importance of the Kennedy Center to Washington. To grasp it fully, one must take a look at the place itself.

Washington, DC is not a city of natural origin. On its site there never was a small settlement of people who came there to rest, water their horses and eventually settle down. The quadrangle of a few square miles on which it lies on the estuary of the Potomac was detached from the territories of the states it borders and made "stateless" in order to house the government of the country. It was named the District of Columbia.

In order to shelter its government from the lures and sins of the big cities, the States of the Union placed most of their governing bodies not in their greater metropolises, but in small townships, segregated or, so to speak, quarantined, to preserve their purity. Whether or not this idea was successful is another story.

Those small cities never developed beyond their role of housing an administrative body; cultural, commercial development took place in the surrounding "natural" cities. So Albany remains permanently in the shadow of New York City, Springfield in that of Chicago, and so forth.

Unfortunately – or rather, as an optimist sees it, fortunately – the seat of the Federal Government of the USA has no shadow in which to hide. There cannot be a skyscraper tall enough, a bridge wide enough, a factory large enough to overshadow the

284

capital of the United States, which stands there open, naked, for all the world to behold. Washington does not "belong to", it "represents", its country.

It has no choice: it must develop from a housing project into a real city; that is, into a multi-purpose place with all the necessary attributes of an *urbs*. It is a long process, and Washington is well along the road. In its present state the development of its cultural life is of crucial importance.

The yardstick by which the life standards of any epoch are measured is its cultural status. As one cabaret artist of sharp wit and tongue put it in my youth, "We all know where the Raphaels, Titians, Leonardos of the Renaissance are hanging. Where its politicians hang – who cares?"

The need for cultural expansion in Washington has long been felt, and with reason. The exquisite National Museum, the Smithsonian Institute and many other institutions are answers to that need. The John Fitzgerald Kennedy Center for the Performing Arts was a further step forward and, as it proved, a giant one.

It is well-nigh incredible that one building, one roof, could bring about such a change, such an upswing, in the cultural life of a city.

The Kennedy Center, splendidly situated on the banks of the Potomac, is not a dominating architectural structure, which is why it is *simpatico*. Its much – and to my mind too severely – criticised exterior will blend well into its surroundings when the landscape is ready, the trees have grown tall enough, and other buildings have risen nearby.

It is a lucky building, for all three of its public halls – the Opera House, the Eisenhower Theater and the Concert Hall – can boast of good acoustics.

It is not only the face but also the spirit of Washington that the Kennedy Center has changed. It represents the greatest success of its kind I have ever encountered. From the day of its opening, it has upgraded the cultural appetite and taste of the city, given it a focus and, so to speak, a "digestive tract". It is well on the way to increasing its influence, and because of its existence one can now seriously consider Washington as, in the very near future, a potential national and even international centre of culture.

That a heap of masonry can have such effect is almost unbelievable. Well, it is not the bricks and mortar alone that do the trick.

Roger Stevens as overall boss is by himself a super power. He

285

has at his side Martin Feinstein, director of all three halls and in direct charge of the two theatres, dramatic and lyric, who is as brilliant as he is dynamic. A dreamer of big dreams, endowed with energy and patience, he inspires confidence that the dreams will come true.

For the success that the National Symphony, the local orchestra of Washington, had during my time, the Center's good acoustics were a deciding factor.

Perhaps there was an inner, unintended meaning in the fact that the first music that sounded in the nearly completed Concert Hall was Verdi's overture to his opera *La Forza del Destino*, "the power of destiny".

The first pair of hands that applauded that first sound were the hands of a great American artist, himself a hero of the lyric theatre, who in his meteoric career had acknowledged the applause of millions and millions of hands.

Long ago – in 1946 – I wanted to perform Verdi's "Manzoni Requiem" in Dallas, Texas. Three of my quartet of vocal soloists were fine young singers of the American contemporary scene, Francis Yeend, soprano; Winifred Heidt, contralto; Gábor Carelli, tenor. For the basso part I had invited the phenomenal Mihály Székely to come from Hungary.

At that time, soon after the end of the war, it was not easy to travel from Hungary to America, but my singer had a year to arrange his trip so I was not worried.

At least, not at first. When about three-quarters of the year had passed without a word from Székely I began to be apprehensive. After a while I thought it better to look around for an understudy. When asking the agencies for a young basso who would undertake the thankless job of covering for my star singer I was told about one who was just starting out, had sung, until then, very little in public, but had a fine voice and was enterprising and talented. I listened to him, liked him, and engaged him.

The date of the performance approached. Still no word from Székely. The young understudy did well at rehearsals. On the very day of the first concert, who should appear but my friend Székely. He quietly marched in and announced in his best, booming, basso

286

belcanto, "Here I am." When I asked him why he had not given any sign of life during a whole year, he simply repeated, "I am here. I told you I would be."

But I thought matters over and found that it was too late for him to step in. His understudy had by then been announced for the evening and showed indeed great promise. If he were to be dismissed at the last minute, after rehearsing, this could easily have discredited him and done perhaps irreparable damage to a budding, fragile, promising reputation.

So I told my star friend that to my regret I would not let him sing (in compensation I arranged another appearance for him two weeks later) and the young understudy had a huge success, probably the first great professional success of his career, which from that time onward rocketed spectacularly.

There is no one, I believe, connected in any way with vocal music and the world of opera who does not know the name of George London.

They were his hands which met in the first sign of approval at the Kennedy Center Concert Hall.

He was at that time in an executive position at Kennedy Center, helping Roger Stevens. Since 1946 we had met, intermittently, mostly professionally. He sang a splendid Prince Bluebeard in Bartók's opera at the Northrop Auditorium in Minneapolis under my direction; his powerful musical and dramatic portrayal of Wagner's *Flying Dutchman* is fortunately preserved on gramophone records as another instance of our collaboration. There were more. When my appointment with the National Symphony was announced, he came to visit me at our home in Switzerland. From that time dates our close friendship. Our artistic collaboration has continued. He appeared with me several times as narrator after he had to abandon singing in consequence of a disastrous illness, paralysis of one of his vocal chords; a great personal tragedy borne with strength and an unimpaired positive outlook, even with humour. Our latest momentous and perhaps most important collaboration has been a performance of Wagner's *Walküre* at the Kennedy Center Opera House in 1974. This was a historic event: the first performance of any Wagner opera by an all-American company in the capital city of the USA. This George produced and directed while I led it musically. Soon after that

George was named director of the Washington Opera Society. That organisation, after some years of struggle, has thus received the kind of leadership which would have assured its standing and its future. Unhappily, severe illness has struck George again and his friends are now praying for his recovery.

Kennedy Center opened on September 8th, 1971. The opening of the Opera House preceded that of the Concert Hall by one day with Leonard Bernstein's Mass, written for the occasion. The work made a deep impact upon the emotionally pre-charged audience, not least because of the re-emergence of the Kennedy name and the Kennedy tragedy. This worked-up state of mind of the public was, perhaps, detrimental to a true appreciation of the work, and the fixed date of the production was perhaps detrimental to the work itself, for in my opinion it is quite outstanding and would have merited a première unconnected with any occasion whatever.

It represents a dramatic study of the drama of worship and thus also an exploration into the nature of the religious Mass as we know it.

For this reason, I think, the name of the piece is a misnomer. If the word "Mass" was placed within quotation marks, then the title would be correct and significant. But how many ordinary members of the public could be expected to read as carefully and thoughtfully as that? The best would have been to use in a sub-title the words that most correctly describe the nature of the piece and to call it:

"Mass"
(A Mystery Play)

The work depicts, movingly, the evolution from the improvised *laudatio* to the ceremony and its subsequent decadence, ending in the hope of a revival, the return of spontaneous, wide-eyed, grateful rejoicing in life's blessings – the true origin and true primary content of all worship.

Be that as it may, the Kennedy Center Opera House succeeded in presenting at its opening a truly original work – not only an original specimen but, as I see it, a species quite new in our age and times. For mystery plays have been missing from our stages for centuries.

The opening of the Kennedy Center's Concert Hall on the next evening, September 9th, 1971, was more conventional in its conception, but the programme was right for the purpose of the evening.

Whereas the Opera House only had to exist (there had been nothing like it in Washington before), the Concert Hall had to *prove* its worth, and its superiority to the former hall. Further, the much belittled, even maligned National Symphony Orchestra had to pass the hard test of being found worthy to become the resident orchestra of the new Center.

I chose a programme that showed the acoustical properties of the hall in as many different ways as it was possible in one single evening, and also the orchestra's prowess by asking it to master some of the most demanding works in the repertory from classical to contemporary.

We performed:
> Beethoven's Overture, "Consecration of the House"
> Mozart's Violin Concerto in G major (K 216) with Isaac Stern as our soloist
> Stravinsky's *Rite of Spring*
> and
> William Schuman's American Song for Tenor Solo, Chorus and Orchestra

Both the orchestra and the concert hall passed their tests brilliantly and it can truthfully be added that the success of both became permanent.

The success of Washington's National Symphony was one of the most gratifying experiences of my professional life so far. Once released, the potential talent of the group blossomed out with incredible speed and force. Stimulation was hardly needed; the best way to help was with the kind of daily care that a gardener gives to his plants.

As the orchestra to begin with had no style or profile whatever, I was, so to speak, on virgin ground, free to impart the kind of music making I was brought up with and am deeply convinced about.

Thus the NSO became within less than two years a close-knit performing group, making an elegant, "lean" sound, and possessing an almost chamber-music-like clarity. The next step was to develop within this style, to make the players intensely familiar with it, and to imbue them with the collective personality of a first-rate orchestra. This was merely a matter of time.

I reckoned that ten years would be needed for the task ahead, and was prepared to give a decade of my life to helping to accomplish it.

Actually I stayed seven years at the helm of the NSO. Orchestra and audience were not happy to have me leave, and my farewell to them was equally emotional. But in fact I was relinquishing merely my music directorship, not my contacts. I had already agreed to stay on for an additional three years as so-called principal guest conductor for a sizeable part of the season.

When I decided to leave my Washington post, my intention was to remain as principal conductor of the Royal Philharmonic Orchestra in London, a position I had held since 1974, simultaneously with my post in Washington, and to give some more time to guest appearances.

But here also, as so often, the great truth, as expressed by my eminent compatriot, the playwright Ferenc Molnár, prevailed: "Everything, always, happens differently." In the spring of 1977, the directors of the Detroit Symphony Orchestra appeared on my horizon, inviting me to the motor city as their music director. At first I turned down the idea, but the directors pursued me relentlessly, and presented the job in such challenging terms that once more I succumbed to temptation. So, there I was again, with an entirely new world opening up before me.

All my previous plans became suddenly obsolete. New ones had to be made, and there are few things as pleasant as making them. They come so willingly to mind: every new task, every new challenge, is a fresh spring.

Going back in time by a few springs:

In 1974 I had resigned from my post in Stockholm, reduced my conducting there to a yearly guest appearance, in order to retrench a bit, with the idea of devoting myself to the steady care of one orchestra only, that of Washington.

But, as usual, destiny intervened, and soon I was again to be connected with two orchestras.

This time it was the Royal Philharmonic Orchestra of London that knocked at my doors, as I have already mentioned.

We were old friends: through the years I had conducted quite a large number of their concerts in London, also going with them on two tours through the USA.

It was easily and happily agreed that I would give them the time I had previously given to the Stockholm Philharmonic. Thus, for some years I was heading symphony orchestras in both capitals of the English-speaking world; an amusing distinction for a person whose native tongue is Hungarian.

Of the London orchestras I have spoken already in these notes. The Royal Philharmonic is the youngest of the four self-governing ones. It was founded by Sir Thomas Beecham after the Second World War, and he remained at its helm until he died in 1961. His associate, Rudolf Kempe, took over and headed it for the next thirteen years until 1974. I am its third conductor (I took up my appointment in July 1975) and, as I can add with pleasure, now appointed for life as its Conductor Laureate.

Beecham was a character around whom legends clustered. One account has it that the Royal Philharmonic was born because his old orchestra, the London Philharmonic, was annoyed with him for having deserted them during the war (it is true that Beecham spent the last years of the war in America) and refused to perform under his baton. Legend also has it that not only his old orchestra, but his old public in London was angry with him too. When he appeared at the start of his first concert with the newly formed RPO the audience in the packed-out Royal Albert Hall – which, unlike the old Queen's Hall, had emerged unscathed from the Blitz – greeted him in stony silence. Beecham marched imperturbably to his place on the rostrum, turned round to face the hostile, silent ranks, slowly folded his hands and said, "Let us pray."

The spell was broken. The people laughed and clapped and Beecham was in their good books again.

He was that sort of man. He gave the impression of a musical gourmet, a genial, splendid amateur, but in fact he was far from that. His music-making had the rare quality of spontaneity, so enchanting when natural and not overdone. His style was one of organised, well thought out improvisation. Perhaps in the strictest

291

sense he was not a "professional" musician. His taste was rarefied and had the aura of the "exquisite".

The first time I saw him was at the Opera House in Budapest in 1922. The first time we met and started to talk to each other was in 1934, when the Ballets Russes de Monte Carlo came to Covent Garden with myself as conductor. The orchestra which played for those long ballet seasons was Beecham's London Philharmonic – a fine orchestra indeed – and Sir Thomas himself conducted a few performances of Tchaikovsky's *Swan Lake*, *Les Sylphides*, and maybe a few more.

During that period Sir Thomas and I often worked side by side and between the older and younger man a cordial relationship developed that was to be permanent.

Sir Thomas' legendary wit shot its arrows in every direction. Some of them came my way.

At that time I went in for overlong conducting batons, which I thought were supremely elegant. One morning Sir Thomas and I had shared rehearsal, with myself taking the first half. When I had finished, I left the pit and sat down in the front row of the stalls to watch Beecham's half. He entered the pit, climbed up on to his rostrum, exchanged greetings with the orchestra and then took a long pensive look at the oversized baton I had left on the stand. He took it up, extended his arms, and started waving it about. Then he turned to me and said, in mock admiration: "Mr. Doráti, I didn't know you were a fisherman!"

Jokes against himself were received rather less well.

When his memoirs appeared, under the title *The Mingled Chime*, I naturally bought a copy. When I received the bill from the bookstore I saw that the typist had made a mistake and, thinking the book was a whodunit, quoted its title as: "The Mingled Crime". I thought this very funny and showed it to him at the next opportunity, with great hilarity.

His smile was frosty.

In 1940 we met in Australia. On his arrival in Melbourne he was interviewed by an awed young reporter, who asked him what new works he was going to perform.

He announced with an Olympian gesture: "I have a rather interesting novelty for you. A tenth symphony by Beethoven."

The young man was astounded. Here was his scoop.

292

"You have found a new symphony by Beethoven, Sir Thomas? Where did you find it? Is it genuine?"

Sir Thomas, without blinking an eyelid, replied, "Oh yes, I found it in the British Museum. And inasmuch as it comes from the British Museum, it *must* be genuine."

The young man wrote feverishly.

"And is this the only novelty you bring, Sir Thomas? Or are there more?"

"An eleventh, a twelfth symphony by Beethoven . . . I don't even remember . . ."

The reporter departed at lightning speed to tell the world.

Fortunately, he never did.

The few of us who stood around listening to this remarkable interview became concerned that it really might get printed and word was sent to the editor to take it easy.

In Sydney, a week or so later, Sir Thomas agreed to serve as auctioneer at a war-benefit sale. Amongst the objects he auctioned was a large caricature of himself drawn by me. (I also drew one of myself, to even things up.) It went for £50. He was not satisfied.

"I did my best, and the model certainly could not have been bettered. Perhaps a more – hm – conventional interpretation of my features would have fetched a higher price."

My own face fetched £30.

No more – luckily.

My own collaboration with the RPO is now in its fourth season. It started most auspiciously with a Beethoven cycle in the Royal Albert Hall. It continues well, and the orchestra keeps its very high performance standard, in spite of certain organisational and managerial problems which plagued it for a long time and have only recently been resolved by the appointment as general manager of my old friend Peter Diamant. The way is now clear for a new ascent into even higher spheres.

It was only natural that, after the recording of Haydn's symphonies, I should reach out further in the same field.

I did not have to look far for another project – the enormous reservoir of Haydn's output was, even now, scarcely tapped, and there are many treasures still awaiting re-discovery.

In the realm of instrumental music, we went on first to record

293

the rest of Haydn's purely orchestral works. At this time of writing, two records of these have already been made (the enchanting "Twenty-four Minuets", a light yet mature late work) and two more are still to come.

Works for orchestra and solo instruments were the obvious next step. Haydn wrote a great number of concertos for keyboard instruments. These are now all recorded. So are the six large piano concertos which Ilse and I performed together, she playing the Steinway. The eleven concertini have been recorded by Ilse on the fortepiano with a chamber ensemble without a conductor. With the RPO, the Brighton Festival Choir and an array of excellent soloists, we have already recorded two of Haydn's great oratorios, the *Creation* and the *Seasons*: the third, *Il Ritorno di Tobia*, is on its way.

I also decided, while still working on the symphonies, to try recording the complete operatic output of Haydn, a complex and difficult task, and even riskier than the symphony project from the commercial point of view. For while the general public knows the symphonies by reputation (however little it knows them in fact) Haydn's operas, although two or three of them are sporadically performed, are hardly in the public's mind at all.

Therefore, would it be possible to kindle the interest of a recording company in such a doubtful undertaking?

It was.

I went about this new venture in the same way as I had with the symphonies, making a detailed plan – more complicated in this case, as the operas themselves are long, complex works and there was the new dimension of the stage to be reckoned with.

The company which took up the project was Philips – now called Phonogram – of Baarn, Holland. W. H. Zalsman, now head of another department in the same corporation, gave the signal to go ahead; his successor Ernst van der Vossen supported us when he took over. The director of the recordings is Erik Smith, a splendid partner indeed. Our sound engineer is Hans Lauterslager, an equally excellent collaborator. And as our orchestra is the fine Chamber Orchestra of Lausanne, we have the added pleasure of making the recordings in the near-paradisal landscape of the Lake of Geneva.

The musical treasure these operas yield is enormous. It surpasses even the highest expectations. It is true that reading the scores had already given one a good idea of their exceptional quality. But, as I said while talking about the symphonies, Haydn's music is so entirely auditive that it can fully take possession of us only through our ears.

It must be heard to be believed.

At their greatest these operas are not only forerunners but worthy companion pieces to Mozart's best lyric works. The whole undertaking is one great voyage of discovery, and as such utterly new in the history of recording.

Amongst the many millions of existing records there are almost none of "unknown" musical works. Recordings, as a rule, don't anticipate but follow successful live performances.

In the case of the Haydn symphonies and even more so of Haydn's operas, that order has been reversed, to the everlasting credit of the recording companies concerned.

28

IT HAS BEEN SAID OF ME THAT I WAS "THE MOST RECORDED conductor". This is merely a PR phrase, the truth of which nobody bothered to verify, least of all myself.

It's true, however, that I have been one of the much recorded and recording musicians for over forty years. From this look-out post I can perhaps offer a few observations, recollections and thoughts on that fascinating new realm of musical life in our days.

I made my first recording back in 1934. The place was London, the company His Master's Voice, the orchestra the old London Philharmonic. The moving spirit in the company at that time was Fred Gaisberg, a fabulous little man who looked like the wizard in a children's story. It was said that he once went talent-scouting in Italy and gave a lifelong contract to a young, unknown singer on such generous terms that he was nearly fired when he returned. The young singer turned out to be Benjamino Gigli. Gaisberg stayed on. True or false, this story fits him like a tight bathing suit (God forbid!).

He was, no doubt, only one of the pioneers of that fast expanding industry, which burst so suddenly into full bloom with the invention of the long-playing record at the end of the 1940s.

As I heard it, the inventor or developer of the long-playing record was an American of Hungarian extraction, in fact a nephew of Karl Goldmark, a very fine and in his time very well-known composer.

The invention was essentially that of the micro-groove. This permitted the recording of approximately thirty minutes of sound on one twelve-inch disc, as compared to four minutes in pre-LP times.

The situation on the appearance of the new record was at first chaotic. I witnessed its start in America, where two huge recording companies, RCA Victor and Columbia, had the market. It was the latter that bought and brought out Goldmark's invention. RCA at first manufactured its own version of it, a smaller record, turning more slowly than the old one (forty-five revolutions per minute, compared to seventy-eight) and giving about fifteen minutes of recorded sound as against the old four. But Columbia's (Goldmark's) LPs, with thirty-three revolutions per minute and twenty-five to thirty minutes of recorded sound on each record, prevailed, and RCA soon converted to the new system. In Europe, the thirty-three-turn-per-minute LP was developed at practically the same time.

The convenience thus offered – that of being able to listen to reproduced sound uninterruptedly for half an hour instead of having to turn over the records every four minutes – worked a miracle, and an immense, worldwide market for the new LPs opened up.

An incredible number of new recording companies also sprang up out of nowhere. Until the advent of the LP the three large companies, EMI (which controlled His Master's Voice), RCA and Columbia, were practically alone in the field. Then, almost from one day to the next, there were hundreds of smaller and larger record makers, from "Nonsuch" to "Unicorn", from "Ariola" to "Zenith", from "Alpha" to "Omega". The recording fever had started and soon grew to epidemic size. It has remained that way ever since.

A new type of artist, the recording artist, has been born in the wake of the micro-groove revolution, and a new record public, not to be confused with the concert-going, opera-going or theatre-going public, has also come into being. We have the recording expert, the record critic, the hi-fi addict. And even our old way of music making has received a new distinction: it is now "live" music instead of being just music as it was before.

The enjoyment, appreciation and evaluation of recorded music are also of a different kind from that which applies to live music. There are new criteria – for instance, noises.

In a "live" performance a sudden mass outbreak of Spanish influenza with all its coughing, sneezing, and wheezing will spoil enjoyment of Beethoven's Ninth Symphony to a much lesser degree than one tiny scratch on an LP of the same work. Reading record reviews, one is astounded at the minute differentiations made between one performance and the other, distinctions never observed when live performances are compared. And so on.

Does this mean a greater immersion in music itself, whether

recorded or live? A finer sense of observation and discrimination? I don't think so. For listening standards of evaluating live music have changed little if at all.

Is this new type of listening worthwhile? I do not think there is a clear answer to that question. From the record listener's point of view, it surely is, for it not only arouses his greater interest in the detail but also helps him to develop this interest further. And it is indeed worthwhile if we consider the "play" element in music. It is not for nothing that music is "played" in every language in the world (except the Italian in which it is "sounded" and the Spanish in which it is "touched"). Those who manipulate a gramophone record in a way perform – "play" – the music for themselves and thus, thanks to the machine, up-grade themselves from passive listening to active participation. For instance, they can change the volume of the music, making it louder or softer to suit their whim; or they can stop the record at any point with one movement of one finger: things which they cannot do in a live concert.

On that level, at which they are primitive "co-performers", any discovery, any further novelty around the next corner, is welcome. But from a purely musical point of view, more precisely from the point of view of music itself, this picking around in detail has precious little meaning.

I made just one experiment in this direction: one day, after reading the comparative reviews of a newly released record of mine – it was the Second Symphony by Brahms – in which the reviewer compared, with admirable patience, my performance with that of about fifteen others, I decided to listen myself.

So I went to the record library of the BBC and got out the records of the same work as conducted by all my great, greater and greatest colleagues of past and present: Furtwängler, Walter, Klemperer, Beecham, Weingartner, *et al*. I listened hard and con-scientiously, hardly eating and sleeping, keeping my attention closely focused. When I had finished I had heard the splendid Second Symphony by Johannes Brahms twenty times in two days. I could not remember one single difference between the many performances. They were all well played, well conducted, well presented, in good taste, honestly offered. One louder accent, one shade of a different speed, did not matter at all. But the sound of the piece *itself,* Brahms's masterwork, was not fresher in my mind than before the twenty hearings.

The quantity of music recorded to date is enormous. It is no exaggeration to say that the primary *and* secondary repertoires of the past three hundred years are now almost completely accounted for. Almost – but not quite. It will still be possible, for some time to come, to find music, even by the greatest masters, that has not yet been recorded.

The catalogue is less rich in the department of contemporary music. The great composers of our century are of course fully represented on records. There is less recorded music by the younger composers of today. But that is hardly surprising in view of the mixed nature of the works available. It is almost more surprising to find as much of it on disc as we do. One must not forget that records are merchandise.

Another question is whether there are not too many recordings of certain works. We see in the catalogues twenty to thirty different performances of, say, Beethoven's or Tchaikovsky's Fifth Symphony and other such popular works.

Are those recordings really too many?

I think not.

One of the greatest attractions of a musical performance, perhaps its most magnetic quality, is the element of improvisation – the inspiration of the moment that occurs even – no, especially – in the most carefully thought out, balanced performance. No two performances are alike. We not only know that, we also expect it; we look forward to the inevitable novelty at the next hearing of the same piece by the same performer or performers. It is the expectation of that pleasant, often exciting, combination of new ingredients in a familiar, cherished substance that kindles the desire to re-hear a piece of music and so makes it "popular".

The recorded performance of a composition has the built-in drawback that it remains always the same. This is also why recordings will never *replace* live music. The freedom, the "gesture", the "allure" of a concert performance would become stale if exactly repeated – like the smile of a beautiful woman in a photograph which, looked at repeatedly, turns into a grimace.

It follows that the only way to escape from the grimace quality of records is to listen to more than one recording of the same piece in turns. This may seem an expensive way of keeping recorded music fresh. But is it really? After all, we do not expect to get into a second performance of a concert or an opera on the ticket we used for the first.

One species of human beings who should *not* listen regularly to records are young, would-be or budding conductors, pianists, violinists, 'cellists, singers – in short musicians of all kinds who really mean to learn their profession. If they do they run the danger that they will try, even involuntarily, to use those well-prepared, often superlative performances as "short-cuts". That would be fatal. There are no short-cuts for professional musicians. They must use their own lives to master their art and it will take them all of their lives to do it – if they are lucky. (What these young people should listen to, as much as possible, are live performances given by master musicians. In my student days we had, in our last years of study, full access to all concerts given at the Academy and all opera performances throughout the season.)

What is the interrelationship between recorded and live music? Do they influence each other? Does one of them help the other or are they mutually harmful?

By and large it is my experience that while a successful performance may stimulate the sale of a record, a successful record will not sell concert tickets.

It was in the 1950s that I conducted the first recording of Aaron Copland's Third Symphony. The record turned out well, was much praised and sold in quantity. The composer and I were both delighted. About two years afterwards we met in New York and talked about the record. It was still doing very well. Copland even mentioned the latest sales figure, which was exceedingly high. I asked him what this had done to the work's performances. (Mine in Minneapolis was, I believe, the second or third after its Boston première.) Copland's reply was that it had not changed the normal, rather slow, progress of the work through the concert halls at all.

This would mean that the many who bought the record of Aaron Copland's symphony were content to listen to it at home.

On the reverse side of the coin, when I gave the first American performance of Messiaen's *Transfiguration de Notre Seigneur Jésus Christ*, many people asked me when the work would be available on records. But – back to the face-side – when, two and a half years later, the record had become available and was selling well,

300

there were no letters or 'phone calls requesting a repeat live performance.

To conclude: the record public seems to be a new species of consumer, just as records and recordings are a new type of music distribution.

29

About my own profession, orchestra conducting, I could not help writing throughout these notes. So a brief summing-up will suffice here.

Conducting is the youngest of the musical arts. Indeed it emerged in its present form less than two hundred years ago. Before that time it was a purely mechanical action confined to its most basic function, that of keeping a group of instrumentalists or vocalists together.

At first one of the instrumentalists or singers gave appropriate signs to the others to start and stop at the same time. (What happened in between was nobody's business.) This custom prevailed for a long time, even after the non-playing or non-singing conductor had appeared. Johann Strauss, who lived almost to see the dawn of the twentieth century, conducted his own music as a *Stehgeiger* (upright fiddler), standing in front of his orchestra with his violin, alternately playing and beating time with his bow.

That basic activity of time beating was not always silent as it is today. The conductor beat the measure loudly, tapping with a music scroll on any object nearby (the top of the clavichord, for instance) or with a long, heavy rod on the floor. The story goes that Jean Baptiste Lully (1632-87) died from blood poisoning, having wounded and infected his big toe with his "baton" while conducting.

The first person whom we hear of as conducting in the modern sense is Joseph Haydn. Contemporary reports from London, where he went in his later years, described him conducting his symphonies during his second stay there, around 1794. He probably did not stand, but sat at the keyboard, hardly ever touching it, and was occupied not only in holding the players together but also in instructing them *how* to play, requesting dynamic, agogic nuances, ordering the phrasing according to his taste, and so on. Remarks which he wrote into some of his scores (interestingly, many of them into those of his operas) and a few sentences in his letters allow us to think that he was exacting these "fineries" from his orchestra as early as the 1770s. Unfortunately, while his development as a composer is uniquely documented, we have no means of following his progress as a conductor. But what we know about his personality gives us a clue. His strong will, his patience, his care for detail, his wide and constantly widening musical and human horizon, his way with people, his friendly but obstinate manner of getting things done as he wanted, all these are conductor's qualities. And what we do know about Haydn's conducting is that he had long and intensive experience of it. He conducted not only his own symphonies and other orchestral works, his own operas, masses, oratorios, and other sacred choral works at their first performances and then at later ones, but also many works by other composers as well. In one year that we know about he conducted as many as 120 opera performances – to say nothing of other concerts – more than any conductor of our time could contemplate, let alone master. And we know, as I say, that he conducted successfully in London in the 1790s.

So it is quite probable that we can regard Haydn as the first (or one of the first) of modern conductors, and probably also as one of the great conductors.

There are other composers who were also noted for their conducting. Mendelssohn was an excellent conductor. Wagner also was evidently a good one, though no less controversial in this capacity than as a composer: *The Times* in 1855 reported of a concert conducted by him that it was "one of the most disastrous in the London Philharmonic's history". But the general consensus of opinion as handed down to us, and what we can see from his own markings in scores, confirm that this must have been an unfortunate exception, if true at all.

Richard Strauss, whom I heard, was a first-rate conductor, and Mahler's brilliant conductorial gifts were a handicap to his being recognised as a composer. By contrast Beethoven, Bruckner, Ravel, Kodály and others were noted for their very poor conducting. Bartók told me that he tried conducting once in his life (he did not say when or where). But he added emphatically, "That was enough – never again!"

Not until well into the second half of the nineteenth century do we hear of conductors who were that and nothing else, or rather, whose conducting was not secondary to some other musical activity.

One of the first of these "exclusive" conductors whose name comes to my mind is Hermann Levi, one of the original conductors in Bayreuth. He was born in 1839. Hans Richter, whom many regard as the father of today's art of conducting, and who began as a horn player, was born in 1843.

It may not be without interest to list, chronologically, some of the most famous conductors on the road to the present day. It throws a sharp beam of light on the rapid development of this art.

Hans von Bülow	born in 1830
Charles Lamoureux	" 1834
Edouard (Judas) Colonne	" 1838
Hermann Levi	" 1839
Hans Richter	" 1843
Vasily Ilytch Safonov	" 1852
Gustav Mahler	" 1860
Felix Weingartner	" 1863
Arturo Toscanini	" 1866

At first, the presence of the professional conductor was in order to save time in the preparation of the performances where large enough ensembles were involved to warrant such help.

The results pleased the public and encouraged composers to write works of greater complexity than they had dared to do before, through fear that the music would have been impossible to perform.

Now nothing is impossible in that sense any more, and in that context the conductor has become indispensable.

But here let us pause to reflect. There is no music, no matter how great its complexity, or for however large an orchestra or other combination it is written, that could not be learned and prepared without a conductor – in theory. However, in practice, the time needed for adequate preparation without a leader would be so great that it would render any such endeavour futile. Two concert performances a year, or one opera performance every four or five years, is about as much as any musical community would get – and how would that serve? It would not satisfy the public and not only would the performers starve but their talents would be stifled by the unbearable monotony of their daily work.

And let us suppose a situation in which large groups of musicians for some reason did decide to rehearse without a conductor. How would the rehearsing proceed? It could not take place in a Babel of discussion. Rather, a few members of the group would emerge with more authority or powers of persuasion than the others, and ultimately one leader would take over.

So we see that the main asset an orchestra conductor must possess is the quality of leadership. This is a rare, but not all too rare, gift. All herd-animals develop it – wolves, elephants and humans. Human leadership in its healthy manifestation is not a quality that exists by itself; it is always balanced by others. If the gift of leadership appears alone, the person cursed with it will be in the best case a bore, in the worst a monster.

Thus, there are leader-scientists, leader-priests, leader-soldiers and so on. The conductor is a leader-musician. Or rather he is either a leader-musician or a musician-leader. The first is someone who would be a leader in any case; if not in music then in some other realm. The second is a musician from head to toe who, if he could not be a musician-leader would be a non-leader-musician.

If anyone is interested, I belong to the latter category. I abstain from classifying my colleagues. Perhaps some readers of these notes will be interested in doing so. It's an intriguing game.

Leadership has no rules, no patterns. It cannot be learned as it requires no special knowledge. Its secret, its force can be put epigrammatically:

"A leader is someone who can make another person love to do what he has to or could be forced to do anyway."

Leadership can assume absurd dimensions in soldiering, when a good general can enthuse his troops to face their very death euphorically.

What havoc, what catastrophes a leadership quality can cause when not accompanied – mitigated – by any *other* talent was all too well demonstrated in the incredible case of Hitler.

All a conductor can know is music. Ideally, he would like to know all of it – the entire immeasurable eternity of it; failing that, as much as it is possible to cram into a lifetime. For while knowing will not make him a conductor, not knowing would disqualify him as a musician, which is his only determinable, basic and indispensable requirement.

305

Conducting schools, therefore, are of little or no use. A conductor's certificate, if it indicates no more than what was learned in class, is worthless. For conducting "technique", of which one hears so much spoken in a highfalutin', superficial way, can be dismissed as hardly existing. It is an elementary set of signals which can be explained in a few minutes, and understood in less. It is much simpler, as well as much less dangerous, than driving a car; something every half-wit can learn, alas.

Indeed, this simplicity of the conductor's outward activity, coupled with the fact that it entails no physical danger, makes it an easy lure for the non–gifted. And they come in shoals.

It may be thought that the task of sound producing, that is, the task of the instrumentalist, or singer, would be twice as hard as that of the conductor, who, besides his mental task – which is not to be depreciated – has no physical problems of consequence to cope with. Curiously, it does not work out that way. The burden of the instrumentalist or singer gives him a certain natural balance which the conductor has to gain out of nowhere – or, if we decline to accept that "nowhere", then from a certain moral force, gathered from sources other than musical.

The conductor has, in fact, no means of his own to make his feelings, ideas concerning the piece he conducts come through in musical sounds. (This was very astutely observed by my daughter, then three years old, who once said to me after listening to a rehearsal, "Daddy, you are the only musician who makes no noise!") Indeed, the conductor produces no sound (some occasional grunts discounted). He has to rely on his instrumentalist and/or vocalist colleagues to produce the sounds in a manner conforming to the patterns he silently imagines and suggests.

This will be willingly done for him, for the process of ensemble performance has jelled solidly enough by now for the roles to be clearly divided: the initiative is that of the conductor. He is *expected* to convey to the players how to employ their skills. It has become a matter of course that the conductor is the one who knows the whole piece: the players only have to know their parts. If both of these conditions are fulfilled, there exists a basis for a satisfactory performance. If the conductor knows his business and the players do not, the situation is bad; if it's the reverse, the situation is worse;

306

if neither side is prepared, disaster ensues. (Every one of these situations has been known to arise.)

The complete mastering of a score, as it has to be mastered by the conductor, is a complex affair that cannot be properly described. It entails not only knowledge of the notes written on the pages but also their "checks and balances" – the form of the piece, its emotional content, its possible extra-musical implications, its style within a larger, aesthetic and historical scope, its special place and meaning in the composer's œuvre, and so forth. All this must have entered into the conductor's mind and *body* so deeply that it is stored in the subconscious and emerges on the occasion of the performance as ingredients of an "improvisation", that is, spontaneous re-creation.

In order that the performing group should be able to follow the conductor's mind and execute his ideas, a two-fold process must be gone through.

First, the rehearsal period, during which the conductor explains in words and indicates with movement his intentions, and the players try them out.

Second, a rapid "control and correction process" during the performance, when the conductor first reminds the players, with gestures, of the agreed details, and gives them quick signals of corrective intent when he hears anything that is contrary to what was arranged, or (on a higher level of co-operation) feels that in the heat of the performance a small change of emphasis, speed, and so forth can be achieved.

There are two schools of thought. One is that the conductor's work is done during rehearsals. Hans Richter said, "*Der Dirigent hat sich wahrend den Proben zu bewähren.*" ("The conductor must prove himself during the rehearsals.") To prove this, it was his habit, from time to time, to have one piece in his concert programme played by the orchestra alone: he would give the sign to start it and then stop conducting. My father told me of this, adding with some pride that he and his colleagues could play without conductor such difficult pieces as the second movement of Tchaikovsky's Sixth Symphony, in 5/4 time. (It seems that in those days – around 1900 – that uneven measure was still quite a problem, although *Tristan*, Liszt's Dante Symphony and other works employing it were already being performed.)

The other viewpoint is that it is at the performance that the conductor has to do his main job, inspiring the players, getting their best out of them.

The truth is midway between the two. Without adequate preparation no amount of inspiring will do any good. But a wise conductor will "leave room" for spontaneous additions or alterations from the rehearsed pattern during the performance. The conductor's task is more to prevent his and his colleagues' rigidity than to insist upon spontaneity which, by that very insistence, can easily cease to be just that.

The conductor who did not allow scope for his players' fantasy and initiative would miss – or abdicate from – a great deal of variety, spontaneity and overall liveliness in his performance. In fact, no performance is "his", all of them are "theirs"; and it is important that the conductor should know that.

In a good orchestral performance there is a surprising amount of "give and take" between the conductor and the players, and if both are worth their salt, in both professional and human terms, the results can be exquisite.

Conducting an orchestra – like every act of leadership – is a human, man-to-man activity. The contact is strictly and invariably from one person to the other. Between the conductor and his orchestra there exists the same relationship as between the animal herd and its leader. As long as the leader is strong and is leading, the herd follows him; as soon as he shows weakness – that is, if he does not lead – he is trampled over.

For quite a long time my idol among conductors was Toscanini, although he ultimately had less influence on my development than other great examples, such as Furtwängler or Busch.

By and large, orchestra conductors fall into two types, the "pros" and the "magicians". Hans Richter and Fritz Busch, for instance, belong in the former category, Hans von Bülow and Arthur Nikisch in the latter. Arturo Toscanini was probably the only conductor I knew – and certainly the one I encountered – who in his person united all the qualities of both.

His magic made him irresistible and his professionalism made him great. His role in the history of performing music was crucially important, for it was he who established – or rather re-established – the maxim of "faithfulness to the letter". After a period in which far too many liberties had been taken with composers' scores, this new approach hit the young among us like fresh air on the first day of spring.

Meticulous to the last detail, in fullest command of the music he performed and of the orchestras he conducted, he was able to release orchestral sound directly from the page in such pure substance that it seemed to happen without any kind of mediation.

This kind of music-making I had never heard before. I became completely devoted to it and learned only later that it did not quite suit my own temperament and led me towards rigidity. In fact, the "Toscanini approach" was only valid for Toscanini himself, and while its principle was available to nourish kindred schools of thought, his way of implementing his convictions was inimitable.

It is very difficult to convey Toscanini's conducting personality in words. The best characterisation of him – a phrase of epigrammatic penetration and humour – I heard uttered by an otherwise unremarkable, lisping youth, who said, "The overwhelming exthperienth with Tothcanini ith the ONE."

Meaning his downbeat.

Nothing more true could have been said: that incomparable, inimitable Toscanini downbeat decided the entire piece of music that was to follow; "contained" it, so to speak, in a capsule.

The visual aspect of his conducting was – thank God – not exhilarating; the exhilaration was in what one heard. Large, clear, forceful beats; very few cues perceptible to the audience. Evident were the total energy, the total dedication given to the performance and the total authority with which he handled both music and musicians.

As a man, he was a curious mixture of attractive and unattractive traits. His rehearsal manners were rude. Today they would not be tolerated even by a minor orchestra and not even from someone of Toscanini's unparalleled eminence. But there were extenuating circumstances. Those were different times. It has to be admitted that, since the turn of the century, the educational and professional standards of orchestras have developed far more than those of conductors. While the former are now infinitely better schooled and prepared, the same cannot be said – generally – about the latter. In the early 1900s energetic, even despotic, handling of orchestras was not uncommon and not entirely unjustifiable.

Toscanini's rudeness was, moreover, not planned misbehaviour. He was very short of temper and easily lost control over himself, while always controlling others. During his tantrums he threw and tore scores, broke his batons, trampled on his wristwatch, shouted and swore vigorously. All these things were endured in silence and accepted without controversy because both his purity of purpose and the sublime results obtained were so obviously evident.

I first heard Toscanini with the New York Philharmonic Orchestra in 1930, on their historic first European tour in Berlin. The programme was Haydn's Symphony No. 101, Pizzetti's Rondo Veneziano and the "Eroica" Symphony by Beethoven. My sister was with me at that concert. We were completely overwhelmed. Never had we heard anything like it. Out of our minds, we "applauded" frenetically, hitting our own heads with both hands.

From then on I listened to him whenever possible. Later, several times, he invited me to conduct his famous NBC orchestra in New York, but we never met until, one morning in the late 1940s, I found myself facing him on the deck of the transatlantic liner *Vulcania*, on a voyage from New York to Genoa. We met, formally, the same afternoon at the captain's cocktail party, and the ten days of the crossing that followed were the most affable one can imagine in the illustrious company of "the maestro". (In those years, when a musician said "the maestro" without adding a name to it, this meant Toscanini – no one else.)

He travelled with his son, Walter, I with Klári and Tonina, who was then eight or nine years old. The maestro was kindness itself with the child. It was amazing to see how his mood would change back and forth in an instant: deeply immersed in a tender, grandfatherly conversation with little Tonina he would suddenly straighten up, turn to a passenger who was about to take a clandestine snapshot of the scene, knock the camera out of his hands, stamp on it, breaking it into smithereens, let out a roar, then turn back with an angelic smile to Tonina and continue his talk at the very syllable he had interrupted it.

How he saw that would–be–photographer at all was a miracle, for he was myopic in the extreme. But his was a strange kind of handicap. To read a score, he had to hold it three inches from his face; a pretty young woman he could spot round a corner.

With me he set aside a daily period for conversation, and would appear for our appointment unfailingly, on the dot.

His main topics were three:

First and foremost, misprints and other faults in well-known, world-famous scores, with explanations as to how he corrected them and why he did so in this way and not in that. This was an unexpected treasure to fall into my lap. Not only did he thus direct my attention to many faulty readings which I had passed over or accepted without criticism; he also made me, from then on, read scores with new eyes, and a much increased alertness.

Second, his many trans-oceanic crossings to both South and North America over the past forty years or so with all particulars of the weather, the sea, the names and other details of the ships, their captains, chief pursers and so forth. This was, evidently, more interesting to him than to me, but in any case I could not but marvel at his phenomenal memory.

This unique memory seemed, curiously, to fail him when it came to his third theme – other conductors. He could not remember their names. He thought and thought – they just did not come to mind.

"You know, my colleague in Boston. He plays the double bass. He is . . . he's called . . ."

"Serge Koussevitsky," I prompted.

"Ah – yes – of course – Koussevitsky – he wrote to me – I forgot . . ."

Then:

"The Englishman, you know, with the small goatee. His father made pills. Let me think, his name is . . . is . . ."

"Sir Thomas Beecham," I supplied.

"Certainly, yes, indeed" – sighing – "he wrote to me – I have not yet had time to reply . . ." And so on.

Like all ocean liners of the period, the *Vulcania* had aboard a small "salon orchestra", consisting of five or six players, led by a pianist. It was rather a poor band, dutifully entertaining the passengers with thin, threadbare sounds at tea time, cocktail time, suppers, evening dances, and so on.

I missed these events whenever possible. Almost the only times I heard the sounds of the band were during my afternoon walks on the promenade deck, when most of the other passengers were inside having tea and I had that lovely, broad gangway all to myself. The strains of the music would reach me for a minute or so every time I strode briskly by the large salon.

One day the sounds from the salon were particularly feeble and tremulous – so much so that I became curious to know what had happened to *"la banda"*. So I interrupted my walk and entered the room.

Looking around, I saw the passengers at their table, having their five o'clock tea or drinks; and on the rostrum, facing them, a white-faced, trembling group of musicians barely able to touch the keys or hold their bows. In front of the players, perhaps three or four paces away from them, was a single chair. On it, turned towards the band, sitting with folded arms, grimly biting his moustache, was Maestro Toscanini. He sat motionless, listening intently.

Greater artists than those of that band have been scared out of their wits by that Olympian, majestic presence.

From that occasion, however, a great friendship between Toscanini and the pianist of the band sprang up. They discovered that both of them were from Parma. That made them brothers. Henceforth Toscanini had two daily appointments for conversation, one with me and one with "the maestro", as he called his minor colleague respectfully and affectionately.

Soon after that first occasion, once more walking on deck, I heard confused musical sounds intermingled with yelling, shouting and banging from the hall inside. I looked in.

There was Toscanini with the band, holding a score two inches from his face, gesticulating, cajoling, cursing:

"Ma no! – Mamma mia! – Questo mai! – Santa Madonna! – No! No! – Così! – da capo! – ignoranti!"

They were in rehearsal.

Next morning, Toscanini sought me out at an early, extra-curricular time, took me aside, and said, "Do you know what I did last night?"

When I shook my head he explained, with glowing pride, "I showed the maestro new cuts in the *Norma* medley!"

I have set down this incident in a spirit of affection, as an important addition to the Toscanini portrait. For in no book or essay that I have read about the maestro have I found anything portraying him in such a warm and human light.

Partly but not entirely because of his poor eyesight, Toscanini memorised every piece he conducted down to the last detail, with every smallest inflection, and never used a score while conducting.

Whether in the case of conductors, instrumentalists, singers or speakers, there is no doubt that performance from memory gives increased concentration and an extra dosage of strength. Why, in the matter of conducting (and that only) this obvious truth should have been disputed it is hard to say, but that is the fact. Great and serious conductors sprang to the defence of conducting from the score.

Otto Klemperer once said in mock despair:

"Because that Italian [Toscanini] is myopic, *I* am expected to learn everything by memory." ·

Busch, Reiner and others, both in their talk and in writing, strongly urged the use of the score while conducting. In contrast, Mitropoulos and de Sabata, for instance, made conducting by memory a fetish.

My own view, based on experience, is that neither principle should be carried to an extreme. Conducting from memory can bring no advantage unless the music has been completely mastered, has become, in its entirety, part and parcel of the conductor's mind and body. The question is: how much music can be so assimilated by one brain and nervous system?

Toscanini's memory was fabulous, but he had the wisdom and strength to keep within its limits. Thus his repertoire, while considerable, never exceeded his retentive capacity.

Most professional conductors cannot restrict themselves in this way, but are compelled, for one reason or another, to conduct far more music than can be adequately memorised. It is possible to learn to memorise a score in a superficial way, and some of the conducting-by-memory fetishists do that, invariably to the detriment of the music and of themselves.

To stand on the podium without the score by reason of personal vanity is of no value whatsoever. That vanity will not be served because, since Toscanini, conducting from memory has become so common (it is not so difficult, either) that it has long since ceased to impress the public.

The fact is that one can conduct very well and very badly both with a score and without one. It is best to do what is most helpful to oneself, to use the score when it helps and to discard it when unnecessary. For only one thing counts, and that is the performance.

Here is an instance of how the matter can be handled with simplicity and sincerity.

In the early 1930s an interesting musical event took place in Berlin. Wilhelm Furtwängler gave a concert with the Vienna Philharmonic; the great German conductor with the great Austrian orchestra in the great German capital performed the great Austrian masterworks.

My sister and I went to the concert, which was indeed exquisite. We heard the "Unfinished" Symphony by Schubert and the Bruckner Seventh, both performed breathtakingly. The playing of the orchestra was superb, and Furtwängler conducted masterfully. From memory, of course.

During the concert word got around that, as a rare favour, an "encore" would follow if desired. So the audience stayed and applauded unrelentingly. And as its reward, it witnessed the following:

after several bows by Furtwängler and the orchestra, a richly uniformed attendant appeared on the podium, carrying an immense dreadnought of a music stand and placing it meticulously in front of the conductor's rostrum. He then left, to return with an imposing-looking, fat score, which he carefully opened at a certain page. Then a short pause followed before Furtwängler reappeared, bowed, turned around, bent over the score and, looking at it carefully, bar by bar, note by note, conducted for us Johann Strauss's "Emperor Waltz" – one of the most popular pieces of music ever written, which surely the entire orchestra and most of the audience knew by heart. But Furtwängler didn't – and he was not taking any chances.

The cheers never seemed to end.

The conductor's personal relationship with his orchestra is an enigma – and a very difficult and sensitive matter altogether.

314

There is a story that a prominent conductor of our time, before facing an orchestra which he had not conducted before, spent hours in front of a mirror rehearsing the words with which he would greet them.

"Good morning, gentlemen!"

Jovially.

No, it needed to be more matter of fact.

"Good morning, gentlemen."

Matter-of-factly.

No, a little more humour would be advisable.

"Good morning, gentlemen!"

Humorously.

No, more immersed in the music that was to be played.

"Good morning, gentlemen . . ."

Immersedly.

After much sweat and toil he had it just right. The next morning, at ten a.m. sharp, he stepped on to the podium and said, as he had decided:

"Good morning, gentlemen."

And had 102 new enemies.

By and large, I think the conductor's knowledge of his material, honesty of purpose and clarity of instruction (verbal and gestured) will convince an orchestra, and will produce good and willing collaborators.

Youth is not an asset in communicating with orchestras. What can a twenty-five-year-old conductor say to the first horn player who, after having been asked to play a certain note long, replies: "Toscanini wanted it short." That kind of thing often happened to me in my younger days.

I spoke of clarity of instructions. The rule is: know what you want to say, and say it briefly and, if you can, not dully. If you bore your collaborators, you're lost. Don't ask for anything that you cannot get, but insist on getting what you have asked for. Don't lose your patience or your temper. Let others lose theirs before you do, if they must. Do not try to be omniscient, you aren't. Admit your mistakes. But do not make so many that admitting them would be embarrassing. Do not command, but suggest. Do not order a repeat playing of a section or any other correction without explaining, in a few words, your reason for it.

These are excellent rules. I wish I had always followed them.

It may have been noticed that in all that I have said the conductor's relationship with the public has not figured at all. And this for a good reason. For the conductor does not work "with" the public, nor directly "for" the public. What he does is entirely for and in connection with the orchestra which is in front of him. The sound of the music that emanates, not from the conductor but from the players in the orchestra, is what must hit the public and hit it right.

It has been suggested by purists that the conductor should be hidden behind a screen. I have nothing to say against that idea except, perhaps, that it is too "pure". By the same token, the entire orchestra – or any performer of any music – should be heard but not seen. The contorted face of a tenor singing his high C is no joy to watch, neither are the puffed cheeks of wind players. The quick in-between "emergency" tunings of the harpist, the various attitudes of string players, the flailing arms of conductors are not particularly attractive sights, and are distractions if treated as the main spectacle.

Still, I would leave it to the audience to decide what it wants to look at and when. Every member of it is free to close his or her eyelids for a moment or two if what is on view becomes tiresome.

In fact, looking at the act of music-making on the fringe of listening to it is something that, although secondary, should not be made impossible.

It is the business of the sound-makers, the music-makers, not to divert the attention of the audience from the music by misbehaving on the platform.

Excessive gesturing is misbehaviour. Every performer on every stage should make it his duty not to get in the way; to let his message reach the public and to beware of reaching out for the public himself.

Useless and exaggerated conductorial gesturing is especially disgusting because it is unnecessary. A violinist, 'cellist, percussionist, etc., *must* make certain kinds of movements which are demanded by the playing of his instrument. The conductor plays no instrument. He gives signs to other people. The more discreetly he can do that, the better for them, for himself and for his listeners. What the conductor's movements must be is to be understandable to the players. The clearer the better. Clear beat is a skill – a small skill at that – which has only one problem: it cannot be learned. The clear beat is born into the body, like the colour of the eye, or a fingernail.

The gift of the "upbeat" is elemental and mysterious and an indispensable asset in the art of conducting. I would not encourage anyone to be a conductor who does not possess it. Yet some musicians have become conductors without it – and in rare cases they have become very good conductors: their musicality, intellect, and other strong traits have counterbalanced the failing.

Wilhelm Furtwängler, one of the greatest, most powerful and most poetic conductors of our times, was one who had a bad beat. He struggled manfully with this shortcoming, and won. His performances of works by Beethoven, Brahms, Bruckner and others – his repertoire was not very large – were breathtaking, awe-inspiring at their best.

He had the curious habit of letting his outstretched arms tremble for a rather long time – five or six seconds or more, which can become a "stage-eternity" – before starting a piece. Out of this trembling the first sound of the orchestra burst forth with cataclysmic force.

All young musicians – amongst them myself – wondered how he managed such a spontaneous, razor-sharp attack by the orchestra with that insecure, "mumbling" beat. I was fortunately at the source of information, my father being a member of the Budapest Philharmonic Orchestra with which Furtwängler often appeared as guest conductor.

One day I asked him: "Tell me, Papa, how do you do it, to start all together after that trembling of Furtwängler?"

My father's surprising reply was: "We never start together."

Yet it always seemed so. Such was the strength, the suggestive force, of this man.

He knew about his "poor beat" and took it good-humouredly in his stride. Once when a young conductor asked him about the problem of upbeats, he replied: "Do you have to come to me, of all people, with this question?"

In the foregoing I have described the conductor's art in perhaps too lowly terms. In fact, it is a modest profession; its true pride is in its modesty. Still, one must not think too disparagingly of it, as I

317

did for many years, regarding it as being inferior to all vocal and instrumental arts and skills, and certainly way below creative effort.

I learned the real worth, the special strength, of conducting, one day, on my own skin, so to speak.

When in 1960 I began rehearsing my first (and so far only) symphony, I was, with my long conducting experience, absolutely certain that I could cope with it easily. After all, I had just then written it, and remembered every note of it well. Yet after two or three minutes of rehearsal, I had to stop and tell the orchestra: "Please, turn to the Beethoven overture. Before we rehearse my symphony again, I have to go home and learn it."

What I realised at that moment was that with every piece of music I conduct, I must learn it *from the conductor's angle*. I must know more than just the music; I must *know how to make it sound*. This knowledge is a special one, not identical with "knowing the music". In other composers' works I had subconsciously incorporated that part of preparation into my overall studies, but had neglected to do it for my own work.

This opened my eyes, and especially my ears, once and for all to what a conductor, a performer, must know of the work he is to conduct, and how he must go about knowing it. A simple, but all-important lesson.

A curious misnomer has bothered me for some time: the name "interpreter" that is given to us performers. It is regrettable that this faulty definition was allowed to creep into our consciousness, for it obscures the truth concerning communication in our art. From it would follow several other misunderstandings: first of all the idea that while music needs to be interpreted, the visual arts do not.

This is absolutely false.

Every art needs to be – and is – interpreted. The interpreters are always the receivers: the viewers in the case of paintings or sculpture, the listeners in the case of music; in every case, the public.

The music maker is the "performer" of it. If at all costs another word is wanted – the "re-creator".

In its essence art is nothing else than the confrontation of a human being with Creation. The capital C should show here that what is meant is cosmic creation, the great life-giving force of our universe. The desire to fathom this creative force is an exclusive human trait; no other being has it.

I like to think that it is the first, baffling "why?" which is at the base of *all* human intelligence and achievement. It must have been that yearning for an answer to a vaguely-felt question that made the man-ape get up on his hind legs to begin with – perhaps his greatest feat so far, because with it he left his belly exposed to attack and henceforth was forced to rely upon his brains to defend it.

Everything that millions of years later became worship, science and art originated in that first "why?" that has never been answered and, one hopes, never will be, because an answer to that primal question would kill every further advance, stifle all fantasy, and obliterate the beauty of the unreal, of the dream.

In that human game of trying to fathom Creation, which started with time itself and will end when time ends, the arts are a way of trying to approach the unknown by participating in it, imitating it as it were, with our small human resources and with our greater human fantasy.

It is interesting to note, and a proof of how neurotic our search for artistic creation is, that the only function in which we *de facto* participate in real creation, the begetting and giving birth to our children, has been the target of the most extravagant taboos in the course of our history.

I cannot create a tree – but I can make an image of a tree.

I cannot make thunder – but I can make a noise like thunder.

I cannot plant my exaltation in another human – but I can convey it to him with a gesture or a sound.

If we would dare to define art, we could say that it is the imitation of creation through invented symbols.

These symbols (lines, colours, sounds, gestures) the artist places in some order before his public. That order is his creative contribution. Each member of his public will then decipher or *interpret* that array of symbols according to his own taste and desire.

It is, I submit, this coding and decoding of symbols that give the supreme joy to artistic production and consumption.

By drawing a tree we are almost the creators of one. And by guessing that the black lines and spots on the white paper *do* mean a tree makes us as good – or almost as good – as the man who almost created that tree for us, and we understand and enjoy how it was done.

Our art symbols when placed into space − on canvas or paper or space itself, in the case of a statue − are ready to be interpreted by the onlooker at any time, for space *lasts* and so do the symbols contained in it.

When we place the symbols into time, a new problem arises, for time does not exist in the sense that space does: it does not last.

If we think of a symphony as an organised expression of emotions, feelings, contemplations within, say, half an hour, it is evident that the original half-hour into which the composer "placed" his symphony is long since past. It does not exist any longer. Neither, then, does his symphony. Its score is a worthless piece of paper for the public, because the public cannot read the symbols written on it. So a new half-hour is needed, plus another person, who has the faculty to *re-create* that music within that half-hour which the public provides through its presence.

Thus, the person or persons on the platform are taking the place of the absent composer, so to speak re-composing or re-creating the music for the listeners present. The music thus brought to life for another fleeting half-hour is still a conglomeration of symbols in the moment of its sounding, and will become music only in the ears of the listeners as *interpreted* by them for themselves.

In this light the role of the listener in the composer-performer-public-relationship is sharply brought to the fore. This is to the good: he should know that the music he hears will be valid for him in the end only through his *own* interpretation, and he should also be fully conscious of the contribution he is obliged to make to music, by giving his time to it: the half-hours he gives to the enjoyment of music are particles of his life and unique; they will never return.

30

At several points throughout these notes I have referred to my work as a composer. I feel compelled to add a few more words about it.

To begin with: composing conductors are a suspicious lot; further, my works are very little known at present and it is an open question whether they ever will find a large public.

No matter.

Both as an artist and as a chronicler it is my job to "bring my brick to the building". Therefore I cannot permit myself to pass over the fact that writing music is the very focal point of my life, and that I regard myself not as a "composing conductor" but the contrary: "a conducting composer".

It was in my early childhood that I began to write music. The first composition of mine that I remember is a scherzo for string quartet. I was about seven years of age then.

My next compositions were operas. There were three of them: the first was called *Arion* and was about that Greek mythological poet and lute player who rode on the back of a dolphin to visit his beloved. The second was the *Wieland*, "The Blacksmith". With it I turned to German mythology. Much later I learned that Wagner did consider that subject and wrote a scenario for it. My libretto was most gruesome: everybody in the opera got killed, so in the fifth act only corpses remained on the stage. Noticing that this rendered the singing problematic, I changed the story and had some of the cast only mortally wounded. The music, if memory serves, was rather in the manner of Grieg than that of Wagner.

The third opus was a one act opera buffa with the name *The Faithful Mozart*, who was indeed the hero of the piece. His eulogised faithfulness, however, was not to Konstanze or any other lady, but to Emperor Josef II to whom he speaks although badly treated and although Frederick the Great of Prussia does his best to entice him to his court.

The libretti to all three operas I wrote, of course, myself.

Soon I began to realise the utter futility of this opera writing

321

and began to write smaller works. There came along some symphonic poems, as for instance Richard III (which broke a piano string) and The Nile, written after Goethe's poem. Perhaps the most original was the piece for wind instruments called Bird-whistle, after actual bird-calls listened to in the countryside. (Messiaen was then eight years old.)

Nothing remained of all that except the top layer, until the entire "book" was lost during the Second World War in Budapest. For all these numerous long works were written into one and the same book on top of each other.

This had a reason:
it was my childish – no doubt highly neurotic – notion, that composing music was forbidden territory. Needless to say that was entirely a self-inflicted torture. My elders never thought of restraining me from anything.

Thus I had no music paper to write upon secretly, save some scraps found here and there and what I made myself, a slow, tiresome grind. One day I had some unexpected luck of receiving from my uncle Caesar (the painter) the gift of a big fat nicely bound book of music paper, that he once meant to use but didn't. That volume became my treasure house. It successively harboured my "collected works" all written into it, in pencil, from the first page to the last. When the book was full, I began, cheerfully, from page one again, erasing what it contained before.

When I was about twelve years old, I realised that I simply had to have some instruction to go further. This meant giving up my secret. After nearly one year of torment, I put the manuscript of a piano quintet, on clean, especially bought paper, on my father's birthday table.

He looked at the present severely and said: "Play it".

Thus I had my harmony lessons with Leo Weiner and one year later the coveted studies with Kodály.

After the Academy years my youthful compositions were quite in demand, when something unexplained and unexplainable happened to me that made me withdraw from composing.

That "loss of courage" or "drying up" was no doubt as neurotic as was the earlier "taboo" and probably closely related to it.

Be that as it may: there followed more than twenty years of

creative "exile", my conductor's life was absorbing, exhilarating and rewarding, yet I was – always – "homesick" for what I felt was my natural habitat.

Now how it happened that I started composing again is told earlier in these notes. It is, I think, no less than providential, that the neurotic traumas were finally shed the moment when issues of survival had to be met face to face. I was then about fifty.

The first work I wrote at that time in the mid-1950s was the largest I have composed so far. It is the dramatic cantata, *The Way*, which I have mentioned before. I come back to it now, because it was a turning point, or rather explosion, which changed my life as much as it was provoked by the inner changes within myself. Its subject is biblical: Calvary. But its theme is more than any single event; it is suffering itself. As Claudel puts it: *Il faut que nous portions notre croix Avant que la croix nous porte.* (We must carry our cross before it will carry us.)

This is not the cross of two wooden planks nailed to each other; it is the burdens that we all carry and the carrying of which liberates us to carry more of it – willingly, freely, strongly – through our lives to our death, and further perhaps.

How pleasing it would be to be able to report that it is an immortal master work. All I can say: the piece exists and has reached some of those who heard it. Its time may come. Perhaps.

My symphony in five movements followed immediately. Its material was ready in the sketches made on the S.S. *Comorin* in 1938.

After the symphony, I wrote quite a number of pieces in fairly quick succession. A Missa Brevis, a ballet, or as I called it, a choreographic poem *Magdalena*. This has not so far been per- formed on the stage, but an orchestral suite made from it, named "Seven Pictures", has been played several times. A cantata for baritone and chamber orchestra, *The Two Enchantments of Li Tai Pe*, followed. Then a string octet; a work for chamber choir and orchestra, Madrigal Suite; a song cycle for soprano and twenty-five instruments; *Chamber Music* on poems by James Joyce; *Night Music* for flute and small orchestra; and several pieces for a *cappela* choir. For Ilse I wrote a series of piano pieces called *Capricci*, which is still being added to; a set of variations on a theme by Béla Bartók; and a piano concerto; finally a concerto for 'cello, another for oboe, and a large symphonic song cycle called *The Voices* on texts by Rainer-Maria Rilke; and some more.

What is all this music like?

When asked I always say: listen to it and you will know.

It is difficult for me to describe music in words; I do it better the other way round.

At the start of my life the art of music went through the upheaval of breaking away from the "German yoke" as Bartók put it. At about the same time German music itself underwent a complete change, breaking away from its old self.

This was the more complicated and the more destructive revolution for it tended to change basic values, whereas the former breakaway, while not timid in innovations, kept those intact.

Arnold Schönberg's *"So geht es nicht weiter"* ("this way it cannot go on any longer") was a cry of the intellect, not of the instinct. He himself remained an unhappy romanticist, a prisoner of his own system, a pope in his Vatican. From it, forays into the world were made, reconciliations effected, as for instance by Alban Berg, a strong talent, who could carry the "system" on his shoulders – a modern musical St. Christopher.

The twelve-tone system came and went, serialism in other forms remained somewhat longer; in a general vacuum many other "isms" are still vacillating, in apparently stagnating waters, like jellyfish.

Schönberg's cry opened floodgates, but did not direct the waters anywhere – it did not show "how it *could* go on".

The problem of that movement was perhaps that it happened in Germany, where the force of musical creation itself was at a low ebb. The tragedy of two world wars, the increasing speed of communications, unnatural to the tempo of human life itself, further confused the logical development of the arts, including that of music.

Where is it heading today?

It could be that it is going in two different directions.

Not everything we hear nowadays as music can be called by that name, if we apply it to that very specific sound art that we are accustomed to call so.

For a long time now, I have felt increasingly convinced that we live in an epoch of musical schism, in a time during which a new art of sound is gradually emerging. It has no name for itself yet, it is not clearly defined, so it can easily be held as a misbegotten aberration of the "mother art". In reality it might not be that, but a budding, young constellation of sound art, born yesterday and ready, or almost ready, to fly in its own orbit.

The art of sound that we call music employs only a very small, select number of the unlimited quantity of sounds that exist around us. These are the tuned – or tunable – sounds. Our tempered scale – a compromise, bowing in the direction of the mechanical and leaving the human ear somewhat frustrated – has twelve of these sounds in one octave, around one hundred sounds that we can readily perceive or differentiate. The non-tempered ear has more, but the number of "musical" sounds is modest.

But modest does not mean poor. Art is discipline, and discipline entails economy. Therefore the art which is capable of the most powerful expression with the minimum of means is the richest.

To the number of our tuned, musical sounds we then add, as seasoning, a few noises borrowed from the "outer world" of untuned sounds. These are made by cymbals, drums, castanets, triangles, bongos, maracas and a good number of other instruments.

So why could not the reverse exist – a sound art based upon the multitude of untuned sounds and using as its seasoning a few tuned notes?

In a jumble, a chaos of unidentifiable, untunable sounds a sudden bell of an A could have the same shattering effect as has a cymbal crash that interrupts a C major chord.

This, of course, is fantasy. What I often hear nowadays presented as electronic, concrete or other "music" led me to dream it up, as an explanation of a phenomenon I otherwise would not be able to understand.

But I have a curious, true story to tell which could suggest that my speculation may not be so far from reality.

During one of my summer vacations, a few years ago, I made the casual acquaintance of a German scientist, then professor at a well-known university.

He was working with computers, but was also an amateur

325

'cellist, an ardent enthusiast of music. We went together on several long walks in the beautiful forests that surrounded our hotel, and on one of them he confided, with many profound apologies, the following – as he called it – sin.

Combining his musical enthusiasm and scientific zeal he had decided to conduct an experiment that included both his passion and his profession. He fed a programme into his computer that consisted of one hundred pages of scores by one hundred composers over about three centuries. The pages were of about the same density of notes. (It was at this point that his apologies began to verge on the hysterical: he knew that the samples should not have comprised "about" three centuries but *exactly* that period; he should not have been satisfied with "about" the same number of notes on each page, but should have seen to it that they were *exactly* the same number. But it was just a game – *sua culpa, sua culpa* – he was descending for relaxation from his scientific pedestal and was very sorry about it.)

The machine was programmed to determine the number of *identical* notes on each page, that is to find out which composer repeated any one note most often, and thus used, on average, the *fewest* notes. The computer was to produce a graph to show just that one special quality on each page, in chronological order of composers.

It was an interesting idea, he felt, to have a glimpse into the composer's mental workshop through that little window: which one of them needed the fewest and which the most notes to fully express himself.

It was not difficult to guess which great composer used the fewest notes, or rather, repeated his notes most often. It had to be Beethoven, as the computer duly confirmed.

The graph that came out from the machine showed first Bach using more notes than Mozart, then Mozart using more than Beethoven; then, after Beethoven, Schubert, Brahms, Wagner, Strauss, in that order, using more and more notes, with Stravinsky, Bartók and others as maximal note users.

But the surprise information of the graph was that at the tail end (chronologically) of the timetable a new graph appeared, running way below the main line and approximately parallel with it, featuring unknown names of the youngest composers he had fed in.

The complete graph must have looked somewhat like this:

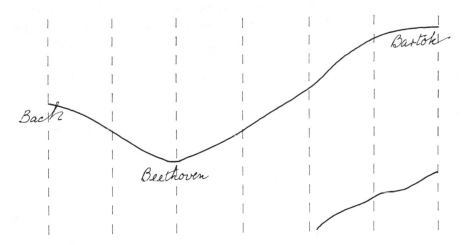

Unfortunately, the professor did not remember the names of the composers who produced the second graph. Obviously they were some of those who do not write many notes, but lines, circles, etc., to indicate sounds of indeterminate pitch.

The interesting features of this experiment were:

First, that the machine registered some of our latest music products on another graph than previous music pieces – that is, refused to admit them as belonging to the same art category as the others.

Second, that it registered these recent pages on the low part of the graph.

Third, that the new graph was shown rising almost parallel to the old graph, indicating:

(a) that the "new art" is becoming more complex;
(b) that the "old art" itself moves along in the same direction.

What startled me in the professor's description was that his experiment and my fantasy were leading to the same possibility – I even say, strong probability – that a new art of sound is being born.

I leave it at that. I am not trying to prove anything. But I cannot get rid of the thought of the "two arts".

That, friends tell me, is an "easy way out of the problem". It is not. It is not a way out at all, but it could be a "way with". It would explain how it is possible for one sort of music-making to go calmly on its own way, undisturbed by the stirrings of another.

But we started out a few pages ago with myself, and I owe the reader a statement of where I stand in the realm of musical creation.

I hold that Schönberg's verdict that music has reached an impasse and has to be started anew is an error. It was true only so far as he himself was concerned, but not for music itself. The infinite possibility of combinations, variations, relationships of one hundred odd notes of our tempered (or untempered, natural) scale are far from being exhausted.

The new should have its source in the challenge it offers, not in its inability to continue the old.

This is my credo, both as a composer and as a performer.

In both realms I am open to new impulses, impressions. I am ready to experiment, to explore new territories to the limit of my emotional world. Where I cannot follow is into the regions where demands are made only on my brain and where my temperament and my emotions, my impetuous, intuitive qualities, are left to idle.

How good my works are I do not know. They are the best I can write.

Compulsion to compose should not be resisted. I think every musician should at least try to compose and, if he is driven to it, continue as long as he lives. He will be a better, more complete musician, a better, more complete person for it. The inevitable, stern, and most of the time just process of natural selection will take care of the vast amount of creative outpourings, and leave only a handful in each century to survive, anyway.

But nothing is a waste; all of what is being produced is necessary to nourish, to make come about that top handful that will shape the century's profile.

And anyone who has succeeded in composing one worthwhile bar – this is Goffredo Petrassi's lovely phrase – has not lived in vain.

I treasure one critical statement concerning my music: "Doráti's music is much more contemporary than it sounds."

If the reviewer knew what he was saying, and if it were true, then this would be high praise indeed.

For what I want to say in my music is definitely of our own time, deriving from impressions gained in it, problems, joys, sorrows lived through in it. I am a child of my century.

But I do not feel the twentieth century to be as monstrous, crude and cruel as it appears through our unspeakably vulgar information system. True, our time is full of unprecedented brutality and horror. Nevertheless, I found and continue to find in it much to enjoy, to cherish, to admire and to respect. So the mixture that makes the soil for my music is not altogether forbidding or abhorrent.

Mozart wrote to his father that "music must never offend". It should also, if it can, console a little.

Also: I never write anything "instead" of something else, either in content, form, or technique.

And finally: I do write for people – real, existing listeners. I imagine them, almost bodily, when I write. They have no faces, no identities, but they are there, watching, taking part in what I do. I explain, I plead, I insist. But I am not "alone" when I write music, and I definitely wish to be understood by lay people, on *my* terms.

31

SOME QUESTIONS THAT I AM OFTEN ASKED ARE PERHAPS TOO pertinent to be shrugged off lightly:

How does it feel to be me? How does it feel to hear my music performed, to walk out on to the platform to conduct a concert? What do I feel during a performance and what do I feel after it?

First – I think absolutely nothing of me being "me". In about my eighth year I lived through a short period when my identity became a great problem. I brooded sombrely:

"Why am I me?"

"Why is my father my father?"

"Why am I not my father and not my father me?"

"Why must I see with my own eyes, why must I hear with my own ears? Couldn't I see just once what my father sees?"

"When I see something blue, is it the same blue that my father sees? Or are we seeing different things but have only the same word for them?"

After a short while, these worries yielded to others and I accepted my identity. I have never had the same problem since.

Never have I had any notion of being somebody of importance. True, I was saved from having to choose my profession, I always had a calling. That would make me one of the chosen, a privilege that has to be accepted, or borne with humility. Even a small talent is an enormous responsibility on one's shoulders; one has to live up to what one was given. I have tried to do that, throughout, first with impatient crudeness, later with growing enlightenment and serenity. Never for a moment have I ever had the feeling – let alone the certainty – that I have achieved that goal. But never, I must add, have I felt frustrated, dispirited or deflated for longer than a few minutes at a time. I have lived, and am still living, in a sort of preparatory period, looking forward to some arrival, some time, somewhere.

And now, the other three questions:

330

When I hear music that I wrote performed by others, I am interested, but not affected personally. When I conduct my music, I give it the same attention and dedication that I give to all the music I perform. I have neither listened to nor conducted my music often enough to be bored by it. It would be quite nice to be able to think, "Oh God, not that bloody piece again!"

When I walk out on to the podium, I do feel the tension of the moment. Not in the form of anxiety, however; more like a horse approaching a jump. I did some riding in my youth, have felt the horse between my knees, and know well the sudden tension of the galloping animal, the sudden aiming of its entire body towards the fence, the change of pace, the flaring of the will, the purpose of the charge. That's about it. All the attention, every nerve, every bit of the brain is focused on what is going to happen, all that one had studied, thought and prepared, is now in that energy, that thrust, which has to conquer the moment that approaches.

During a performance, I am pure concentration. All that I feel is the music, nothing else. That concentration restrains every unnecessary function of brain and body. In my fifty-four years of conducting, I have never coughed or sneezed during a performance, even if I have had 'flu or a bad cold. Itches, pains, aches – all are obliterated. The submersion, the dedication, physical and mental, is complete.

And after it's over, release, a happy moment; then, right away, even before I have left the podium, a severe self-appraisal, almost invariable discontent – and a vow to do better next time.

Now that I have replied to these questions, may I answer one of my own: What would I *like* to be?

I always wanted to be a musician. And that is still what I want to be now – a musician, and a good one; a better one tomorrow than I am today. I do not want to "excel", just to be very, very good.

And I would like to keep increasingly interested in the fine arts, literature, the theatre, geography, history – everything to do with my times.

To be what is called a "Renaissance man". That is what I would like to be.

32

MY TASK IS COMPLETED. I HAVE PUT DOWN ON PAPER THE MAIN events of my musical life, my observations, my beliefs, as they have developed and changed during my time, as life itself has changed during it. What pleases me most is that this last page is written in the turmoil and excitement of a new beginning. I look over calendars, sketches of compositions waiting to be completed, correspondence. I observe that my plans solidly cover the next four years with new ideas, enterprises cropping up all the time.

How far will God's grace allow me to carry on? At my age the question is natural. I ask it in confidence and without anxiety.

I remember the proud sentence that "a fine work of art is in every one of its states complete". My life, then, is no "fine work of art" because, whenever it ends, it will still be a fragment, much more unfinished than finished.

Ilse has just come into the room, asking what I was doing. When I told her, she tactfully departed, leaving me alone to finish the book.

She need not have, for her presence in whatever I am doing is constant. So, too, she is in every letter of these notes. She never encouraged me to start them, never prodded me to continue or to finish them, yet without her presence they would not have been finished, never even been begun. As, without her being, and being for me what she is, I should be in every respect a much inferior man to what I am, and especially to what I still hope to become.

Throughout these notes I have refrained from this kind of very intimate, very tender reference. I leave this one as a loving "Good morning" at the start of a new day. Nothing more, nothing less.

It is wonderful, exhilarating, to look expectantly into a new dawn.

Maybe, next time, the figure in the sand will come out right.

October 30th, 1977

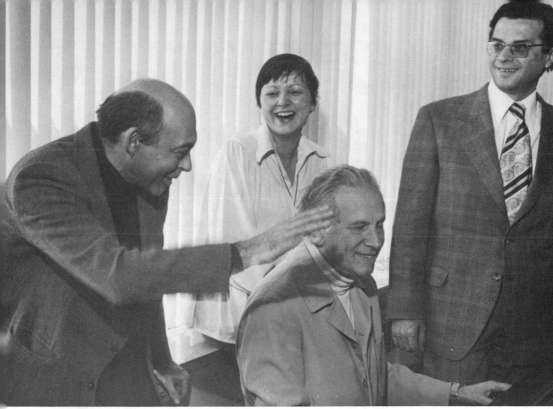

Antal Doráti at the piano and some fellow Hungarian musicians in March 1978. *Left to right,* 'cellist Janós Starker, cimbalom player Marta Fabian and composer Zsolt Durko.

Soprano Elisabeth Søderstrom and tenor Curtis Rayam perform with pianist Antal Doráti during the Soirée musicale, part of the Detroit Symphony Orchestra's 1978 Schubert and Vienna Festival.

Maestro Doráti rehearses the Detroit Symphony Orchestra for the March 1979 staged performances of Strauss's *Elektra*.

Antal Doráti during an informal question-and-answer period at Detroit's Orchestra Hall in March 1979.

Soprano Gwyneth Jones and Antal Doráti rehearse for the April 1979 concert performances of Strauss's *Die aegyptische Helena*.

Maestro Doráti, the Detroit Symphony Orchestra, the Kenneth Jewell Chorale and soloists respond to applause following the Carnegie Hall performance of *Die aegyptische Helena*. *Left to right*, Antal Doráti, Willard White, Curtis Rayam, Barbara Hendricks, Matti Kastu and Gwyneth Jones.

Aaron Copland and Antal Doráti during the Detroit Symphony Orchestra's birthday celebration of the composer's works in October 1980.

Antal Doráti poses with some distinguished fellow Americans before the October 1980 performances of Schuman's cantata *Casey at the Bat. Left to right,* former Detroit Tigers baseball star Al Kaline, composer William Schuman, Maestro Doráti and former Detroit Tigers baseball star Charlie Gehringer.

Antal Doráti in Paris in 1964. Photo by Jacques Aubert-Philips.

Giacomo Manzù's *Nymph and Faun,* in the courtyard of Wayne State University's McGregor Memorial Conference Center, Detroit. Photo by Wayne State University Center for Instructional Technology.

Giacomo Manzù's *Porte della morte* at St. Peter's, Rome. Photo by Oscar Savio.

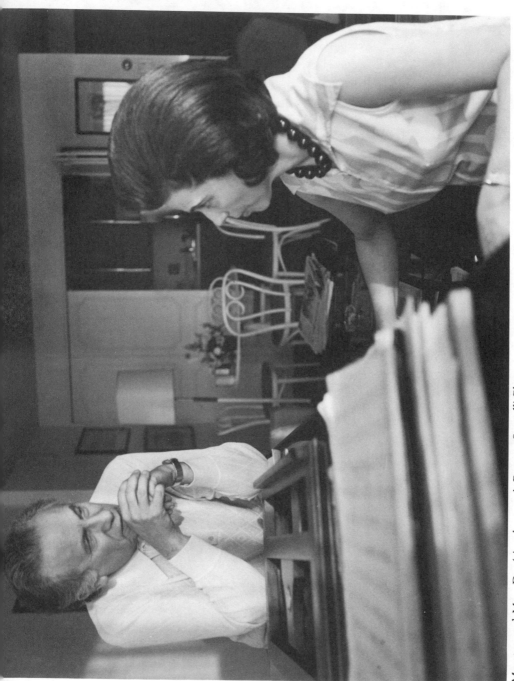

Maestro and Mrs. Doráti at home. A Ramon Scavelli Photo.

33

"BUT, NONNO! IT IS TOMORROW ALREADY!"

This golden sentence was minted by my grandson, Nicky, at the age of six ("Nonno" is the Italian word for grandfather) when, on one of our regrettably rare visits together, I gave him seven pieces of candy, one for each day of a week. The goodies were placed in full view on my desk, and he was to pick them up, daily, one by one. The second day he came to my study at the ungodly hour of five in the morning – when only grandfathers may be up and about – and the above little jewel was his reply to my quizzing the reason for his welcome but unexpected appearance. With that, he took his health-food candy bar of the day with majestic aplomb and departed.

And left me to deal with the tomorrow, which was, indeed, already at hand. Very much so.

This little scene comes to mind as I begin to write additional chapters for the American edition of my *Notes,* which I brought to a close just three years ago, at exactly the same spot where I am sitting now, looking out from my desk at the pleasant garden landscape with its still bright green grass and ample trees, their thick foliage showing the first spots of rust, slowly shaking in the soft autumn breeze. A car passes now and then. No sign of any passers-by.

It is one of my rare free mornings in Detroit, which is very welcome, for I have many things to do. To write this chapter, for instance. But also other things, such as finishing the finale of my string quartet, which should have its first performance in Paris in November. And a full basket of correspondence to attend to. And, of course, the programmes of the many concerts during the next weeks to study.

Ilse's piano-playing sounds faintly from downstairs.

Our living quarters in Detroit are in the very lovely and agreeable garden suburb called Grosse Pointe, which has the reputation of harbouring the very exclusive aristocracy of the era. If this is so, we do not see any of it, as we live with good friends in a uniquely hospitable, free and democratic arrangement. This once-in-a-lifetime relationship is one of the most cheerful and memorable of our recent years and should be recorded here.

Once, when I came as a guest conductor to Detroit – I believe in 1975 – my management failed to book hotel rooms for us in time. When it woke up and began to inquire, it found out that not a single room was available in or around the city for that particular week. The Detroit Symphony's Junior Women's Association rose to the emergency in the person of Mrs. Maralyn Domzalski, who offered lodgings in her house to Ilse and me. We accepted very half-heartedly, preferring in a strange city a hotel room of our own, where we could do as we pleased. As we heard later, the offer was made with just as little enthusiasm, for it is not an easy matter to harbour two complete strangers in one's home, and what's more, two artists, musicians. Who knows how disagreeable, how unbearable they can be? But our prospective hosts heroically decided that for one week they could put up with almost anything. We, too, made up our minds that for one week we would put a good face on whatever might come.

The lady who fetched us at the airport, was, to begin with, extremely good to look at, with a blondish aura of easiness, a certain elegant, carefree openness that presaged well. At my arrival I had a slight throat problem. Thus, knowing that my host was a medical man, en route to our future quarters I asked our gracious driver: "Madame, is your husband perchance a throat specialist?"

Whereupon, with an irresistible smile, she replied: "No, I'm afraid it's rather the other end."

Dr. Henry Domzalski is a noted urologist.

With her utterly enchanting sentence, a lasting friendship was started and sealed.

The week spent in the Domzalskis' house was one of the most agreeable in our memory. So, when I next came to Detroit, we halfway expected another invitation, which did not fail to arrive. Then, in 1977, when we were to make our headquarters in Detroit, their very hearty offer to share their house for the weeks of our presence was too tempting to refuse. Since then, whenever Ilse and I are in Detroit, the four of us live at Windmill Pointe Drive in brotherly-sisterly harmony, without a single disturbing incident; this is a very, very rare companionship to come about.

(Henry, as I know him, is not likely to write his memoirs, so what *he* has to say about us will be known in less definite terms. I always was lucky in such situations.)

The entire neighbourhood is serene and lovely. Ilse and I have long walks in this tranquil landscape every day. We do not meet many people. Those few, who also walk, we know and exchange greetings with. Most of the drivers of the cars that pass us also say hello. Some stop and ask, concerned for our well-being, if they can help us, "give us a ride", thinking it improbable that people would just walk about the landscape by their own free will.

This is Detroit, then, the Motor City.

Obviously an important part of this chapter will be devoted to Detroit, although not because I have spent most of the last three years here as Music Director of the Detroit Symphony Orchestra. Far from it: because of what has happened to the post of symphony orchestra director in our days, I have been in the city proper for no more than thirty-four weeks during the last three seasons. With the orchestra itself I have spent only a little more time (six additional weeks) on tours.

These meager statistics go to show how sadly the times have changed. In those days when great orchestras were emerging, they came about through the extended collaboration of a good conductor with a good orchestra. Their association lasted for decades and bore heavenly fruits of highest culture. To mention but a few, there were the forty-five years of the Concertgebouw Orchestra with Willem Mengelberg, about the same length of time as the Chicago Symphony with Frederic Stock. The last of these heroic epochs has just ended: Eugene Ormandy's directorship of the Philadelphia Orchestra.

It is not just the number of years that makes the difference. Even more important is the number of months, weeks, days, hours during those years in which the combined talents, energies and ambitions of conductors and players are forged together into the supreme amalgam of a great orchestra. But even as late as during my own Minneapolis times, I was together with my orchestra for only about six months each year.

How did this change occur? And why?

I think that, basically, it is today's public which has shifted its attention to a large degree from music to the music-makers, and as

335

those are of less enduring interest than music itself, the public needs a greater variety of them. Actually, it is not *our* wish to travel so much and to be so little with the orchestras for which we are responsible. The entire situation is so perverted that, if we did have more time to offer, we would not be welcome any longer at all, anywhere. Our real strength has become, ironically, not our presence, but our absence.

When I came to Detroit, I gave its orchestra as much time as was left over from previously accepted engagements, mainly in London with the Royal Philharmonic Orchestra, and elsewhere. That was accepted, and miraculously it proved to be enough to produce deeply satisfying results – at least musically. In fact, the DSO has, in a way, "outflanked" its home community. It is in danger of not being recognized by it commensurately with its value to the city and the service it renders to it, not only with music-making, but also as Detroit's cultural standard-bearer, or, to change the metaphor, as its umbilical cord to the outside world.

For Detroit is rather isolated. Supplier of automotive vehicles to the thoroughfares of the world, it is not itself located on the world's main arteries. Then too, its geographical situation, on the shores of Lake St. Clair and the Detroit River, although potentially beautiful, is unhappy in that its various districts and suburbs are quite separated from each other. This situation is not helped by the absence or insufficiency of public transport (no streetcars or subways at all, an altogether too thin network of bus lines), a circumstance which, although a natural outgrowth of the entire area's "automobile mentality", has a very negative effect upon its social development in the long run.

How much Detroit's "seclusion from itself" contributed to the extreme severity of the racial upheaval that took place in 1967 may be hard to establish. At any rate, perhaps no other large American city suffered so much damage, so great a setback from that kind of unrest as did the Motor City. Its once flourishing, attractive downtown district has been all but abandoned completely, and allowed to go to shambles – a sad, melancholy array of run-down streets without the sweetening touch of antiquity. Yet the more admirable and encouraging is the present effort to restore it to what it was: the center of a great city. Detroit has undertaken a civic movement true to its chosen name, "Renaissance". Scarcely a decade old, the courageous initiative has borne great, more than merely visual results.

Besides the great renaissance of Detroit itself, several other renaissances are now taking place within the city, and there were several in the past. The very *raison d'être* for my presence here, the Detroit Symphony Orchestra, has already had two re-births and is presently going through another renaissance period. The complete reorganization of the Chrysler Corporation could be called and is probably amounting to a re-birth. Then, there is the story of Orchestra Hall, a smallish concert hall of miraculous acoustics, built in 1919 for Ossip Gabrilowitsch, who was then the Music Director of the Detroit Symphony. This unique building was allowed to fall into complete disrepair and is now being reconstructed, step by step and inch by inch, by a stalwart and brave group of culture-conscious citizens.

All of this is a curious testimony for a certain thoughtlessness and carelessness on the one side, and for an inherent heroic strength, a will to re-build, on the other.

Detroit was never known as a cultural center; it was satisfied with being the automobile capital of the globe. Nevertheless, it has valuable cultural assets and a great and so far not fully developed potential of using and enjoying them. Its Institute of Arts is an excellent museum, housing first-rate collections of paintings, sculpture and other products of the fine arts, of a value and quality much above their general reputation. It also has had a symphony orchestra since 1914, which, although disbanded for two brief periods since its founding, has become far better than has been admitted by its own public or elsewhere in the United States. By and large, the Detroit Symphony Orchestra had become a competent performing body, without special distinction, respected but hardly cherished, accepted rather than admired.

It was to remedy this situation that I was called upon. When I was asked to join the orchestra as its Music Director, I was given the mandate to upgrade it into what is called, for want of a better name, a "world-class" orchestra.

Alas, the group of fine citizens who took over responsibility for the destiny of their orchestra failed to plan providently for its ascent into the world-class category, probably more through the *laissez-faire* attitude in which great wealth can indulge than through negligence.

They did not realize, or at any rate did not anticipate, the fact that the upgrading of an orchestra means budgetary expansion commensurate with the orchestra's rise in quality and scope.

My constant admonitions were royally disregarded. "All the bills are paid, aren't they?" was the almost curt reply I received to my warnings. They were indeed, promptly and generously. But paid from what? From deeper and deeper dippings into the smaller and smaller reserves.

Perhaps the Detroit Symphony Orchestra's Board of Directors did not really believe that their orchestra would – or could – become part of the world's elite, but I did. And thus I proceeded to go on with the task with which I was entrusted in 1977. This task was, by and large, completed within two years. It turned out that the orchestra had far greater reserves in talent than I, even optimistically, had anticipated. Therefore, there was nothing else to do than to make the performers feel, individually and collectively, that they were artist-musicians rather than musician-workers. Once they truly recognized their real status, their playing shone in new, splendid colours, overnight, as it were.

By 1979 we had an orchestra second to none triumphantly touring the music centers of Europe. I must therefore say that, within my multi-faceted Detroit experience, the most gratifying single feature was the emergence of the orchestra itself from routine satisfactoriness to overall excellence. The evolution was of the same kind as happened during my Washington years, although starting from and leading up to higher levels. The truly exceptional accolade which the orchestra received on its European tour in 1979 – as a much touring musician, I am well in the position to have a judgment on that – was fully merited.

The public of London, Paris, Berlin, Brussels, Madrid, Stockholm, Oslo, Zürich and sixteen other European cities turned out in droves to hear the Detroiters. Practically every concert was played to sold-out houses and a more than generously appreciative audience. About eight-five per cent of the many reviews were full of the highest praise. It can truly be said, not without some irony, that the Detroit Symphony Orchestra so far has been accepted and acclaimed at its full value only in Europe.

The New York press, when the orchestra appeared in their city in a series of three concerts in the spring of 1980, was not yet ready to accept the newcomer from the American Middle-West totally. If it had arrived from England or Mexico, it probably would have had an easier time. The public, in three sellouts at Carnegie Hall, embraced it warmly. As yet tender and young within its new high sphere, the orchestra was nervous at these New York concerts, and, thinking back upon those evenings, perhaps even I, with all my years of hardening and experience, was not at my calmest.

The hometown public duly feted its orchestra upon its return from faraway successes. It comes to the concerts at Ford Auditorium in ever-increasing numbers, and a new pride in and loyalty to the DSO is clearly in the making. Nevertheless, the last to recognize the supremacy and full value of its orchestra will be Detroit itself. "No one is a prophet in his own land", says the proverb. True enough. Especially when – as in this case – someone wasn't exactly a prophet in his homeland for a long time.

34

THE GREATEST ENEMY OF THE FINE THINGS IN LIFE IS ROUTINE. LIVING with it is like living inside a room with closed shutters. There is just enough light to get about, to attend to chores; one can even distinguish good weather from bad – *outside*. Sun, rain, shower, breeze, heat, cold – all that is *outside* – always, everything, *outside*. When, after years have gone by in the artificial dusk, a shutter is opened, the light is blinding, downright disagreeable. One has to get used to it. Then life can begin again, on the new level of being part of the outside and the outside being part of ourselves.

Gustav Mahler said: *"Routine ist Schlamperei"*. "Routine is slovenliness" – a truth cruelly but correctly seen and exposed.

What is this routine-slovenliness? And where does it come from?

It is one of the more disgusting human specialities; not a natural phenomenon. Nature is not slovenly; routine is unknown in it. From the beautiful symmetry of a maple leaf, the exquisite pattern of a snowflake, to the pedantic, fastidious arrangement of a peach, from the tidy, acrobatic efficiency of a squirrel (I am just observing one busily, knowingly, hiding something in the ground, hoarding for the winter. How will he ever find it again?) to the leap of a panther, nature is always unique, superlative. Never, never routine.

Yes – *nostra culpa* – we have brought routine – boredom – upon ourselves, we, the supreme *homo sapiens,* by inventing the "everyday". That has never existed before. Our minds gave birth to it, to destroy us. It is the everyday that creates slovenliness, routine; it is the everyday that kills love, ambition, joy, leading us astray from nature, making us lose contact with its creative forces, with creation itself.

Elsewhere in these notes I postulate that art is the outcome of the human craving to confront creation face-to-face. This craving is present in every human being, buried under the ballast of the everydays, of routine. Woe to those who cannot work themselves out of that heavy heap of rubbish.

To some it may seem that I have wandered from my subject. Not to me. I am right here where I was, in Detroit, Michigan, put here by destiny for a good reason: to try, with the help of my splendid colleagues, to reduce the number of everydays, to try to help my fellow humans work themselves out of that heap, to rise above the gray mist of the everydays.

Will we succeed? It is possible, perhaps even probable. Many signs give much hope. But it is too soon to tell. To get out of the mire of the everydays is much more difficult than to give in and sink into it. And takes longer. As my own time is limited, I see myself as the catalyst of the process, a sort of miniature Moses, allowed to lead his people *to* the promised land, but not *into* it.

Now three squirrels scurry about in the garden before my window. Next to the fine orchestral sounds that can be heard hereabouts nowadays, it is these garden surroundings that have gladdened my heart every day. This joy is as great now as it was three years ago, when I first came here.

Whenever I take up a new post, I make my plans to suit the environment. Thus, I looked into the music-making of the city and surrounding area. I found it checkered, on the whole somewhat pale. Every star performer has visited it at one time, as they go to every large city for a day. A good number of chamber-music concerts are being given regularly, to a smallish but faithful and interested local public. Its orchestra has existed for over seventy-five years, and during this time it has had two promising periods, one under the leadership of the Russian pianist-conductor, Ossip Gabrilowitsch, and the other under the French Paul Paray. The involvement of the local giant industries in music is and was unremarkable, with one notable exception: the famous "Ford Hour", which for a number of years was the automobile industry's great contribution to the cultural life of its capital. It not only brought a great array of the finest conductors and soloists of those days to Detroit, but also projected the sound of the Detroit Symphony Orchestra all over the country through its nationwide broadcasts. (The corresponding and rival "General Motors Hour" that sprang up a little later, operating out of New York City, showed less local patriotism.) It was said that this radio hour – which, while doing very good public relations service for the Ford Motor Company, held to such a high esthetic level that it meant a very real cultural contribution to the entire country's musical life – originated from the fact that Henry Ford I was a genuinely musical man. I readily believe this. That the motor king's musical taste was not the highest, that he liked folksy, "easy" music, does not matter at all. What mattered was that *some* kind of music gave him *real* enjoyment. Therefore, music did "exist" for him as a personal experience. A regrettably very rare quality amongst kings, automobile or other.

It is a mystery to me why so very few of the great potentates of the world are musically inclined. Perhaps they forego the joys of music on purpose, to avoid the dubious reputation of Emperor Nero, who as we all know fiddled while . . . and, for themselves, choose to do other things while. . . .

Be that as it may. The fact remains that very few of the high-and-mighty are musical. While this might be some loss to music, the real losers are they themselves.

These and other ruminations – deviations from the main line of my thoughts – come easily here at my window, while I am taking in the beauties of the constantly-changing colors and shapes. This is the kind of flatland-scape that casts its spell not by its grandeur, but by its innumerable details, the kind that fascinated the Flemish painters. When I began to write these last chapters, the landscape was bathed in a hundred shades of green. Now the trees are flaming in a multitude of reds, ochers, yellows. A feast – nay, an orgy of death. We have chosen the black of mourning to mark our passing away. The trees celebrate their death with a volcano of colors. We would, too, perhaps, if we were as certain to be re-born with the coming spring.

It's not a long way to go back to my subject. Music, the art I humbly serve, is for those who are open to be penetrated by it the most excellent celebration of *life,* past, present and future. It is this aura of feasting, be it serious or laughing, aggressive or demure, that I try and hope to convey and create with my music-planning and music-making.

What I have learned of the musical past of the Motor City suggested to me that a disruption of the honourable and orderly subscription seasons would be desirable. Thus, I envisaged yearly music festivals, which proved, on the whole, very successful. The reservation implied in the preceding sentence refers to financial success, which varied according to the nature of the festival. The first and third, dedicated to Beethoven's and Brahms's music, were sellouts. The second, featuring Schubert and Viennese music, was not. The fourth, yet to come, will be a Bartók festival on the occasion of the composer's centenary, and its audience appeal is problematic, being connected with contemporary music, which is still anathema to the largest part of the public all over the world. (As an inveterate optimist, I must add here that we may be in for a pleasant surprise.)

Artistically and morally, however, the festivals were unquestionably great successes, mainly, as I see it, because the festival programmes included not only offerings by the Detroit Symphony Orchestra, but also much chamber music, solo recitals, and pertinent musicological congresses. Thus, many other local musical organizations were involved and manifold musical interests were served. The city indeed became a *music center* for the one- to three-week periods of our festivals. Also, for the first time they made the name "Detroit" internationally known for its cultural assets rather than for its industry.

The same purpose was well served by a nine-part television series called "A Beethoven Festival", which was backed by the Ford Motor Company (much in the spirit, I believe, of old Henry Ford).

The city's name subsequently gained even more lustre internationally by the orchestra's European tour, which cannot be described by a lesser word than the one I have already used: "triumphant".

One look at the garden again. All of a sudden, a gust of wind. Millions of leaves fly from the trees, almost a cloud, like locusts, as many are lifted from the lawn, twirling, yellow, in low, circular sweeps. Naked branches begin to show between the whirlpools of foliage, the first warning fingers of winter's finality. The awesome end of a life cycle.

Back again quickly to the warmer climate of my notes, nearing their goal, too.

I have said before that the Detroit orchestra is only known at its true value in Europe. I come back, somewhat wistfully, to that statement to enlarge upon it a little. What I wrote is indeed true, but it is also true that this orchestra had never before played as beautifully as it did throughout that tour in Europe. What happened has a simple explanation: the Detroit Symphony Orchestra worked itself out of the "rubbish heap" of the many everydays under which it had been buried for too long.

Yes, those who are to give light have to *have* light.

This is one of the very important, very crucial reasons why an orchestra must from time to time travel, feel the contact with the "outside". It will improve immensely with the experience, as did the Detroit Symphony Orchestra, which since its tour has played many times as well and more beautifully than it did in Paris, London, Stockholm, Berlin and so forth. Not quite twelve hours before I wrote these words, it performed Beethoven's Sixth Symphony with a perfection and intensity that only a few ensembles can equal.

This sudden upswing in the orchestra's playing will be most noticeable in the recordings which were made in the aftermath of the tour. We began recording for London Records in the spring of 1978, at the slow pace of three long-playing records per year. Thus far, the orchestra has recorded ten records, of which only four have been released for sale so far. One need not say more about them than that two of the ten are best-sellers, and yet all of them are "pre-Europe" recordings. The great surprise is still to come, when the later ones are released.

35

MY PROFESSIONAL DETROIT STORY IS, OF COURSE, UNFINISHED, AND therefore cannot be summarized. True, my music directorship will end in the spring of 1981, after four, I may say, well-employed years, but that will not put an end to my involvement with the Detroit Symphony Orchestra. Far from it, as I can foresee with an inward smile and as will be evident in time. Yet, the incomplete experience already yields worthwhile and perhaps significant recollections.

At my first press conference in Detroit, one reporter asked: "And what about black players in your orchestra, Mr. Doráti?"

"Well, what about them?"

"Will you have them in the DSO?"

"Of course. First of all, we have already two black string players" (one is still here; the other left for his hometown and is now a member of the Cleveland Symphony Orchestra) "and if more will come to audition for eventual future vacancies, they will have the same consideration as all the others."

This reply provoked further questions, which ended by my declaring categorically that so long as I shall be at the helm of the Detroit Symphony Orchestra, no one will either join or leave it for reason of colour of skin, creed, or any other reason whatever than musical quality. This is certainly as it should be, and that is how it was and is upheld within our group.

Not entirely without problems.

The race issue has touched the arts in America (although not centrally), and that is also as it should be. If the problem has to exist at all, much to our shame, it cannot be confined to any one corner of life; or, rather, no corner can be exempt from it. And, basically, it is not a race – but a minority – problem. It is a regrettable human trait that wherever a population minority exists, sooner or later it will be attacked, often severely mutilated, or in some instances even extinguished, by the majority. At different times and in different places the minorities might be Jews, Christians, blacks, whites, no matter. Invariably these "attack periods" end in reversals similar in force and drama to what came before. These sick cycles did not begin with crucifixions and did not end with gas ovens.

A gradual social readjustment of the black and white populations in North America has been taking place for the last one hundred years or so. It began with the nominal liberation of the once-imported black slaves during the Civil War – the real cause of which was not the slave issue – and has been continuing on its winding, complicated route ever since. It is still far from its final resolution. It was bewildering to me, coming to this country from Europe, where this particular white versus black racial prejudice does not exist (there are plenty of other prejudices abounding there, just as contemptible), to witness the state of affairs in the United States.

During my Dallas years, in the late 1940s, I had invited the incomparable black singer Marian Anderson to be soloist with the orchestra. When I asked her to dinner at my house, not only were my other friends unwilling to join us, but our black maid refused to serve at "that kind" of dinner party. Klári and I did the serving and there were five of us: Miss Anderson, my wife and I, and just one couple of our "other" friends, John and Claire Rosenfield.

It was John, by the way, who told me of a priceless episode, pertinent and very American, which at this point I cannot keep to myself.

The reader may recall that John Rosenfield was at that time the all-powerful art editor and critic of the *Dallas Morning News*. In that capacity, he wrote one day a rave review of a black choir which had given a concert in the city. He was, so he said, truly enchanted by the excellence of the performance, and knowing that a black group did not have the easiest time in the South-West, he was especially generous in his praise. The next morning, to his surprise, a visit by the choir director was announced to him while he was at work in the huge editorial room, with its two hundred desks and as many clattering typewriters. John made a great show of receiving the huge black man in the most gracious manner, offering him his hand, a chair and a cigar. His guest sat down rather timidly, at the very edge of the chair, and hesitantly stated the reason for his visit, which was to thank John from the bottom of his heart for the favourable write-up. Coming from the pen of such a prestigious critic, it would help the choir a great deal.

346

John assured the director that he did no more than his duty as a music reviewer, that the choir was really very good, gave his best wishes for the future and so on, thus engaging his guest in further conversation while secretly looking around the circle of his colleagues, who watched the then rather unusual scene, conveying to them with his proudly blinking eyes: "See here, boys, *this* is the way to receive a black American citizen!"

John indeed succeeded in putting his guest more and more at ease. The visitor occupied a larger and larger part of the chair until he took full possession of it, crossing his legs and obviously feeling more and more comfortable by the minute. When John finally got up, signalling the end of the visit, the man bent forward and said, confidentially: "Just one more question, Mr. Rosenfield. Are you, perchance, Jewish?"

Smiling in mild surprise, John answered: "Yes, why do you want to know?"

Whereupon his guest said, beaming: "Oh, I just wanted to assure you that I have no racial prejudices whatsoever."

This preutopian scene is a period piece. (In a utopian landscape, the conversation never could have taken place.) Times have changed greatly, and today the joke could be understood in several ways.

As for symphony orchestras throughout the country, they search for black musicians like Diogenes with his lamp looking for the true man. Astonishingly, few turn up. Although the black race is by and large very musical – in fact, it has contributed most significantly to the musical traditions of the New World – so far its talents are concentrated much more in the popular music scene than in so-called "serious" music, which is, including its American branch, still intrinsically European. Thus, from the practical point of view, black participation in symphony orchestras lags far behind theoretical calculations. If the black population of the United States is put at around eighteen per cent, it is impossible to think that the racial makeup of symphony orchestras could be distributed even somewhere near that percentage within the next two generations. A large symphonic body is lucky if it can muster three per cent of black musicians.

Why do I say lucky? From the musical point of view – and that is the only one that counts – the skin color of the performer is completely irrelevant. Yet all of our large (and I am sure also the small) orchestras try to employ as many black musicians as they can. For what reason? Bad conscience? Atonement?

It comes to mind that after the Hitler times, each Nazi said that he knew one "good" Jew, whom he "saved". As there were some 13 million Nazis in Germany (not more: a very small number of people to bring such havoc, such devastation and misery into the entire world), there must have been 13 million "good" Jews who were "saved" – many more than exist altogether. On that basis, the United States should have now 200 million splendid black people, which somehow does not add up.

No, that is not the reason. Opportunism? Hardly. Not yet. In Detroit, for instance, the city administration is overwhelmingly black (very efficient, and much liked generally), so it would not be unthinkable that one would be inclined to do favours for it, even to the possible detriment of the orchestra. On the other hand, it must be said that not the slightest pressure was ever applied to force the DSO to employ black musicians; not a single word of even the faintest suggestion of that nature has ever come to my ears, which hear a lot. Still, if today there is any kind of racial "discrimination" in American symphony orchestras, it is in favour of rather than against blacks. Even I have to confess that, in spite of my rigourous principles on quality, I once succumbed to the temptation of being – what? Sympathetic? Helpful? Human? Or just catering to my own vanity by being "good"?

It doesn't work.

In one case I accepted an applicant, not as a regular member of the orchestra, but as an "orchestral fellow", a quasi apprentice position lasting one year, after which the fellow must go through the normal auditioning process if he wishes to apply for a vacancy if there is one. Well – I accepted him because he was black. He was not proficient enough, but I thought that in a year he might make enough progress to attain full professional level, and I took a chance. I was wrong, and did more harm than good by allowing other than strictly professional considerations to prevail.

The fellow did not make the grade, although he was given the fairest possible opportunity. I rooted for him, biting my fingernails throughout the entire audition. A symphony orchestra – as I knew only too well – is not a school, and its members cannot be selected on the basis of future development only. I had hoped to the last minute that my optimistic estimate should be proven correct, but no:

he could not become a regular member. Thus, I had caused, out of what I thought was "goodness" but was in fact nothing but weakness, much heartbreak and embarrassment.

What I have said at the outset – that no one will ever enter or leave my orchestras for any but musical reasons – remains true. Not by my merit, but by the strength of the principle itself. I will reiterate this and stick to it, but much more humbly than when I pronounced it first.

The exact measure of a conductor's work is the quality of the performance of his orchestra. It is to be remembered – as I have already pointed out in these notes – that it is the orchestra and not the conductor that makes the music. Thus, the prime endeavour of every orchestra conductor who merits that name is to lift the performance level of his orchestra to the highest sphere possible. To the superficial observer, it may seem that this is best achieved by firing the bad players and hiring good ones in their places. In reality, it is not so. To begin with, it is not always easy to establish who the "bad ones" are. It takes great skill, experience and a pair of good ears to be able to pinpoint the real weaknesses in an orchestra of one hundred members. Even once that has been done, it is far from being enough. The reasons for the weaknesses must be determined before going farther. In nine cases out of ten, it will turn out that a change in personnel will not be necessary to achieve decisive improvement. Often formerly "useless" elements can be turned into great assets. To bring these transformations about is part of the conductor's talent and skill.

Fortunately, in the case of the Detroit Symphony Orchestra, an enormous mass of superior talent lay quite close to the surface. It is a very special pleasure for a conductor to notice when an orchestra under his baton begins to "fill out" its own potential. This is what happened and continues to happen in Detroit, with remarkably few casualties on the wayside.

In the course of this "musical renaissance", the orchestra's atmosphere changed and is continuing to develop as that of a group of artists, in contrast to what I have called the city's general "assembly-line mentality". A wonderful transformation indeed, for music is not made by the same methods as automobiles. It is to be hoped that this new "music spirit" will prove contagious, for it is as much needed by the entire populace as fresh, unpolluted air, which nowadays may be less readily available than a fine orchestra. Should this newly-acquired attitude and status of Detroit's orchestra remain isolated, not fully embraced by those who should be its beneficiaries and backers, new problems, new debacles, and even catastrophes could happen that would devastate Detroit's cultural realm.

Thus, a sceptic may well ask whether or not those who had the idea of a world-class Detroit Symphony Orchestra – and, even more, those who made this idea become a reality – had inadvertently opened a Pandora's box.

The optimist's answer is: "No! This is as it was ordained to be. The cause of the present suffering and anxiety is strangely belated birthpains, no more."

The neutral observor is waiting, silently.

36

Although the Detroit Symphony Orchestra experience has been the novelty in my life since 1977, I have also continued all of my other varied and rewarding activities in the years since I completed the first edition of *Notes of Seven Decades*. My earlier interests remain undiminished or are even continuing at an accelerating pace. The slowing down becoming to a man who will shortly be seventy-five – I am constantly being reminded of this regrettable "event", so I hope I shall be forgiven for bringing it up – has not come about yet.

When my seventy-fifth birthday is passed, I intend to curtail my work as a performer a little. But not my creative life. There will be no reduction there, as far as I can help it. It is indecent to talk publicly about composition plans, so I only mention that I have them. Since completing my 'cello concerto, I have concentrated on chamber music, except for one small choral work called "Of God, Man and Machine". Five meditations on Hindu texts, for voice, oboe, 'cello and percussion, called "In the Beginning", and a "Sonata for Assisi" for two flutes are the harvest of the last two years. A string quartet, the most ambitious task a composer can undertake, has been finished since I began to write these chapters for my "American" *Notes*.

My prose writing, besides the present task, has consisted of some essays about Bartók and Kodály; the former's one-hundredth anniversary will be in 1981, and the latter's in 1982. Demands for personal recollections have been numerous, and to write them has given me pleasure, as well as a sort of sportive interest in the number of them I could produce without repeating myself.

What else? Oh, yes – I drew and painted quite a bit during these last years – if not better, then not worse than before.

The Royal Philharmonic of London more and more becomes "my" orchestra. Or I should really use the reverse expression, and say that I am getting more and more to be "its" conductor, just as I believe that one should never think or say about one's child, "this is

351

'my' boy", but be content to be "his" father. Our concerts together grow in mutual understanding and scope, and begin to show that intimate knowledge not only of the music we perform together, but of each other, that is the essential asset of *squisitezza*. My recent tour to Italy and Switzerland with the Royal Philharmonic was thus immensely satisfying.

The RPO, as it is known, has financial problems, too, as, indeed, has practically every orchestra everywhere. Only the way they cope with them is different, and the Royals do it with royal grace and dignity.

Another tour took me to the north of Europe with the Orchestre National de France of Paris, an orchestra of rejuvenated vitality. During this time we renewed and intensified our old relationship.

An unexpected call also took me to Hungary, where I was asked to participate in a film about Bartók for his centenary year. In the course of my short visit, the film turned out to be two films, involving much music-making and some talking in English, German and Hungarian.

Ilse professes regret about all these comings and goings. She wishes for me to do less and urges me to "cut down", but I am certain that she would be very upset if I *had* to and is very happy that this is not so, not yet. I have every intention of going on healthy and hale for a long time.

With Ilse's hand in mine, I do not have to ask for God's further help, for I have it already. No more can be asked for, no more can be hoped for.

This is the only aspect of my life which *is* complete. In all others, no matter when it ends, it will be a fragment, as I have said already. It will not be a great work of art, perhaps, for those, as we know, are complete in every one of their stages. But it will be part of one – a sketch, so to say – which, in contrast, is meant to be, destined always to remain incomplete.

I love sketches. I collect them, cherish them. They give to me greater insight into their creators' innermost secrets than do their masterworks. Thus, I like to think of my life as a sketch, as one part of a greater work of art, incomplete and unimportant in itself, but without which the whole would not be quite as complete as it is or aspires to be.

That small part, in its full littleness, is my total contribution. The brick, the one brick in the wall that I brought to the building.

37

And now I have definitely, absolutely, irrevocably arrived at the end of my *Notes*. This is, actually, the second "revised and augmented" edition, for I put some new material in the Hungarian translation (which was not – Heaven forbid! – done by me, but to which I could not resist adding some of my own words in my native tongue) before I wrote these final chapters.

Be it solemnly resolved here, that whenever and wherever another edition of this book be printed, it will appear without another word contributed by me.

The reader who has arrived at this sentence will, no doubt, take a deep breath of relief.

Not too soon, please.

I did not say that I will not write another volume one day.

Nothing autobiographical. Not any more.

Rather something else. Something original. For instance, an idea presents itself already: "Once there was a girl and a boy . . ." A promising start, though it could lead to complications. I will have to think it over.

October 23rd, 1980

Index

354

355

358

363

recording (*cont.*)
  Haydn's complete symphonies, 272–3
    and other Haydn works, 294–5
  popularity of certain works, 299
  role of the listener, 298
Reiner, Fritz, 216, 313
Reinhard, Max, 140, 186
Respighi, Ottorino, 184, 222
Rethberg, Elizabeth, 99
  in *Aegyptische Helena,* 100
Riabouchinska, Tatiana, Ballets Russes, 146
  and Lichine, 147
  in *Graduation Ball,* 163
Richter, Hans, 29, 72, 304, 308
  and conductors at rehearsal, 73, 307
Rigoletto (Verdi), at Münster, 115–16
Rilke, Rainer-Maria, 324
Rimini, early trip to, 83, 84
Rimsky-Korsakov, Nikolai
  Coq d'or, 154, 251
  Shéhérazade, 154, 191
Rite of Spring, see Sacre du Printemps, Le
Rockefeller Foundation, 277
Rodeo (Copland), 184, 203
Rome, 208
  Dorátis move to, 238
  life in, 253–4
Rome Opera House, 239
  productions at, 250–1, 254
Romeo and Juliet (Delius), 184
Romeo and Juliet (Tchaikovsky), 198
"Rosalinda", *see Fledermaus, Die*
Rosenfield, Claire, 199, 346
Rosenfield, John, 215, 346–7
  and Dallas Symphony, 194, 195, 196, 198, 202, 203, 213
Rosenkavalier, Der (R. Strauss), Kleiber conducts, 74
  Strauss conducts, 76
  Suite from, 216
Rostova, Lubov, 147
Royal Albert Hall, 178, 291, 293
Royal Ballet, 153
Royal Festival Hall, BBC Symphony at, 262
  facilities and programme of, 257–8
Royal Opera House, Covent Garden, 131, 132, 133
  Ballets Russes seasons at, 141, 152–3
  Le Coq d'or at, 251

orchestra of, 257
Royal Philharmonic Orchestra, 235, 257, 281
  Doráti with, 290, 293, 294, 336, 351–2
Rubinstein, Arthur, 178, 203
Rudolf, Max, 187
Rumania, 23, 28
Rupe, Gordon, Jnr., 200
Russia, 8
  occupation of Budapest, 210–12, 213

Sacre du Printemps, Le (Stravinsky), 222, 223, 289
  reception of, 178
  revision and copyright problems, 174
Safonov, Vasily Ilytch, 304
Salome (R. Strauss), 136
  Burian as Herod in, 68–70
  Jeritza in, 71
  reorchestrated for Rajdl, 100
  Strauss conducts, 76
Salome (Wilde), and *Miraculous Mandarin,* 52–3
Salzburg, 148, 279
  Kodály in, 11, 47
  Mozarteum, 237
Samuel, Gerhard, 207, 224
San Antonio, opera in, 134
San Francisco, 194
  opera in, 134
San Francisco Symphony Orchestra, 152
Sanromá, Jesus Maria, 59
Santiago, 236
Schalk, Franz, 29
  at Budapest Opera, 73–4
Schauspieldirektor, Der (Mozart), on French radio, 129
Scheveningen, 249–50
Schiller, Friedrich von, *Don Carlos,* 114
Schoeffler, Paul, 91, 99
Schönberg, Arnold, 178
  and the impasse in modern music, 324–5, 328
  Erwartung, 252
  string quartets, 51
  "Transfigured Night" as ballet, 184
Schubert, Franz, 35, 239
  range of notes used by, 326
  Lieder, 37
  "Unfinished" Symphony, 314

369

371